Gender and the Self in Latin American Literature

This book explores six texts from across Spanish America in which the coming-of-age story ('Bildungsroman') offers a critique of gendered selfhood as experienced in the region's sociocultural contexts. Looking at a range of novels from the late twentieth century, the author explores thematic concerns in terms of their role in elucidating a literary journey towards agency: that is, towards the articulation of a socially and personally viable female gendered identity, mindful of both the hegemonic discourses that constrain it, and the possibility of their deconstruction and reconfiguration.

Myth, exile and the female body are the three central themes for understanding the personal, social and political aims of the Post-Boom women writers whose work is explored in this volume: Isabel Allende, Laura Esquivel, Ángeles Mastretta, Sylvia Molloy, Cristina Peri Rossi and Zoé Valdés. Their adoption, and adaptation, of an originally eighteenth-century and European literary genre is seen here to reshape the global canon as much as it works to reshape our understanding of gendered identities as socially constructed, culturally contingent, and open-ended.

Emma Staniland is a Teaching Fellow in Spanish American Studies at the University of Leicester, UK. Her research interests include Spanish American women's writing, Latino/a culture and literature with a particular focus on US writers with roots in the Hispanic Caribbean, genre studies, and feminist literary theory.

Routledge Transnational Perspectives on American Literature

Edited by Susan Castillo, King's College London

1 **New Woman Hybridities**
Femininity, Feminism, and International Consumer Culture, 1880–1930
Edited by Ann Heilmann and Margaret Beetham

2 **Don DeLillo**
The Possibility of Fiction
Peter Boxall

3 **Toni Morrison's *Beloved***
Origins
Justine Tally

4 **Fictions of the Black Atlantic in American Foundational Literature**
Gesa Mackenthun

5 **Mexican American Literature**
The Politics of Identity
Elizabeth Jacobs

6 **Native American Literature**
Towards a Spatialized Reading
Helen May Dennis

7 **Transnationalism and American Literature**
Literary Translation 1773–1892
Colleen Glenney Boggs

8 **The Quest for Epic in Contemporary American Fiction**
John Updike, Philip Roth and Don DeLillo
Catherine Morley

9 **The Literary Quest for an American National Character**
Finn Pollard

10 **Asian American Fiction, History and Life Writing**
International Encounters
Helena Grice

11 **Remapping Citizenship and the Nation in African-American Literature**
Stephen Knadler

12 **The Western Landscape in Cormac McCarthy and Wallace Stegner**
Myths of the Frontier
Megan Riley McGilchrist

13 **The Construction of Irish Identity in American Literature**
Christopher Dowd

14 **Cities, Borders and Spaces in Intercultural American Literature and Film**
Ana Mª Manzanas and Jesús Benito

15 **American Utopia and Social Engineering in Literature, Social Thought, and Political History**
Peter Swirski

16 **Transnationalism and American Serial Fiction**
Edited by Patricia Okker

17 **Nature, Class, and New Deal Literature**
The Country Poor in the Great Depression
Stephen Fender

18 **Travel and Dislocation in Contemporary American Fiction**
Aliki Varvogli

19 **Nabokov, History and the Texture of Time**
Will Norman

20 **The Transnationalism of American Culture**
Literature, Film, and Music
Edited by Rocío G. Davis

21 **Utopia and Terror in Contemporary American Fiction**
Judith Newman

22 **Occupying Space in American Literature and Culture**
Static Heroes, Social Movements and Empowerment
Ana Mª Manzanas and Jesús Benito

23 **Identity, Diaspora and Return in American Literature**
Edited by Maria Antònia Oliver-Rotger

24 **Cold War American Literature and the Rise of Youth Culture**
Children of Empire
Denis Jonnes

25 **Masculinity in Contemporary New York Fiction**
Peter Ferry

26 **Ethnic Literatures and Transnationalism**
Critical Imaginaries for a Global Age
Edited by Aparajita Nanda

27 **Gender and the Self in Latin American Literature**
Emma Staniland

Gender and the Self in Latin American Literature

Emma Staniland

LONDON AND NEW YORK

First published 2016 by Routledge

2 Park Square, Milton Park, Abingdon, Oxfordshire OX14 4RN
711 Third Avenue, New York, NY 10017

Routledge is an imprint of the Taylor & Francis Group, an informa business

First issued in paperback 2018

Library of Congress Cataloging-in-Publication Data

Staniland, Emma.
Gender and the self in Latin American literature / by Emma Staniland.
pages cm. — (Routledge transnational perspectives on American literature)
Includes bibliographical references and index.
1. Spanish American fiction—Women authors—History and criticism.
2. Spanish American fiction—20th century—History and criticism
3. Women in literature. 4. Sex role in literature. 5. Self in literature. I. Title.
PQ7081.5S83 2015
863'.6099287098—dc23 2015016281

ISBN: 978-0-415-70831-9 (hbk)
ISBN: 978-1-138-54767-4 (pbk)

Typeset in Sabon
by codeMantra

Contents

Acknowledgments

There are many people who I need to thank for helping me write this book. On a professional note I wish to acknowledge the receipt of an AHRC grant for the PhD thesis with which it began, the guidance of my supervisor for that project, Dr Sheldon Penn, and the immensely valuable support and encouragement of colleagues (many once teachers) in the School of Modern Languages and other Schools of the College of Arts, Humanities and Law at the University of Leicester. Thank you also to Elizabeth Levine and Nancy Chen at Routledge for their balance of professionalism and personalized support.

That I have the great fortune to do a job I love alongside people many of whom are close friends as well as great colleagues provides an easy segue into the personal thanks I want to give here to those who have directly and/or indirectly contributed to this monograph. Writing a book about the concept and experience of self-development will obviously incite a person to consider all of the elements that have met in their own coming-to-be. As part of that process the completion of this project both the first and the second time around has been a major rite of passage for me, and one during which I have been extremely fortunate to be accompanied by kind, generous, interesting, insightful and motivating individuals without whom I would neither have gotten through the experience or be (the better aspects of) the person I am today. Among you, you bring energy, support and, most importantly, the laughter that opens up a space in which the things that matter are always suddenly more visible, and I thank you wholeheartedly for making me feel like I belong somewhere. Pues gracias a mi peña, Ariane Richards, Anna Vives, Clara Garavelli, Lucía Pintado Gutiérrez, Marc Ripley, Nuria Escudero Pérez, por las cenas, las charlas, los cafés, el tabú y la voluntad de bailar en supermercados. Thank you to other special Tower dwellers and friends Ann Miller (whose wit and empathy with my fear of the blank page are always immensely appreciated), Aurélie Joubert, Corinne Pelton, Liz Jones (with particular mention for calmness, sensitive pragmatism and therapeutic trips to homeware stores), Marion Krauthaker, Martín Agnone, Michelle Harrison, Özge Özkaya and Yvonne Cornejo. Thanks to Rebecca Styler, Scott Freer and Emma Kimberley for dinners, music, encouragement, and company during the tougher moments of both the PhD and this process;

to Jo Mallin, for knowing; to Kelly Woodward for always being there, even when I don't manage it. Thank you to Annette Knight, Chris O'Malley and Sylvia Sanders, with my utmost respect for the very important work they do and gratitude for everything they have helped me to understand. To my wonderful, inspirational Grandad, George Staniland, and much-missed Grandma, Clarice, to Nanny and in memory of Grampy, to Mum and Dad, Abi and Jeff, for all your support.

Lastly, I would like to dedicate this book to my students past, present and future, and thank you for being such great teachers. I sincerely hope it says something meaningful to you that you might carry with you on your travels. Go far!

Introduction

MAPPING THE JOURNEY: GENERIC, THEORETICAL AND CULTURAL CONTEXTS

> 1. *Carácter de la obra.*—¿A qué genero pertenece? a) Novela; b) cuento; c) poesía; d) ensayo.
> Morris vaciló. [...]—En realidad—explicó él—, no estoy seguro de poder contestar exactamente la primera pregunta.
>
> 1. *Description of the work.* To what genre does it belong? a) Novel; b) short story; c) poem; d) essay.
> Morris hesitated. [...] 'The fact is', he explained, 'I am not sure whether I can precisely answer this first question'.
>
> Cristina Peri Rossi, *La nave de los locos* (1984)

To address, as this book does, portrayals of the formulation of gendered selfhood in female Spanish American development novels, demands engagement with questions of gender and genre epitomized by the dilemma of Cristina Peri Rossi's character Morris in *La nave de los locos*. Morris is one of the many marginalized Others that populate Peri Rossi's narrative, and the episode referred to in the epigraph sees him wishing to publish a book that declines to adhere neatly to accepted generic categories. When required by the publisher's submission questionnaire to define the nature of his writing, Morris enters into a humorous exchange with the office receptionist that clearly exposes the ties between dominant configurations of gender and genre—a fact all the more evident in the Spanish language because the same word—*género*—serves for both. When he tells her that he firmly believes his work is androgynous and cannot be categorized according to the options presented, she replies: 'There are Doctors for such problems... [...] You mustn't worry too much'.[1]

Such crises of categorization are a primary concern of this study, which explores Spanish American versions of a literary form whose particular ways of interlinking gender and genre have been of interest to feminist studies since the early 1980s. The Bildungsroman is a subgenre of the novel devoted to narrating the development of the individual in dialogue with his or her social context—the process of *Bildung*—accounting for the mutually informative relationship between individuality and community; selfhood and society. Since its inception in eighteenth-century Germany, the Bildungsroman has grown to become a transnational genre of literature, adopted and adapted by writers from around the world, and its taxonomy has represented a significant contribution to debates within genre studies and feminist literary criticism about the double-edged sword of established conventions for classifying literary works; an act at once clarifying and constraining. Thus, 'identity' and the concerns about belonging and non-belonging always invoked by that term are a central thread in discussions about the Bildungsroman, both in relation to its own historical development and to its thematic concerns and narrative arc.

GENDERED GENRE

> As soon as the word 'genre' is sounded, as soon as it is heard, as soon as one attempts to conceive it, a limit is drawn. And when a limit is established, norms and interdictions are not far behind: 'Do', 'Do not' says 'genre', the word 'genre', the figure, the voice, the law of genre.[2]

As David Duff has explained, from the early 1900s onwards we witnessed the 'steady erosion of the perception of genre' as a term of necessity in Western literary discourse, to a view of it as a word that 'carries unmistakable associations of authority and pedantry' and therefore 'seems almost by definition to deny the autonomy of the author, deny the uniqueness of the text, deny spontaneity, originality, and self-expression.'[3] The subject of Derrida's above-cited piece *The Law of Genre* (1980), for example, this unfavorable view of the constraints of literary form has been important for feminist literary criticism because of the useful parallels that have been drawn between genre's functioning as a straightjacket for creative writing, and the rigidity of other identity categories central to the organization of symbolic and real-world orders. Consequently, the questioning of genre categories can open up broader questions, as Ralph Cohen helpfully expresses in his piece 'History and Genre' (1986), where he reminds us that there are 'value distinctions' at play in the act of labeling a given work,[4] and argues that because 'genre concepts in theory and practice arise, change, and decline for historical reasons',[5] then 'generic transformation can be a social [not just a literary] act'.[6] Hence, because gender is one of those key organizational categories, the interrogation of particularly gendered genres plays a central role in a broader feminist engagement with the politics of representation, and what is seen to be at stake here is the fact that to challenge genre in literature can also be to challenge, as Derrida puts it, 'a biological *genre* in the sense of *gender*'.[7]

The Bildungsroman exemplifies perhaps more than any other literary form the gendering of genre and the potential consequences of this beyond the realm of the text. First and foremost this is, quite simply, because its central interest is the development of a self that is always, inescapably, implicitly if not explicitly, gendered by the vocabulary of our hegemonic systems. Further to this, though, the particular qualities of this genderedness are rooted in the genre's origins in post-Revolutionary Europe; in a time and place feeling the aftershocks of mass social and political changes that inevitably impacted upon notions of selfhood—even if selfhood nonetheless remained firmly masculinized. Indeed, as further evidence of the pervasiveness of this assumed maleness, even in more recent studies we have witnessed oddly insistent attempts by some critics of the genre to delimit its validity as nomenclature in line with that genderedness, as well as in terms of cultural and historical specificities. For example, in his 1987 piece 'Cultivating Gender: Sexual Difference, Bildung, and the Bildungsroman'—contemporary to my chosen corpus—John H. Smith argues that the central concept of *Bildung* is only available to male protagonists and is premised on their unrestricted access to the patriarchal symbolic order, arguing that 'the goal of the Bildungsroman [...] is to represent the self's developmental trajectory within the bourgeois patriarchal social order and thereby to expose the structuration of (male) desire.'[8]

Reflecting the impact of Enlightenment thought in Western societies of the time, it is Johann Wolfgang von Goethe's now paradigmatic *Wilhelm Meister's Apprenticeship* (1795–6) that is credited with being the first to articulate the shift in cultural values that generated this kind of narrative. In his depiction of the eponymous bourgeois hero's attempt to seek a life more meaningfully in tune with his particular sensibilities, Franco Moretti explains, Goethe codifies modern '*youth* as the most meaningful part of life';[9] as a stage where 'apprenticeship' is no longer the slow and predictable progress towards one's father's work, but rather an uncertain exploration of social space',[10] by a self that is now 'perennially dissatisfied and restless',[11] so that self-development takes place through the interaction of the interior being and the demands imposed upon the self from outside; by society. Hence, one of the most frequently cited definitions of the genre, put forward by Wilhelm Dilthey in *Das Erlebnis und die Dichtung* (1913) emphasizes the traditionally episodic and chronological nature of this kind of narrative as follows:

> A regulated development within the life of the individual is observed, each of its stages has its own intrinsic value and is at the same time the basis for a higher stage. The dissonances and conflicts of life appear as the necessary growth points through which the individual must pass on his way to maturity and harmony.[12]

The protagonist of this journey, the *Bildungsheld*

> enters life in a blissful daze, searches for kindred souls, encounters friendship and love, but then [...] he comes into conflict with the

> hard reality of the world and thus matures in the course of manifold life-experiences, finds himself, and becomes certain of his task in the world.[13]

Clearly, the nature of this pivotal conflict and that of its resolution will be key indicators of the ideologies that inform any take on the Bildungsroman, classical or contemporary. Commenting on the inherent message of these narratives as they are defined by Dilthey, Todd Kontje posits that the hero 'engages in the double task of self-integration and integration into society', where, ideally, each task implies the other, until 'the mature hero becomes a useful and satisfied citizen.'[14] In these terms, 'the *Bildungsroman* is a fundamentally affirmative, conservative genre, confident in the validity of the society it depicts, and anxious to lead both hero and reader toward a productive place within that world.[15] And if it is that responsive to the discursive frameworks of its social context, the 'uncertain exploration' of the world that Moretti refers to above appears to retain, in actual fact, a strong element of predictability as a result of the ideological ties between self, text and context. Moreover, and very importantly for my critical interest in the depiction of gendered identities in the Spanish American context, the *Bildungsheld* of the classical Bildungsroman is not aware—*must not* be aware—of the invisible hand guiding his progress from youth to maturity, because, Moretti writes:

> it is not sufficient for modern bourgeois society simply to subdue the drives that oppose the standards of 'normality'. It is also necessary that, as a 'free individual', not as a fearful subject but as a convinced citizen, one perceives the social norms as *one's own*.[16]

The Bildungsroman thus appears as an inherently conformist genre that propagates dominant social hierarchies and perpetuates the subjugation of the individual by disavowing agency. And not least because, according to Kontje, the genre's didactic pretensions are motivated by the aims of the author, who must have conviction and 'confidence in the validity of the society that [he] depicts'.[17]

From the feminist and broadly poststructuralist perspectives of the present study and others like it, both the persistent assumed maleness of the protagonist and the genre's alignment with dominant social mores are clearly deeply problematic, and they beg questions not purely regarding the genre's actual feasibility as a female-centered narrative, but also pertaining to its validity: is the Bildungsroman a genre that facilitates indoctrination into hegemonic discourses? Is it, or could it become, a tool for oppression? And if this is the case, what worth can it have, for example, for the six Spanish American women writers central to this project? Why go to the trouble of recuperating such a generic framework? One really important response to these concerns is found in Smith's separation of the concept of *Bildung* from the issue of *roman*—the distinction between the possibility of self-development and the tenets of the genre that has grown up around that central notion. He writes that

> *Bildung*, and its narrativization in the Bildungsroman [...] leads to the construction of male identity in our sex-gender system by granting men access to self-representation in the patriarchal Symbolic order. As such *Bildung* is a central form of the institutional cultivation of gender roles.[18]

It is not the genre that matters, initially, therefore, but the question of a *Bildung* that is not just a matter of identity, but one of *gendered* identity—and this will be a central concern for the remainder of this study. Because, really crucially, even in its original form the narrative trajectory of the development novel, which must begin and end with *Bildung* however that might be textualized, is concerned with matters of individual empowerment and social agency that are vital acquisitions for the woman writer: Acquisitions that can, and have, been rescued and rearticulated via those new discursive practices that have come into play since the genre's creation, and that have enabled a productive reemphasis of its various tenets, as well as revelation of its more useful qualities in the name of Other versions of selfhood.

In fact, such ideological rigidity as that described above seems in any case deeply incongruous with the period of history that gave birth to the genre: Goethe's prototypical text was written in the wake of the Enlightenment and before the French Revolution had even come to an end. Social mobility had become a possibility for the first time, the nature and importance of education and self-improvement had become pertinent issues in ways previously unseen. All of these values and ideals regarding individual and social progression are clearly embedded in the form and content of the Bildungsroman, and so it seems unlikely that the future towards which its protagonist is moving be constituted by a telos insinuating the complete collapse of the self under external forces; that the antagonism Dilthey highlights could only ever lead to the individual's subjugation to hegemonic systems and the total loss of possibilities for self-definition. It could do, were it synonymous with closure, but this is not the case. In fact, Thomas L. Jeffers points out in relation to the exemplary *Wilhelm Meister* that 'the comic ending is remarkably *open-ended*, with many problems unsolved'.[19]

Instead of being characterized by absolute fixity, the telos guiding the journey of the *Bildungsheld* can be seen as a point of synthesis that is the desired outcome of the meeting between selfhood and society, and which assumes some level of individual agency to be at work. For example, Moretti refers to Gyorgy Lukács's *Theory of the Novel* with regard to this, and the 'attempt at compromise' that is read therein as 'the core of novelistic structure'.[20] In his chapter 'Wilhelm Meister's Years of Apprenticeship as an attempted synthesis', Lukács explores the dualism that is the necessary precondition to 'compromise', emphasizing the important presence of agency in the Bildungsroman, where he sees the nature of the protagonist and 'the structure of the plot' to be 'determined by the necessary condition that a reconciliation between interiority and reality, although problematic, is nevertheless possible; that it has to be sought in hard struggles and dangerous adventures, yet is ultimately possible to achieve'.[21] The *Bildungsheld* is not a passive individual pushed unknowingly towards his prefabricated destiny, but the central character of a story that encapsulates

> on the one hand a wider and consequently more adaptable, gentler, more concrete idealism, and, on the other hand, a widening of the soul which seeks fulfilment in *action*, in *effective* dealing with reality, and not merely in contemplation [my emphases].[22]

What may be interpreted as a rigid, didactic narrative portraying the central protagonist's preordained journey towards a socially acceptable version of maturity, and concurrent indoctrination with hegemonic ideals, is now legible as an empowering genre because neither the interior 'soul' nor the exterior social force becomes dominant—rather, a crucial synthesis is achieved meaning that while the individual may not be in complete control of the world around him or her, s/he does have a level of agency; as much as s/he may be impacted and shaped by his or her surroundings, the individual too can have impact and give shape. Fundamentally, the confrontation between the individual and the social in the Bildungsroman is not characterized by 'philistinism—the acceptance of an outside order, however lacking in idea it may be, simply because it is the given order',[23] a point concretized by Thomas Jeffers' interpretation of Goethe's original central project as that of '*self*-cultivation' (my emphasis):[24] 'Goethe's dominant principle', he asserts, was 'that the individual is born not for society's sake but for his own, and that society is essentially an arena in which individuals can collectively realize their own 'capabilities'.[25]

BILDUNGSHELD/BILDUNGSHELDIN: THE OTHER BILDUNGSROMAN

These ideas further explain the possibilities for the genre's rearticulation as a voice-piece for non-hegemonic selfhood by emphasizing the centrality of the *Bildungsheld* (male) or *Bildungsheldin* (female) as the embodiment of the ideals of self-development, social integration and agency towards which the Bildungsroman drives—a feature explored by Mikhail Bakhtin in his seminal piece 'The *Bildungsroman* and Its Significance in the History of Realism (Toward a Historical Typology of the Novel)' (1979). Focusing on the way in which 'the image of the main hero is constructed',[26] Bakhtin compares the '*ready-made* hero' of the Bildungsroman with protagonists of other novelistic subgenres, highlighting a meaningful contrast between the *Bildungsheld* as 'the image of *man in the process of becoming*' and the more static central figure who is an 'immobile and fixed point around which all movement in the novel takes place' but whose 'change and emergence do not become the plot'.[27] Very simply, the relationship between the individual and the social—the relationship that makes agency matter—cannot be explored in stories about such fixed characters because the potential, mutual impact of individual and society upon one another is made irrelevant by an unchanging character. According to Bakhtin, in the Bildungsroman:

> Changes in the hero himself acquire *plot* significance, and thus the entire plot of the novel is reinterpreted and reconstructed. Time is introduced into man, enters into his very image, changing in a fundamental way the significance of all aspects of his daily life. This type of novel can be designated in the most general sense as the novel of human emergence.[28]

And so the genre reflects social change, because its protagonist comes into view

> along with the world and reflects the historical emergence of the world itself. He is no longer within an epoch, but on the border between two epochs, at the transition point between one to the other. *This transition is accomplished in him and through him* [my emphases].[29]

Effectively then, to be denied the right to *Bildung*, is not only to be denied the right to travel a path of legitimization at the end of which identity and agency are to be found, but also to be denied the right to participate in social change. But, vitally, Bakhtin's underlining of the possibility of 'reinterpretation' and 'reconstruction' that is brought about by the particularities of the role of the *Bildungsheld* indicates a generic pliability that can allow the agency locked within this representative framework to be grasped by individuals previously denied self-expression.

In this way, the epochal cusp upon which Bakhtin sees the protagonist to be standing is a location that insinuates the *moving beyond* dualism; a 'transition point' that recalls Moretti and Lukác's references to the 'compromise' and 'synthesis' reached by the successful negotiation of antagonistic oppositions between self and society, and which comes into play in the structure of this book (to be discussed later). This genre's potential for the expression, exploration, and interrogation of selfhood is thus understood to be in a continual state of evolution, and as a consequence, to disregard the genre as one that imposes a problematic state of closure is to overestimate structural and thematic limitations. Bakhtin stresses the potential that has always been present in even the most traditional examples of the form, but which has been lost through failure to account for the inherent contingency of the *Bildungsheld.* This is 'socialization *as* subjective growth';[30] a journey towards satisfaction through belonging, in which '[o]ne's formation as an individual in and for oneself coincides without rifts with one's social integration as a simple *part of a whole*.'[31] And so what comes to matter most about the Bildungsroman is not the fact of its being structured by a fixed or desired end point, but the nature of that telos, for it is that which will ideologically inform the experiences that make up the journey of formation, and mean that just as the form can be put to work to provide a conservative account of one individual's eventual succumbing to the hegemony, so can it account for the kind of refusal *and* rebellion that is entirely necessary to the Bildungsroman of the Other.

ARTICULATING FEMALE SELFHOOD

All of the above qualities are key indicators of what Joanna Frye has described as the form's 'decided place [in] the experiential base of feminist criticism' and a subsequent 'clear relevance to the urgency of female self-definition.'[32] This characterization is clearly meaningful for its place in the gender/genre debate, and in particular to understanding feminist appropriations of the genre, where the dominant male presence in the Bildungsroman, both as author and protagonist, is a historical bias-turned-catalyst for reenvisioning the Bildungsroman as a valuable site of contestation to artists and scholars interested in the representation—or lack thereof—of female experiences of selfhood. As we will explore, this bias reflects a historical understanding of the differences between the genders so that if, as Paul McAleer has summed up, 'the *Bildungsroman* of the late eighteenth and nineteenth centuries stands as a cultural record of the way in which the self was conceived during this period of history',[33] then it is also a record of how the 'self' at that time was *not* perceived—of the fact that notions of female selfhood were as absent from society as from literature. Or, as Moretti puts it, exclusion of non-white, non-male protagonists in the form's early years

> lies in the very elements that characterize the Bildungsroman as a form: wide cultural formation, professional mobility, full social freedom—for a very long time, the west European middle-class man held a virtual monopoly on these, which made him a sort of structural *sine qua non* of the genre. Without him, and without the social privileges he enjoyed, the *Bildungsroman* was difficult to write, because it was difficult to imagine.[34]

For this reason, the Bildungsroman is a genre very usefully read in light of Cohen's point, above, regarding the value systems inherent to the formulation of generic categorizations, because such a reading keeps in view the potential strength of genre as a legitimizing force and holds onto the ways in which the *narration* of the becoming of the self can make visible the *discursive nature* of gender formation. It underlines intriguing parallels between intra- and extra-textual worlds that move us to consider how the policing of boundaries in one inflects and reflects the policing of those lines in the other.

As Stella Bolaki rightly emphasizes in her excellent book *Unsettling the Bildungsroman: Reading Contemporary Ethnic American Women's Fiction* (2011), the 'resurgence of interest' in the genre 'especially by marginalized subjects, can be explained in part by alluding to phenomena such as the women's and civil rights movement [sic], multiculturalism, decolonization and various experiences and histories of diaspora'.[35] The novels I consider in *Gender and the Self in Latin American Literature* all emerge from a postcolonial context, engage with localized regional and national cultures and histories, and with experiences of exile, clearly responding to the issues that have revitalized the global Bildungsroman canon. It was first during the 1970s, Carol Lazzaro-Weis explains, that feminist writers and literary critics took up the challenge of recuperating the Bildungsroman specifically, drawing into it the focus on gender that would instigate its reimagining as a space that 'proved most useful in analyzing the ways in which nineteenth- and early twentieth-century women novelists had represented the suppression and defeat of female autonomy, creativity, and maturity by patriarchal gender norms'.[36]

What followed was the gradual appearance of a canon of critical works that sought to underline the importance of the genre as a means of expressing ideas about and experiences of female selfhood; to recover a corpus of previously ignored female texts that narrate the experience of female development; and to theorize the thematic and structural features of the newly established female canon in dialogue with feminist literary theory. For example, in their seminal study *The Voyage In: Fictions of Female Development* (1983), Elizabeth Abel, Marianne Hirsch and Elizabeth Langland depart from a critical intention to contribute to what they describe as now a 'tradition among critics of the Bildungsroman'; to 'transform a recognized historical and theoretical genre into a more flexible category whose validity lies in its usefulness as a conceptual tool' for the depiction of female experiences,[37] because 'the sex of the protagonist modifies every aspect of a particular *Bildungsroman*: its narrative structure, its implied psychology, its representation of social pressures.'[38]

Written a few years later, the very title of Esther Kleinbord Labovitz's study *The Missing Heroine: The Female Bildungsroman in the Twentieth Century* (1986), initially seeks out a protagonist whose 'failure to make an appearance in the novels of the nineteenth century when the Bildungsroman was at its height opened up questions of a historical, social, and cultural nature'.[39] The nineteenth century *Bildungsheldinnen* that her search leads her to were most often only traced up to a point of 'physical maturity' (in the event that their development was acknowledged at all), then abandoned by narratives failing to recognize their potential beyond that point—a fact that ultimately 'militat[ed] against their designation as *Bildungsroman* heroines.'[40] However, her subsequent search for the twentieth-century heroine is comparatively more fruitful, and she is motivated by this greater visibility to argue that the Bildungsroman surely does not need to be considered a less 'viable structure for the female heroine by virtue of her different developmental process'.[41] Rather, such a heroine would be 'a vehicle advocating fuller exploration of women's goals and expectations' who thus facilitates 'a redefining of the genre'.[42]

Departing from this perspective, feminist studies of the form have sought to outline the changes that appear in Bildungsromane about female protagonists. Drawing to a close their overview of the female Bildungsroman canon from the nineteenth century through to the early 1980s, the decade during which my chosen corpus of texts starts to appear, Abel et al. conclude that:

> Women's developmental tasks and goals, which must be realized in a culture pervaded by male norms, generate distinctive narrative tensions—between autonomy and relationship, separation and community, loyalty to women and attraction to men. The social constraints on female maturation produce other conflicts, not unique to female characters, but more relentless in women's stories. Repeatedly, the female protagonist [...] must chart a treacherous course between the penalties of expressing sexuality and suppressing it, between the costs of inner concentration and of direct confrontation with society, between the price of succumbing to madness and of grasping a repressive 'normality'.[43]

The essays in their edited volume draw out specific thematic shifts between male and female versions, a number of which are pertinent to the novels that I explore here, in terms of aligning them with recognized conventions, and as regards their adaptation of the genre's shape as a means of adapting also its didactic aspirations and thus pushing for social change, as will be explored in more detail in their respective dedicated chapters. As a result, Abel et al.'s helpful working definition of these narratives highlights issues of gender difference, while also underlining the qualities of the genre that makes its recuperation by women writers a worthwhile endeavor, because '[a]lthough the primary assumption underlying the *Bildungsroman*—the evolution of a coherent self—has come under attack in modernist and avant-garde fiction, this assumption remains cogent for women writers who now for the first time find themselves in a world increasingly responsive to their needs.'[44]

> Our reformulation [transforms] a recognized historical and theoretical genre into a more flexible category whose validity lies in its usefulness

> as a conceptual tool. [It] shares common ground with the presuppositions and generic features of the traditional Bildungsroman: belief in a coherent self (though not necessarily an autonomous one); faith in the possibility of development (although change may be frustrated, may occur at different stages and rates, and may be concealed in the narrative); insistence on a time span in which development occurs (although the time span may only exist in memory) and emphasis on social context (even as adversary).[45]

READING THE POST-BOOM SPANISH AMERICAN FEMALE BILDUNGSROMAN

The Spanish American development novels that this book considers stand as evidence of the transmutability and persistent vitality of the Bildungsroman and constitute a clear challenge to purist regulation of generic categories on a number of levels. In all, I bring together here six novels encompassing a period of ten years of Spanish American women's writing in the twentieth century, and five of the countries of the region: from Argentina, *En breve cárcel* (Sylvia Molloy, 1981), from Chile, *Eva Luna* (Isabel Allende, 1987), from Cuba *La nada cotidiana* (Zoé Valdés, 1995), from Mexico, *Como agua para chocolate* (Laura Esquivel, 1989) and *Arráncame la vida* (Ángeles Mastretta, 1985) and from Uruguay, *La nave de los locos* (Cristina Peri Rossi, 1984). This is a transnational corpus of texts that affirms, through stylistically diverse accounts of individual experiences in a variety of social settings, the narrative possibilities opened up by the reassessment of the tenets of the novel of development discussed above. Written by female authors with no stake in upholding dominant principles literary or social, these works' interactions with the Bildungsroman as generic framework expose connections between genre and gender that are, in turn, revelatory of the immensely meaningful dialogue taking place between cultural and social domains. Their stories recount the lives of women in a variety of national, historical and political settings, and are each part of a literary output that speaks of important sociocultural shifts in the Latin American region; ones that not only facilitated but made important the Bildungsroman as a vehicle for advocating social change via the portrayal of female experiences of selfhood and a growth towards social agency.

The need to recognize the interconnections between gender and genre as organizational systems with which this Introduction has begun is, therefore, also generated by the broader sociohistorical and sociopolitical contexts and ambitions of these texts. *Gender and the Self in Latin American Literature* explores the value of the Bildungsroman form to the writers and novels studied specifically by examining its role as a vehicle for the critique of gendered identities that, in turn, endeavors to encourage growth towards female empowerment. As has been made evident by previous studies of both its original and contemporary forms, the *relato de formación*, to use a common Spanish translation of the original German, is an important symbolic vehicle for voicing the individual's desire to be recognized by, integrated into, and valued as part of, a wider community. And as in the above studies on European literature, narratives of the Spanish American canon at large that inflect the shape of the Bildungsroman have begun to be outlined. Writing in 1996, for example, in the first of what remains only a handful of studies on the genre, María Inés Lagos explained in *En tono mayor: Relatos de formación de protagonista femenina* (1996) that her work departed from a point at which the Spanish American Bildunsgroman had not yet received 'systematic' consideration, so that there was no sense of a recognizable corpus, only renowned examples such as *Don Segundo Sombra* by Ricardo Güiraldes, *Las buenas conciencias* by Carlos Fuentes or *Las batallas en el desierto* by José Emilio Pachecho—notably all by male authors.[46] Her volume was followed by Leasa Y. Lutes's *Allende, Buitrago, Luiselli: Aproximaciones teóricas al concepto del 'Bildungsroman' femenino* (2000) and Julia A. Kushigian's *Reconstructing Childhood: Strategies of Reading for Culture and Gender in the Spanish American Bildungsroman* (2003). More recently, Yolanda A. Doub has underlined in her work *Journeys of Formation: The Spanish American Bildungsroman* (2010) that the genre has 'flourished' in Latin America during the last century, and explored regional examples for their use of the travel motif.

These studies contribute to the genealogy of the Bildungsroman a blueprint of its Spanish American canon that is, as expected, revelatory of similar issues of gender bias, and a similar understanding of the value of its female versions to that expressed in the European studies discussed above. For example, Kushigian makes the significant point that as the 'grand narrative of coming of age', the Bildungsroman is responsible for iterating a 'traditional paradigm of normative human development', and begins her critique of it with the clear premise that 'the theory of the Bildungsroman—self-realization, identity, and development—would look different if you took the female or marginalized experience as the norm'.[47] Lutes, in turn, makes the important statement that:

> el examen de las fuerzas formativas en la construcción de un sujeto femenino sacará a la luz las restricciones y frustraciones encontradas por la mujer en su desarrollo. Una articulación de la problemática de la realización femenina parece imprescindible para adelantar el proceso de liberación de la mujer de los límites superimpuestos por su contexto.

> examination of the formative forces at work in the construction of the female subject brings to light the restrictions and frustrations encountered by women in their development. An articulation of the problems involved in female self-realization seems vital to forwarding the process of liberating women from the limits imposed by her context.[48]

They have also helped to address any canonical gender imbalance in the Spanish American field by drawing together a variety of female Spanish American narratives under the Bildungsroman umbrella: Lagos takes Teresa de la Parra's *Ifigenia* (1924) and *Las memorias de mamá Blanca* (1929) as the earliest regional examples, and considers versions from the 1940s through to the 1970s before focusing on works from the latter half of the 1980s.[49] Lutes observes that it was during the 1970s that the form was claimed by women writers and became one of their preferred kinds of narrative—a reflection of the growth in impact of the feminist movement.[50] Doub, in turn, concurs that 'there has [...] been a veritable boom of novels of female formation since the 1980s',[51] and this view is of particular relevance to the corpus of this study, as shall be discussed shortly.

Given my interest in a doubly marginalized (non-European and non-male) version of the Bildungsroman, and the relationship between that genre and women as a marginalized social and literary group, the present study shares with Kushigian's and Lutes's work the desire to question the untenable delineation of the Bildungsroman in terms that have limited its potential for narrating the *Bildung* of protagonists not native to the context of its inception. I adopt here a revisionist approach inspired by the fact that the Bildungsroman's now very visible transnational canon tells us that its bracketing-off in such ways is not only unnecessarily narrow, but actually unachievable. However, although I will consider and refer to generic tenets borrowed from the original generic frame in question, my predominant interest lies in the thematic issue of *Bildung* as a gendered and gendering process.

I will return to that issue again shortly, in conjunction with the introduction of the structure of this book. But firstly, it is useful to take the time to position the six novels examined here on the Spanish American literary landscape: all were published post 1980 and therefore all are identifiable as 'Post-Boom' novels in line with the now broadly accepted understanding of that literary wave having been formulated during that decade. An in-depth overview of the (ever-contentious) tenets of the Post-Boom is beyond the scope of this book, and has been extensively carried out by such seminal works as Donald Shaw's *The Post-Boom in Spanish American Fiction* (1998) and Philip Swanson's *The New Novel in Latin America: Politics and Popular Culture After the Boom* (1995), but I will briefly outline here those aspects of its literature that seem to have made the Bildungsroman an especially pertinent form for writers of that generation—and it is here that Doub's point, above, bears relevance to my work. The first, and for me most intriguing, of the commonalities between the Post-Boom novel and the classical Bildungsroman is their inception in revolutionary contexts. The Post-Boom writers' generational identity derives in large part from their having been inspired to develop 'a sense of a different relationship between fiction and its sociopolitical context' by the political atrocities of the 1970s and 1980s; decades scarred by authoritarian regimes, human rights abuses of horrifying proportions, and guerrilla warfare.[52] In essence, then, the Post-Boom came to life just as the Bildungsroman did: at a time when social shifts necessitated new understandings of the relationship between the individual and their social context. It is therefore perhaps not surprising, but nonetheless compelling, that the genre and the movement also come to share ideological interests expressed in their thematic focus: the articulation of new kinds of selfhood.

Of especial relevance to this project is the fact that the Post-Boom's answer to the Bildungsroman's then radical introduction of the white middle class bourgeois voice,[53] was the introduction of a female literary voice and the portrayal of female experiences of life in the region; what Uruguayan writer Ángel Rama famously referred to as the 'great eruption of women writers' that has come to be recognized as one of the wave's major characteristics,[54] and a change whose 'powerful' value Argentine Post-Boom writer Mempo Giardinelli reflected on in a lecture delivered at the Americas Society in 1994, remarking:

> I do not believe in feminine or feminist literature (literature has no sex), but I think that one of the most noteworthy and original aspects of Latin American literature is the sudden materialization of a remarkable generation of writing women. It is they who are introducing the most original changes in theme, point of view, writing techniques and experimentation.[55]

In a postcolonial region where the artist/writer has been attributed a crucial role in post-independence society, the significance of this evaluation should not be underestimated. For example, Edwin Williamson has posited that from the Latin American postcolonial arena grew 'two great themes': 'first, the aspiration to found a just social order' and 'secondly, the quest for an authentic American identity.'[56] The latter concern, he suggests, 'gave the artist a major role in society', so that 'in times of great crisis the creative writer seemed best qualified to articulate the destiny of the nation' and, as a result, the 'successful creative writer in Latin America [has] enjoyed a moral power and public status' that literary figures in Europe have 'rarely, if ever, been accorded'.[57] Quite simply, the political significance afforded to literature in the Spanish American cultural sphere means that for women not to be participating in the regional canon means not having access to a highly privileged, powerful form of self-expression and social interaction. The recovery of that realm of communication was essential both to the entrance of women into the public sphere, and to the introduction into the region's cultural history an interest in identity politics that engaged specifically with gender. In its discontinuation of that gender bias, the Post-Boom further paved the way for the portrayal of female experiences of selfhood and society whose expression has equally been an aim of the writers and critics engaging with the question of the female, or otherwise non-hegemonic Bildungsroman.

Stylistically, the Post-Boom's revised understanding of the connection between art and life is often negotiated through a neo-realist style that counters the Boom writers' more 'writerly' (rather than 'readerly') texts and perceived assumption that artistic innovation in and of itself constituted a challenge to social norms and could effect change.[58] Instead, the literature of the new generation, according to Chilean writer Antonio Skármeta, would be 'vocationally anti-pretentious, pragmatically anti-cultural, sensitive to the banal, and rather than re-ordering the world [...] it will simply present it.'[59] The nomenclature '*neo*-realism' acknowledges the continuation of some of the ambiguity with which the Boom generation had approached the question of 'reality', as opposed to a simple return to the traditional realism common to Spanish American literature of the first half of the twentieth century.[60] In relation to this, Shaw credits Swanson with having made the point that when considering the role of realism in the Post-Boom, 'we must always ask [...] what ingredient it is that they add to a realistic style or outlook to carry it beyond old-style realism':[61] in its confrontation with 'the tragic impact of events in Argentina, Chile, Uruguay and Central America' the Post-Boom narrative was shaped by 'a greater emphasis on content, directness of impact, denunciation, documentality or protest'.[62] So that even with what Roberto González Echevarría has described as the '*retorno del relato*' ('return of narrative'), 'a rediscovery of linear storytelling without the fragmentation and the unexpected shifts in time sequence, undermining patterns of cause and effect' that were key features of Boom experimentalism,[63] the realist illusion is not simply once again upheld. Instead, the Post-Boom is typified as realist in its intentions to 'present' its sociopolitical and temporal locality to the reader, but the legacy of the previous generation's work influences a still profound interrogation of what reality is, how we perceive it, and how it can be explored, and *changed* through literature.

These thematic interests and stylistic qualities come together in another key shared feature of the Bildungsroman and the Post-Boom novel: that of an investment in the subject and experience of 'youth' as the 'period, *par excellence*, for illustrating the attempts of humankind to know itself'.[64] Other critics of the female Spanish American Bildungsroman have also noted this thematic interest and its aptness to the broader context of these writers. For example, Lutes comments in her volume on a 'resurgence of interest of themes associated with the development of the adolescent' during recent decades; an interest that is unsurprising

> puesto que la misma sociedad sufre de crisis de identidad. Ella se ve metida en un proceso que se dirige hacia la toma de conciencia, o bien étnica o bien de tipo de auto-valoración como en los casos de los varios grupos marginados por la sociedad tradicional.[65]

> given that society itself is suffering an identity crisis. It finds itself moving towards a grasping of consciousness, be it of an ethical nature or of the kind of self-evaluation experienced by the various groups that have been marginalized by mainstream society.

And certainly this focus on youth (possibility), as opposed to maturity (closure), was incarnated by the Post-Boom writers in the young protagonists they deployed as the 'basic nucleus of experience and capture of reality',[66] and which allowed them to respond to 'the fiasco of 1968, of Vietnam, of the loss of the Latin American social revolution and the so-called death of utopia' as the backdrop to writing that, Giardinelli has emphasized, 'contains a heightened charge of frustration, of pain and of sadness for everything that happened to us in the 70s and 80s, a charge of unease, rage and rebellion'.[67]

The exploration of such crises, and above all the resultant, cathartic, engagement with their impact, then, is enabled by the recuperated linear narrative and neo-realism of the Post-Boom text, and its investment in symbolic value of youth. That investment is then furthered by adding into the mix an interest in the popular culture that, in turn, is one of the qualities that informs an association of the Post-Boom with the postmodern. For example, Santiago Colás writes in *Postmodernity in Latin America: The Argentine Paradigm* (1994) that one of the

> criteria most often agreed upon for distinguishing between the modern and postmodern cultural sensibilities is their respective attitudes towards mass culture. Modernism defined itself in opposition to mass culture. Postmodernism embraces its form and contents, incorporating them within new artifacts that blur the distinction between high and low culture.[68]

Portrayals of 'television and films, pop music, sport, casual sex, and drugs: a fun culture that provides the context of the *rites of passage into adult life*' [my emphases], thus becomes commonplace in the literature of this generation.[69] In the four texts from my corpus that most closely approach the traditional Bildungsroman arc—those of Esquivel, Allende, Mastretta and Valdés—a linear but retrospective narrative enables a close examination of the coming-to-be of the female protagonist. (In all except Esquivel's novel, the narrative voice used is the first person, and the impact of such features is explored further in my analytical discussions.) In these novels such elements are represented via the use of postmodern genre-mixing that engages localized literary and cultural forms previously denigrated as 'low canon', many of which, of course, are associated with women: in Esquivel the use of recipes as a structuring device is key to this strategy, and is accompanied by the use of the melodrama and high romance borrowed from the *novela rosa*. In *Eva Luna*, Allende infuses her *novela* with the Latin America *telenovela*, making of that typically kitsch and immensely popular visual art form a political tool, when her protagonist's screenplay is used to denounce the authoritarianism and human rights abuses of the government. Mastretta's title *Arráncame la vida* is borrowed from a Mexican bolero, and this popular music form is used, for example, in a key scene in the text, where protagonist Catalina deploys that song as a way of expressing her feelings for Carlos—the man with whom she has the affair that catalyzes her willingness to bear witness to her politician husband's corruption. Lastly, in Valdés's *La nada cotidiana*, popular culture is represented by references to cinema in particular; U.S. films whose watching in secret denounces the censorship of the Revolutionary government of which she and her novel are fiercely critical.

The remaining two novels of my corpus, those by Peri Rossi and Molloy, fit less neatly within the frameworks for identification provided by the Bildungsroman's key tenets, in large part because they also represent what can be considered the more radically postmodernist and poststructuralist dimensions of Post-Boom literature. These works are highly fragmented, with a much more nebulous sense of both the chronology and the location of their story, and with what are, at least in the orthodox terms they seek to challenge, more 'problematic' characters: in *En breve cárcel*, a lesbian protagonist and in *La nave de los locos* an impotent male who is accompanied on his travels by a range of 'othered' characters, like Morris, mentioned at the start of this chapter. It is their inclusion in this project, therefore, that presents the greatest challenge to the tenets of the Bildungsroman proper, and one of the key factors in making this study not a revision just of examples of the genre from Spanish America, but a revision of how *Bildung* as the genre's main interest is depicted by writers from the region, and for what purpose. I have approached these two works as 'anti-Bildungsromane', but not deploying the term as David Miles did in 'The Pícaro's Journey to the Confessional: The Changing Image of the Hero in the German Bildungsroman' (1974), where he used it to describe texts that *parody* the classical generic frame.[70] Because, as discussed above, for women writers and their interests the reclaiming of this generic framework has been of extreme relevance, and deemed necessary in spite of the complexities of the steps required to achieve it, for them to undermine its structure to that extent would be unhelpful. Here, therefore, I apply the term as a way of describing how it is that Peri Rossi and Molloy retrace the journey of development undergone by the gendered self, using the analytical perspectives afforded by experiences of exile to reveal and unpick the discourses through which their *Bildungsheld/in* were formulated. They thereby enact a deconstruction of both self and society that is a necessary prerequisite to the 'reformulation' of a selfhood along different lines, and the prefix 'anti' is intended to denote that, as opposed to the demise of a (masculinized) concept of *Bildung per se*.

While the relationship between the Post-Boom and postmodernism is not central to the aims of this project, what is vital is the relationship between the Post-Boom, postmodernist literary techniques and feminism, because the value systems and critical perspectives of all three are united within the Post-Boom Bildungsroman's continuation of the original form's didactic objectives. For as Patricia Waugh explains:

> Postmodernism is usually presented as an art of the marginal and oppositional and as such would at least seem to offer women the possibility

> of identity and inclusion [...] In literary terms, both have embraced the popular, rejecting the elitist and purely formalist celebration of modernism [...] Both movements celebrate liminality, the disruption of boundaries, the confounding of traditional markers of 'difference'.[71]

Giving evidence of the important links between these three literary and ideological arenas, Williamson aligns 'the prominence of women's writing in the years following the Boom' with 'the true historical significance of the general flowering of Latin American literature since the 1920s'.[72] He emphasizes how the deeply engrained masculinist ideologies of Latin American societies led to the establishment of authoritarian regimes that were eventually driven to a 'terminal crisis of authority' during the 1970s,[73] and explains how literature served as the chronicle of these sociopolitical developments, so that, in hindsight,

> it can be appreciated that from the late 1960s the writers of the Boom and the post-Boom had been registering the progressive impotence of Hispanic patriarchy—in the subversive language games of novelists[,] in the dictator novels of the mid-1970s, in the new fascination with the egalitarian ethos of international mass culture, in the literature that bore testimony to the repressions of the authoritarian state, and finally, *in the burgeoning of women's writing* [my emphases].[74]

In effect, the Manichean worldviews of the dictatorships and the other sociopolitical upheavals represented in the works studied here (the Chilean, Venezuelan, Uruguayan and Argentine dictatorships, the Mexican and Cuban Revolutions and their aftermath), served to level social playing fields, exposing the deeply engrained binary oppositions that enabled the formulation of social subjects as either marginal or empowered; as belonging or not belonging; as winners or losers; as appropriately 'male' or appropriately 'female'. And it is the potential for change exhumed from such disruption of accepted orders that my selected corpus expresses. Williamson's study thus ends at the point at which this one begins, in the 1980s and with the Post-Boom generation who took up the task that he envisages as the most essential to the possibility of change in Spanish American society: the 'critique of patriarchy [that] may point to an eventual reconciliation of Latin American national identities with the inescapable pluralism of modern culture.'[75]

Emerging from this synopsis of the qualities and characteristics of Post-Boom writing is an image of a dynamic movement that wishes to engage with as much immediacy as possible with a knowable and experienced social reality (however unstable such a concept may be), with the political, social and cultural issues that are at play in that reality, and with their effect on the lives of the individuals living that reality as their own. Yet more concretely, what becomes apparent here is the need for an artistic form that can encapsulate the experience *of change and development*. For, in essence, the great theme of identity identified above by Williamson as a key feature of Spanish American writing since independence is now engaged with again here in its contemporary guises. Youth (that which youth can symbolize—the potential for change) and gender become central vehicles for this literary interaction with identity, and plurality is championed in the interrogation of the relationship between individual and social context. The renegotiation of the Bildungsroman via engagement specifically with contemporary processes of *Bildung* as discursively enacted, provides the ideal framework for such questioning.

ARCHETYPE—EXILE—BODY

My readings of Allende's, Esquivel's, Peri Rossi's, Molloy's, Valdés's and Mastretta's novels see them as Post-Boom works that exploit the possibilities for adaptation of the Bildungsroman via a reencoding of conventions that, to borrow McAleer's useful words, 'molds and reshapes the form to the extent that its manifestations and functions, while still recognizable, operate in a very different way'.[76] As far as it is represented by these selected works, then, the Spanish American female Bildungsroman is a geographically, culturally, and gender-specific form of the novel of development that stands as evidence of the flexibility and subsequently greater possibilities for agency that it has to offer, underlined in the earlier sections of this chapter. Both the novels and my readings of them engage a revisionist perspective that underscores the importance of this symbolic form as one that illuminates the role of compromise in identity formation, but which simultaneously elucidates potential for agency and empowerment. In part, this agency lies in expression, in literature, and in the reclaiming of a voice with which to recount the *Bildung* of the Other: that of women and of non-orthodox gendered identities. Most specifically, I see the narrative course of the Bildungsroman echoed in these authors' focus on the developmental trajectories through which gendered identities come into view within the social orders and ideological regimes of Spanish American patriarchies. They narrate socially, culturally and historically specific experiences of the 'becoming' of the self, putting in evidence the discourses by which gendered identities are formed. The conflicts found in the texts are the result of the difficulties inherent to this process, which requires the internalization of an order that can survive only through the subordination of its female and/or feminized elements. The critique that these writers present is born of the interrogation of that conflict; of the struggle between internal and external pressures that characterizes the process of *Bildung*. And the result of their critique is the expression of processes of development that moves beyond the frustrations of a Manichean world and into a creative third space characterized by desire and agency. In this way, the perhaps more problematic notion of 'compromise' can be reconceived as a more hopeful synthesis—not a negative giving up of the self in the name of conformity, but a combination of qualities and possibilities that projects forward, towards positive change.

Starting out from a point at which the existence of both a female and a Spanish American canon has been highlighted by preceding studies, this book approaches the genre from a new angle. As I have already implied, rather than directly deploying previously established generic categories to justify the inclusion of the chosen novels, or as paradigms against which to compare them, my approach is stimulated by the textual interests of the novels. As such, I am above all concerned with adopting the narrative arc provided by *Bildung* as an overarching frame by which to structure my study as a whole, and any challenges the texts under consideration pose to predominant descriptions of the Bildungsroman as generic structure are understood only as valuable adaptations: magical realism, metafiction, oneiric portrayals of fragmented selves, poststructuralist riddles, and postmodern inclusions of popular culture, all make a valid contribution to the overall process that is rendered visible by my cross-corpus approach, because they serve to depict experiences crucial to the growth towards the kind of self-knowledge and subsequent agency that my project seeks out. In effect, then, what this book offers is a comparative reading of Allende's, Esquivel's, Peri Rossi's, Molloy's, Mastretta's and Valdés's novels that engages with them not just as individual variations on the Bildungsroman, but as a set of texts that work together to form a transnational Bildungsroman, depicting a journey of development that takes place through the literary topoi of fairy tale and mythical archetypes, experiences of exile, and female embodiment.

The threefold structure of this study comes from the fact that I locate each text within one of three phases of identity development inspired by the triadic form of the Hegelian dialectic and its stages of thesis, antithesis, and synthesis—each of which constitutes one necessary step on a longer journey towards a desired goal. Elaborated in his work *Phenomenology of Spirit* (1807), published just over a decade after Goethe's paradigmatic novel, the resonant similarities between Hegel's philosophical mode and the Bildungsroman's own narrative shape have been noted by scholars such as Meyer H. Abrams, who suggests that Hegel's work in itself is, in fact, a Bildungsroman.[77] Here, that similarity in shape has been adopted as an analytical structure that facilitates a critical reading of the *Bildung* of gender by retextualizing Hegel's three phases in terms germane to gender studies: as stages of 'construction', 'deconstruction', and finally 'reconstruction' of gendered identities. This cross-corpus approach enables me to read the narratives individually, accounting for their historical and national specificities, but all the while placing them in relation to one another in order to appraise the cultural spectrum they present, too, for what it reveals about how the complexities of gender formation are perceived, narrated, and challenged by Spanish American women writers in the late twentieth century.

The Hegelian dialectic model is invaluable to facilitating a reading of discursive identity construction because it does not, contrary to assumptions often made of it, envisage a teleological endpoint that would fix gender identities into a circumscribed time or place. Rather, as Sara Salih points out

> Dialectic is the mode of philosophical enquiry [...] in which a thesis is proposed which is subsequently negated by its antithesis and resolved in a synthesis. This synthesis or resolution is not, however, final, but provides the basis for the next thesis, which once again leads to antithesis and synthesis before the process starts all over again.[78]

Pushing through the phase of dualistic opposition, this philosophical mode facilitates a drive forward that is given momentum by the antagonism of oppositionality, rather than allowing opposition to instill stasis. As such, the dialectic is a model that lends itself well not only to poststructuralist critical approaches that push for change through uncertainty and lack of closure, but also to notions of growth and development. And if, in its destabilizing of antagonistic dualisms, the Hegelian dialectic is in tune with the poststructuralist endeavor to undermine the binary organization of Western symbolic orders and the damaging effects of that structure, it is also this quality that allows an understanding of the dialectic as a useful mode for feminist criticism. Kimberley Hutchings advocates this grasping of Hegel's mode as a feminist critical tool, writing that

> Hegel is battling with the same conceptual conundrum which is constitutive of feminist philosophy in the Western tradition. This is the conundrum of how to escape the conceptual binary oppositions (between culture and nature, reason and emotion, autonomy and heteronomy, universal and particular, ideal and real) which have associated women with the denigrated term and prescribed the exclusion of women from the practices of both philosophy and politics.[79]

If we apply the dialectic narrative pattern to an understanding of gender as social construction, then on this particular trajectory the concept of 'Absolute Knowledge' that was Hegel's defined goal, and which Jonathan Singer explains as the point at which 'the mind realizes that *what it seeks to know is really itself*',[80] is the gendered self coming to know itself as *gendered*; to fully recognize the discourses by and through which it is produced. Most importantly, it is upon arrival at this point of self-recognition that agency is achieved, because without an understanding of the discursively produced identities that we embody, these social constructions, which Judith Butler has argued can—precisely because they are *constructions*—be deconstructed and reconstructed, can never be questioned or reconfigured. In this sense, what the application of a dialectic model as a framework for reading the

Bildung of gender can facilitate, is the exemplification through literature of Butler's point that

> [p]aradoxically, the reconceptualization of identity as *effect*, that is, as *produced* or *generated*, opens up possibilities of 'agency' that are insidiously foreclosed by positions that take identity categories as foundational and fixed. For an identity to be an effect means that it is neither fatally determined nor fully artificial and arbitrary. [...] Construction is not opposed to agency; it is the necessary scene of agency, the very terms in which agency is articulated and becomes culturally intelligible.[81]

Here, just as for Hegel, 'Absolute Knowledge and true freedom are inseparable'.[82] According to Sarah Salih, Butler understands the *Phenomenology* to 'be characterized by open-endedness and *ir*resolution which contain more promise than teleology',[83] and the application of Hegel's dialectic as conceptual framework, and as a lens through which a rejuvenated reading of *Bildung* can be made, is precisely the kind of further appropriation of Hegel that Butler indicates is possible.

Aligning itself with that belief, this project works with Butler's redefined dialectical model, characterized as one in which 'knowledge *proceeds through* opposition and cancellation, never finally reaching an "absolute" or final certainty, but only positing ideas that *cannot be fixed* as "truths"'.[84] My reading of the topoi of female archetypes, experiences of exile, and the female body as localized rearticulations of Hegel's three stages allows me to focus above all on the primary thematic concerns and literary techniques of the six writers, but is also informed by significant contributors to Latin American studies such as Deborah Castillo, who has warned against both the casual and rigid application of European and Anglo-American approaches to Latin American writing. In her seminal work *Talking Back: Towards a Latin American Feminist Literary Criticism* (1992), Castillo espouses a flexible approach to feminist analyses of Latin American literature, adopting only those theoretical approaches that help our understanding of the position of women as social subjects in Spanish America, rather than applying one critical approach in reading the region's literature. In order to achieve this, Castillo says, she

> borrow[s] advisedly from both first world and Latin American(ist) criticism what is pertinent and insightful, while trying to avoid the pitfalls of adhering too closely to the unsatisfactory recipe of combining Anglo-American and French theory in equal parts and seasoning with a dash of Latin American fiction.

Not wishing to replicate this kind of misprioritization, I am not heavy-handedly applying the Hegelian dialectic here as a systematic epistemological framework through which to extract meaning from these texts, but instead deploy it as a scaffold that facilitates a particular kind of engagement with localized feminist concerns and the areas of gender studies to which they, in turn, speak. The color and texture of the literary texts remain strongly at the forefront of my study, generating useful readings of social critique that are responsive to Latin American specificities.

Following on from this Introduction, in Parts One, Two and Three, the six novels are read in pairs, as stories that together portray a progression from a point of imposed gendered identities, towards a form of self-knowledge that is informed by Hegel's concept of Absolute Knowledge, as described above, and perceived as the first crucial step towards personal and social agency. Part One focuses on the role of fairy tale and mythical archetypes in *Eva Luna* by Isabel Allende and Laura Esquivel's *Como agua para chocolate*, novels whose bestseller status has not only led to film adaptations but has also attracted much scholarly interest. The popularity of these two narratives suggests that their portrayals of female experiences of selfhood were meaningful for an immense readership. It therefore seems equally meaningful to examine what it is that they say, and I do this by evaluating the numerous ways in which the writers engage with archetypal female tropes from the worlds of fairy tales and myths. Reading those as resonant topoi for female gendered identity construction and via Latin American feminisms and feminist literary criticism, I engage with the scholarly critiques made of these two writers on the grounds of essentialism, and work to reposition that criticism in light of localized understandings of womanhood.

Part Two considers exile in guises both literal and metaphoric, as a space of entrapment and as a space of liberty, exploring its function as a topos in which orthodox gendered identities may be deconstructed, interrogated, refuted. Here, *En breve cárcel* by Sylvia Molloy and *La nave de los locos* by Cristina Peri Rossi provide the focus of analysis. These novels are much more experimental than the other four that accompany them in this study and, as mentioned above, because they are narratives in which social constraints are shown to derail the natural progression of a coming-to-know the self, since that self is rendered unspeakable in the vocabulary of the hegemonic social order, I have termed them 'anti-Bildungsroman'. Molloy's and Peri Rossi's novels are a fascinating combination of texts, portraying two journeys towards selfhood that take very different trajectories: Peri Rossi's work depicts a movement outwards, an exploration of the world at large that entails a search for the social self as a way back to personal selfhood, whereas Molloy's text takes the opposite route, turning inwards and unpicking the individual in order to grasp the social dimensions by which the self is inescapably defined.

Part Three turns to *Arráncame la vida* by Ángeles Mastretta and Zoé Valdés's *La nada cotidiana*, and to representations of the female body. These last chapters, in which the cumulative impact of the stages of development explored in the previous two 'stages' also becomes evident, I argue that Mastretta's and Valdés's novels depict the body as the site upon and through which a usable and active female gendered identity is recuperated. The myriad references to the body in these two novels function as textual strategies by which to explore issues of class identity and its interactions with versions of womanhood, women as national and social subjects in post-Revolutionary Mexico and Cuba, and female sexual autonomy as a means of defying dominant versions of femininity. This reconstructed body is, for now at least, the site of individual and social agency—the point towards which the three-stage process of self-development explored here has been progressing. This new relationship with the body as a key site in the discursive construction of gendered identities and a vital component of selfhood and social agency is, I argue, made possible by the progression through the stages of construction and deconstruction seen in Parts One and Two. This final stage of the threefold journey towards agency, I will show, is one at which self-empowerment is made possible by metacognition of the body as the location of a performative agency whereupon the material and the symbolic come together. As such, I read the female body as it is depicted in these texts as the point of Hegelian synthesis—a term whose relevance to the Bildungsroman is echoed throughout the studies of it explored earlier in this chapter—where the mythical construction and the exilic deconstruction of gendered identities meet in the reconstruction of an active female body.

Overall, the view of the *Bildung* of gender permitted by the critical explorations offered in this book is a panoramic one that accounts for issues specific to the national, historical and political contexts portrayed, while enabling a cross-corpus engagement that reveals the generalized discourses by which gender is inscribed within the Spanish American cultural context. As a consequence, my study sheds light on the processes by which an individual agency created at first in fiction is brought to life through writing and representation, showing the texts in question to 'dwell on that dangerous cutting edge of possibility, stringing out bridges of words into the uncharted future'.[85]

NOTES

1. Cristina Peri Rossi, *La nave de los locos* (Barcelona: Biblioteca del Bolsillo, 1984), p. 129. 'Hay médicos para eso... [...] No se preocupe demasiado'. All subsequent references are taken from this edition. With the exception of citations in English from Sylvia Molloy's novel *En breve cárcel*, all translations into English provided in this study, of both primary and secondary sources, are my own.
2. Jacques Derrida, 'The Law of Genre', *Glyph*, no. 7 (1980) 202–213, p. 203.
3. David Duff, 'Introduction', *Modern Genre Theory*, David Duff (ed.) (Harlow, UK: Pearson Education Ltd., 2000), p. 1.
4. Ralph Cohen, 'History and Genre', *New Literary History*, 17.2. Interpretation and Culture (Winter 1986), 203–218, p. 206.
5. Cohen, 'History and Genre', p. 204.
6. Cohen, 'History and Genre', p. 216.

7. Derrida, 'The Law of Genre', p. 203.
8. John H. Smith, 'Cultivating Gender: Sexual Difference, *Bildung*, and the *Bildungsroman*', *Michigan Germanic Studies* 13.2 (Fall 1987), 206–225, p. 215.
9. Franco Moretti, *The Way of the World* (New York: Verso, 2000), p. 3.
10. Moretti, *The Way of the World*, p. 4.
11. Moretti, *The Way of the World*, p. 4.
12. Wilhelm Dilthey, *Das Erlebnis und die Dichtung* (1913), p. 394, cited in Elizabeth Abel, Marianne Hirsch and Elizabeth Langland, *The Voyage In: Fictions of Female Development* (Hanover, NH; London: University Press of New England, 1983), pp. 5–6.
13. Cited in Todd Kontje, *Private Lives in the Public Sphere: The German Bildungsroman as Metafiction* (Philadelphia, PA: Pennsylvania State University Press, 1992), p. 12.
14. Kontje, *Private Lives*, p. 12.
15. Kontje, *Private Lives*, p. 12.
16. Moretti, *The Way of the World*, p. 16.
17. Kontje, *Private Lives*, p. 12.
18. Smith, 'Cultivating Gender', p. 216.
19. Thomas L. Jeffers, *Apprenticeships: The Bildungsroman from Goethe to Santayana* (London: Palgrave Macmillan, 2005), p. 24.
20. Moretti, *The Way of the World*, p. viii.
21. Gyorgy Lukács, *The Theory of the Novel: A Historic-Philosophical Essay on the Forms of Great Epic Literature* (London: Merlin Press, 1971), p. 132.
22. Lukács, *The Theory of the Novel*, p. 133.
23. Lukács, *The Theory of the Novel*, p. 134.
24. Jeffers, *Apprenticeships*, p. 13.
25. Jeffers, *Apprenticeships*, p. 34.
26. Mikhail Bakhtin, 'The *Bildungsroman* and Its Significance in the History of Realism (Toward a Historical Typology of the Novel)', in V. W. McGee (trans.), Carol Emerson and Michael Holquist (eds.), *Speech Genres and Other Late Essays* (Austin, TX: University of Texas Press, 1986), p. 10.
27. Bakhtin, 'The *Bildungsroman*', pp. 20–21.
28. Bakhtin, 'The *Bildungsroman*', p. 21.
29. Bakhtin, 'The *Bildungsroman*', p. 23.
30. Moretti, *The Way of the World*, p. 233.
31. Moretti, *The Way of the World*, p. 16.
32. Joanne S. Frye, *Living Stories, Telling Lives: Women and the Novel in Contemporary Experience* (Ann Arbor: University of Michigan Press, 1986), p. 79.
33. Paul McAleer, 'Transexual Identities in a Transcultural Context: Jaime Bayly's *La noche es virgen* and the Comic *Bildungsroman*', *Journal of Iberian and Latin American Studies*, 15.2/3 (August/December 2009), 179–198, p. 179.
34. Moretti, *The Way of the World*, pp. ix–x.
35. Stella Bolaki, *Unsettling the Bildungsroman: Reading Ethnic American Women's Fiction* (Amsterdam; New York: Rodopi, 2011), pp. 10–11.
36. Carol Lazzaro-Weis, 'The Female "Bildungsroman": Calling It into Question', *NWSA Journal*, 2.1 (Winter 1990), 16–34, p. 17.
37. Abel et al., *The Voyage In*, pp. 13–14.
38. Abel et al., *The Voyage In*, p. 5.

39. Esther Kleinbord Labovitz, *The Missing Heroine: The Female Bildungsroman in the Twentieth Century: Dorothy Richardson, Simone de Beauvoir, Doris Lessing, Christa Wolf* (New York: Peter Lang, 1986), p. 4.
40. Labovitz, *The Missing Heroine*, p. 5.
41. Labovitz, *The Missing Heroine*, p. 8.
42. Labovitz, *The Missing Heroine*, p. 5.
43. Abel et al., *The Voyage In*, pp. 12–13.
44. Abel et al., *The Voyage In*, p. 13.
45. Abel et al., *The Voyage In*, pp. 13–14.
46. María Inés Lagos, *En tono mayor: Relatos de formación de protagonista femenina en Hispanoamérica* (Providencia: Editorial Cuarto Propio, 1996), p. 9.
47. Julia A. Kushigian, *Reconstructing Childhood: Strategies of Reading for Culture and Gender in the Spanish American Bildungsroman* (Lewisburg, PA: Bucknell University Press, 2003), p. 15.
48. Leasa Y. Lutes, *Allende, Buitrago, Luiselli: Aproximaciones teóricas al concepto del 'Bildungsroman' femenino* (New York: Peter Lang, 2000), p. 11.
49. Lagos, *En tono mayor*, pp. 55–56.
50. Lutes, *Aproximaciones*, p. 4.
51. Yolanda A. Doub, *Journeys of Formation: The Spanish American Bildungsroman* (New York: Peter Lang, 2010), p. 5.
52. Donald Shaw, *The Post-Boom in American Fiction* (Albany: State University of New York Press, 1998), p. 13
53. Jeffers, *Apprenticeships*, p. 34. Jeffers underlines that 'In the era of the French Revolution it was cutting edge to declare the rights of a burgherly man like Wilhelm [...] Equality of opportunity, was (and actually still is) the beckoning ideal'.
54. Ángel Rama, 'Los contestatorios del poder', *La novela latinoamericana 1922–1980* (Bogota: Instituto Colombiano de Cultura, 1982), p. 468. 'La masiva irrupción de escritoras'. This does not, of course, signify that women's writing did not exist in Latin America prior to the Post-Boom era. The meaning of the female presence in the Post-Boom is not a straightforward question of the appearance of women's writing, but rather their appearance as a dominant, not marginal, presence that actively shaped the qualities and characteristics of the movement. See Brígida M. Pastor and Lloyd Hughes Davies's recently published *A Companion to Latin American Women Writers* (London: Tamesis, 2012) and Elzbieta Sklodowska, 'Latin American Literature' in Philip Swanson, ed., *The Companion to Latin American Studies* (London: Arnold, 2003), for a discussion of the marginalization of women authors during the nineteenth century, and of their gradual appearance as significant contributors to a variety of genres.
55. Mempo Giardinelli, 'Reflections on Latin-American Narratives of the Post-Boom' (1994) in *Review: Literature and Arts of the Americas*, 29.52, 1996, 83–87, p. 83.
56. Edwin Williamson, *The Penguin History of Latin America* (London: Penguin Books, 1992), p. 286.
57. Williamson, *History of Latin America*, p. 513.
58. Shaw, *The Post-Boom*, p. 13.
59. Antonio Skármeta, 'Al fin y al cabo es su propia vida la cosa más cercana que cada escritor tiene para echar mano' (1979), quoted in Shaw, *The Post-Boom*, p. 9. 'Vocacionalmente anti-pretenciosa, pragmáticamente anti-cultural, sensible a lo banal, y más que reordenadora del mundo [...] simplemente presentadora de él'.

60. Philip Swanson, *The New Novel in Latin America: Politics and Popular Culture after the Boom* (Manchester, UK: Manchester University Press, 1995), p. 3.
61. Shaw, *The Post-Boom*, p. 19.
62. Shaw, *The Post-Boom*, p. 13.
63. Shaw, *The Post-Boom*, p. 21.
64. Lutes, *Aproximaciones*, p. 1. 'La adolescencia es reconocida como la etapa por excelencia para ilustrar los intentos del ser humano para conocerse a sí mismo'.
65. Lutes, *Aproximaciones*, p. 2.
66. J. A. Epple, 'El contexto histórico-generacional de la literatura de Antonio Skármeta', cited in Shaw, *The Post-Boom*, p. 17. 'núcleo básico de la experiencia y la aprensión de lo real'.
67. Mempo Giardinelli, 'Variaciones sobre la postmodernidad o ¿Qué es eso del posboom latinoamericano?', cited in Shaw, *The Post-Boom*, p. 12. 'el fiasco del 68, de Vietnam, de la pérdida de la revolución social latinoamericana y la llamada muerte de las utopías' 'contiene una elevada carga de frustración, de dolor y de tristeza por todo lo que nos pasó en los 70s y 80s, una carga de desazón, rabia y rebeldía'.
68. Santiago Colás, *Postmodernity in Latin America: The Argentine Paradigm* (Durham, NC; London: Duke University Press, 1994), p. ix.
69. Shaw, *The Post-Boom*, p. 17.
70. David H. Miles, 'The Pícaro's Journey to the Confessional: The Changing Image of the Hero in the German Bildungsroman', *PMLA*, 89.5 (October 1974), 980–992.
71. Patricia Waugh, *Feminine Fictions: Revisiting the Postmodern* (London: Routledge, 1989), pp. 3–4.
72. Williamson, *History of Latin America*, p. 563.
73. Williamson, *History of Latin America*, p. 563.
74. Williamson, *History of Latin America*, p. 563.
75. Williamson, *History of Latin America*, p. 566.
76. McAleer, 'Transexual identities', p. 180.
77. Meyer H. Abrams, *Natural Supernaturalism: Tradition and Revolution in Romantic Literature* (New York: Norton, 1973), p. 228.
78. Sara Salih, *Judith Butler* (London: Routledge, 2002), p. 3.
79. Kimberley Hutchings, *Hegel and Feminist Philosophy* (Cambridge: Polity Press, 2003), p. 2.
80. Jonathon Singer, *Hegel: A Very Short Introduction* (Oxford: Oxford University Press, 2001), p. 92.
81. Judith Butler, *Gender Trouble: Feminism and the Subversion of Identity*, 2nd edn. (New York: Routledge, 1999; 2002), p. 201.
82. Singer, *Hegel*, p. 88.
83. Salih, *Judith Butler*, pp. 4–5.
84. Salih, *Judith Butler*, p. 3.
85. Jennifer Browdy de Hernandez, *Women Writing Resistance: Essays on Latin America and the Caribbean* (Cambridge, MA: South End Press, 2003), p. 9.

BIBLIOGRAPHY

Abel, Elizabeth, Hirsch, Marianne and Langland, Elizabeth, *The Voyage In: Fictions of Female Development* (Hanover, NH; London: University Press of New England, 1983).

Abrams, Meyer H., *Natural Supernaturalism: Tradition and Revolution in Romantic Literature* (New York: Norton, 1973).

Bakhtin, Mikhail, 'The *Bildungsroman* and Its Significance in the History of Realism (Toward a Historical Typology of the Novel)', in V. W. McGee (trans.), Carol Emerson and Michael Holquist (eds.), *Speech Genres and Other Late Essays* (Austin, TX: University of Texas Press, 1986).

Bolaki, Stella, *Unsettling the Bildungsroman: Reading Ethnic American Women's Fiction* (Amsterdam; New York: Rodopi, 2011).

Browdy de Hernandez, Jennifer, *Women Writing Resistance: Essays on Latin America and the Caribbean* (Cambridge, MA: South End Press, 2003).

Butler, Judith, *Gender Trouble: Feminism and the Subversion of Identity*, 2nd edn. (New York: Routledge, 1999; 2002).

Cohen, Ralph, 'History and Genre', *New Literary History*, 17.2, Interpretation and Culture, Winter 1986, pp. 203–218.

Colás, Santiago, *Postmodernity in Latin America: The Argentine Paradigm* (Durham, NC; London: Duke University Press, 1994).

Derrida, Jacques, 'The Law of Genre', *Glyph*, no. 7 (1980), 202–213.

Doub, Yolanda A., *Journeys of Formation: The Spanish American Bildungsroman* (New York: Peter Lang, 2010).

Duff, David, 'Introduction', *Modern Genre Theory*, David Duff (ed.) (Harlow, UK: Pearson Education Ltd., 2000).

Frye, Joanne S., *Living Stories, Telling Lives: Women and the Novel in Contemporary Experience* (Ann Arbor: University of Michigan Press, 1986).

Giardinelli, Mempo, 'Reflections on Latin-American Narratives of the Post-Boom' (1994) in *Review: Literature and Arts of the Americas*, 29.52 (1996), 83–87.

Hutchings, Kimberley, *Hegel and Feminist Philosophy* (Cambridge: Polity Press, 2003).

Jeffers, Thomas L., *Apprenticeships: The Bildungsroman from Goethe to Santayana* (London: Palgrave Macmillan, 2005).

Kleinbord Labovitz, Esther, *The Missing Heroine: The Female Bildungsroman in the Twentieth Century: Dorothy Richardson, Simone de Beauvoir, Doris Lessing, Christa Wolf* (New York: Peter Lang, 1986).

Kontje, Todd, *Private Lives in the Public Sphere: The German Bildunsgroman as Metafiction* (Philadelphia, PA: Pennsylvania State University Press, 1992).

Kushigian, Julia A., *Reconstructing Childhood: Strategies of Reading for Culture and Gender in the Spanish American Bildungsroman* (Lewisburg, PA: Bucknell University Press, 2003).

Lagos, María Inés, *En tono mayor: Relatos de formación de protagonista femenina en Hispanoamérica* (Providencia: Editorial Cuarto Propio, 1996).

Labovitz, Esther Kleinbord, *The Missing Heroine: The Female Bildungsroman in the Twentieth Century: Dorothy Richardson, Simone de Beauvoir, Doris Lessing, Christa Wolf* (New York: Peter Lang, 1986).

Lazzaro-Weis, Carol, 'The Female "Bildungsroman": Calling It into Question', *NWSA Journal*, 2.1 (Winter 1990), 16–34.

Lukács, Gyorgy, *The Theory of the Novel: A Historic-Philosophical Essay on the Forms of Great Epic Literature* (London: Merlin Press, 1971).

Lutes, Leasa Y., *Allende, Buitrago, Luiselli: Aproximaciones teóricas al concepto del "Bildungsroman" femenino* (New York: Peter Lang, 2000).

McAleer, Paul, 'Transexual Identities in a Transcultural Context: Jaime Bayly's *La noche es virgen* and the Comic *Bildungsroman*', *Journal of Iberian and Latin American Studies*, 15.2/3 (August/December 2009), 179–198.

Miles, David H., 'The Pícaro's Journey to the Confessional: The Changing Image of the Hero in the German Bildungsroman', *PMLA*, 89.5 (October 1974), 980–992.

Moretti, Franco, *The Way of the World* (New York: Verso, 2000).

Peri Rossi, Cristina, *La nave de los locos* (Barcelona: Biblioteca del Bolsillo, 1984).

Rama, Ángel, 'Los contestatorios del poder', *La novela latinoamericana 1922–1980* (Bogota: Instituto Colombiano de Cultura, 1982).

Salih, Sara, *Judith Butler* (London: Routledge, 2002).

Shaw, Donald, *The Post-Boom in American Fiction* (Albany: State University of New York Press, 1998).

Singer, Jonathon, *Hegel: A Very Short Introduction* (Oxford: Oxford University Press, 2001).

Smith, John H., 'Cultivating Gender: Sexual Difference, *Bildung*, and the *Bildungsroman*', *Michigan Germanic Studies* 13.2 (Fall 1987), 206–225.

Swanson, Philip, *The New Novel in Latin America: Politics and Popular Culture after the Boom* (Manchester, UK: Manchester University Press, 1995).

Waugh, Patricia, *Feminine Fictions: Revisiting the Postmodern* (London: Routledge, 1989).

Williamson, Edwin, *The Penguin History of Latin America* (London: Penguin Books, 1992).

Part I

Construction

Archetype, Fairy Tale, Myth

1 Como agua para chocolate/ Like Water for Chocolate *by Laura Esquivel* (1989)

In *Como agua para chocolate*, Laura Esquivel presents her reader with a female Bildungsroman recounting the life—from birth to death at the age of thirty-nine—of Tita de la Garza, youngest daughter of the fearsome, widowed Mamá Elena, and youngest sister of Rosaura and Gertrudis. The fulcrum of the plot is the family tradition that dictates the youngest daughter must remain unmarried until her mother's death, essentially functioning as her personal servant. Tita's 'true love', Pedro, accepts to marry the eldest sibling Rosaura instead, so that he can at least remain close to the heartbroken protagonist. From this seminal moment onwards, a series of fantastical events punctuate and motivate the storyline and, as is clear from just this brief summary, the formulaic nature of the plot and the cast of characters recall the structures and archetypes of fairy tales and their antecedents—ancient myths and folklore both indigenous and postcolonial. My critical interest in gender in this novel brings together the Bildungsroman and these archetypal narratives because of their common didactic imperative, and for their shared role in the socialization of the individual. By reading it within the broader framework presented by *Gender and the Self in Latin American Literature*, and considering its contribution to the formulation of gender the novel is given a new context within which to be explored. In terms of how this is mapped out as a narrative of self-development, Tita is denied from the outset experience of the rites of passage that the traditional womanhood of her historical and sociocultural context would engage. As a consequence of this, if she is to avoid being emptied of personhood she must cut her own path. Tita seeks a way to self-actualization via recourse to the dominant models available to her, and is depicted as doing so through innovative and subtle manipulations of her situation, as well as via more outright challenges to the forces of oppression by which she is subjugated.

This portrayal of a character who at once achieves and fails to achieve liberation has been key in inspiring a deeply dichotomized critical response to Esquivel's novel. In broad terms, the work was 'universally panned by the male-dominated literary establishment as "lite lit"',[1] to quote Debra Castillo, and has also garnered disapproval among feminist literary critics for failing to challenge stereotypes. As an example of the former kind of critique, in her very useful summary of the wide range of academic studies on, and varied approaches taken to, Esquivel's oeuvre in general, Elizabeth Moore Willingham rightly highlights Antonio Marquet's extremely negative 1991 essay '¿Cómo escribir un best-seller? La receta de Laura Esquivel' ('How to Write a Bestseller?: Laura Esquivel's Recipe'),[2] as one that 'quickly took its place as the model negative review of *Como agua para chocolate*'. In it, Marquet levels at Esquivel accusations of presenting to her reader 'a flat world, observed from an angle—unjustifiably biased towards the protagonist—in which only black and white exist, with no nuance at all'.[3] As an example of negative feminist critiques, in turn, Diane Long Hoeveler's assessment of the novel speaks very clearly, also adopting a terminology derived directly from the narrative features of the text itself, which is structured around twelve cooking recipes (one for each month of the year). Like Marquet, she characterizes its 'ideological agenda' as the presentation of a 'recipe [...] for the construction of femininity'; 'the notion that women need to be the nurturers of both their culture and their families',[4] and summarizes the novel as recounting

> an old platonic story mediated by down-home recipes and Mexican kitsch. It is a hybridized commodity, a text that attempts to mediate and therefore obviate the insoluble dilemmas that both Western and Mexican patriarchies have constructed for women. But it is ultimately a depressing saga of women defeated by their bodies, and as such I think that *Like Water for Chocolate* is, at best, problematic as feminist fiction.[5]

Hoeveler's concern for the role of the female body here is interesting in light of the literary topoi with which this book is concerned, because it underlines the significance of that body as a locus for identity, an issue that is the primary concern of the final two chapters of this study. More immediately though, it also emphasizes the body as the site of definition in essentialist approaches to gendered identities, and an unease about the integration of such perspectives into Esquivel's novel.

In direct contrast to this reaction, but also extremely indicative of the roots of consternation about the novel's portrayal of normalized gendered identities and gender roles, we can take the example of Tony Spanos's reaction to the novel. For him it is an 'extraordinarily original' piece of writing generated

> as from a second uterus, which is the kitchen [space that] becomes different conflicting metaphors throughout the novel. Although this type of novelty may appear highly incompatible to many feminist critics, other women writers and women in general whose message is to reject patriarchal dominion and to move beyond the confines of domestic life, Esquivel reclaims the kitchen as a very serious domestic sphere

> which is the most sacred place in the house, and from which the protagonist controls her destiny through her recipes.[6]

It is rather difficult to grasp precisely what Spanos means when he says that Esquivel wrote the text 'as from a second uterus'. But his conceptual choice embraces as openly as the above critics reject the alignment of female identity with the domestic realm that makes the kitchen setting of the story one of its most hotly debated features.

My own approach to this story is akin to that of María Teresa Martínez-Ortiz, who neatly summarizes the issues at stake by saying:

> one can argue that Laura Esquivel's text is neither feminist nor anti-feminist but a complex hybrid novel that both resists and embraces traditional Mexican patriarchy. While the text cannot fit within the limits of radical feminism, it would also be problematic to remove [it] from feminist shelves.[7]

We also have in common an interest in archetypal and mythical references in the novel, an approach that necessarily entails engagement with the polarized responses to Esquivel's work, for they stem in large part from the text's intertwining of archetypal characterizations with the intention to instigate reenvisionings of social orders and symbolic economies. Interpreted by voices such as Marquet's as the creation of a 'flat' world, I find the myriad intertexts and intertwinings of archetypal, fairy tale and mythical points of reference for female identity found in the story to be precisely what generate within it a world of great depth and nuance. The simplicity of the narrative structure and fairy tale-esque writing style belie greater complexities framed therein. It is true that *Como agua…* does not provide answers to all the questions it poses, but the fact is that to ask questions at all is a vital first step in the identification of any problem, and in beginning to formulate responses to it.

It is noteworthy for me that Moore Willingham signals in her review chapter the need for 'a re-examination of reductionist efforts on Esquivel's fiction' and, as part of this, further applications of the perspectives of fairy tale criticism as a pertinent avenue of critical analysis,[8] for this chimes with my approaches to Esquivel's story within the threefold framework of this study. I believe it is particularly valuable to approach this narrative as one about the foundations of female identity both in terms of its revelation of platforms and constructions, and its initiation of their critique. The novel represents important first steps on the overall journey of *Bildung* engaged in by all of the works studied in this book, and this chapter explores the key rites of passage experienced by Tita as the heroine of this female Bildungsroman, and their interspersing with fairy tale and mythical archetypes: birth, loss and grief, motherhood, and madness or loss of self, are examined here through an approach that accounts for the story of development of selfhood that *Como agua…* tells, as well as for the foundational narratives of female selfhood upon which it draws, into which it feeds, and which it challenges.

SETTING UP CINDERELLA

Como agua para chocolate begins at the very beginning, with its protagonist's birth. Read against the frame of the classical Bildungsroman, this is a narrative shift that belies an interest in the earlier formative years; in the period when children are most reliant on adult intervention for survival and for an initiation into the project of selfhood. So rather than begin in early adolescence, when she has already undergone a number of important developments, as would a prototypical Bildungsroman narrative,[9] Esquivel accounts for her main character's entrance into this world, and establishes thereby a set of qualities the reader quickly grasps as tinged with fairy tale qualities:

> Tita arribó a este mundo prematuramente, sobre la mesa de la cocina, entre los olores de una sopa de fideos que se estaba cocinando, los del tomillo, el laurel, el cilantro, el de la leche hervida, el de los ajos y, por supuesto, el de la cebolla […] [L]a consabida nalgada no fue necesaria pues Tita nació llorando de antemano, tal vez porque ella sabía que su oráculo determinaba que en esta vida le estaba negado el matrimonio. Contaba Nacha que Tita fue literalmente empujada a este mundo por un torrente impresionante de lágrimas que se desbordaron sobre la mesa y el piso de la cocina.[10]
>
> Tita made her entrance into this world prematurely, upon the kitchen table, amidst the smells of the noodle soup that was cooking, of thyme, of bay leaf, of coriander, of boiling milk, of garlic and of course, of onion […] [T]he usual slap on the bottom was not necessary because Tita was already crying, perhaps because she knew that her destiny in life was to be forbidden to marry. As Nacha used to tell it, Tita was literally pushed into this world by an immense torrent of tears that overflowed onto the table and floor.

The youngest daughter confined to the kitchen space and kept removed from social rites of passage usual to her culture and class, Tita is established from the start as a Mexican take on Cinderella. And of course this is further compelled by the hyperbolic depiction of her arrival into this world upon a flood of tears—a key motif in early versions of Cinderella, as I shall discuss—and through references to mystical notions of 'oracles' and 'destinies'.

Given Esquivel's training and work as a kindergarten teacher before embarking on her writing career, it is perhaps not surprising that she found in fairy tales a compelling resource for her depiction of Mexican female

Bildung. The clearly evident Cinderella intertext has been noted in numerous studies of the novel, and discussed in some depth by critics such as Cherie Meacham in her interesting article '*Como agua para chocolate*: Cinderella and the Revolution'. Meacham encapsulates the dualistic nature of critical reactions to this aspect of the novel by considering 'the tension between elements [of it] that inscribe patriarchal tradition and those that transcend and transform it in Esquivel's Mexican version of the European folktale'.[11] In fact, this facet of Esquivel's narrative has become one of the most widely critiqued elements of her writing, informing negative perspectives on the novel along the lines of Marquet's, cited above, for being a simplistic work filled with the kind of stock characters whose dichotomized portrayals allow no room for nuance, and therefore problematize any engagement with the complexities of non-essentialized gender identities.

Whether deemed positive or negative, however, the fairy tale intertext remains important at the levels of both genre and gender: as far as the former is concerned because it establishes a literary and canonical frame to which the narrative can speak, thereby articulating its generic identity as well as its fracturing of that mold. Here, however, I wish to develop the application of the Cinderella reference as a frame of analysis specifically for gender and within the context of the narrative of self-development, because it is so key in terms of how we engage with the female protagonist. It locates Tita and her *Bildung* within the domestic sphere and informs it with all of the issues that this implies when seen from more radical feminist perspectives: a life of confinement and drudgery, a lack of autonomy and recognition, limited power, and expectations of passivity. It establishes, or at least appears to, a destiny of precisely the type that women writers have long sought to challenge, and for that reason, as Meacham neatly summarizes, 'while recognizing subversive elements in the original content of these stories, most feminists tend to view their more contemporary versions as vehicles of traditional engendering'.[12] Leading on from this, of course, the integration of the Cinderella framework also sets up the roles of those characters who accompany Tita throughout her self-development, allocating the role of 'Wicked Stepmother' to Mamá Elena, establishing Rosaura as the 'Ugly Sister', Nacha as the 'Fairy Godmother' and Pedro as the 'Prince Charming'. It also, therefore, establishes another important dimension of the narrative—the romance plot that has, too, been deemed especially problematic by feminist critiques, because it is that dimension of the fairy tale genre that most strongly infuses it with conservative gender ideals.

Clearly, the split critical reaction to Esquivel's fairy tale intertext is partly informed by the broader context of feminist fairy tale studies that Meacham refers to; a field that has itself generated readings as polarized as the reactions incited by Esquivel's novel. These debates have been examined in detail and very usefully summarized, for example, in Donald Haase's edited volume *Fairytales and Feminism: New Approaches* (2004). In a debate that Haase traces back to the 1970s, the tales have been seen as stories that either perpetuate essentialist notions of femininity, implying a limited range of expectations both social and individual of what role women can, and should, play in their own lives and communities, or as texts that function 'as a mirror of the forces limiting women [that then] makes it possible to project alternative ways of constructing lives'.[13] Thus, while Meacham is absolutely right to underscore the existence of different responses to the stories, I am wary of the claim that 'most feminists' focus on the negative repercussions of later incarnations at the expense of seeking out the meanings of the original folk tales. In contrast, and given my interests here in notions of origins and legacies, my focus will be on excavating the foundations of the original tales as they appear in Esquivel's multigenre, multilayered story.

For these reasons, Jack Zipes's more optimistic work on the fairy tale genre provides an important analytical frame of reference here. Zipes clearly sees these narratives as capable of instigating social change, not simply as tools for the propagation of damaging and restrictive stereotypes. He writes in his seminal study *Fairy Tales and the Art of Subversion* (1983; 2012), that 'Fairy tales are predicated on a human disposition to social action—to transform the world and make it more adaptable to human needs while we try to change and make ourselves fit for the world'.[14] His description immediately calls to mind the dialogue between self and society that is at the center of the Bildungsroman narrative also, and this is furthered when he goes on to explain how the tales 'can be both provocative and traditional' and have been 'used by different social institutions, writers, artists, to either bring about conformity or to question conformity to the dominant civilizing processes of a society'.[15]

To my mind the fairy tale inferences of Esquivel's text need appreciating as an element of her more general Post-Boom, postmodernist technique of genre-blending and subsequent deconstruction of canonical norms, furthering her social critique far more than it plays into the hands of dominant ideas on gender. I do not challenge the claim that the story is populated with archetypes, therefore, because I see this as purposeful, not problematic:

> The term *archetype* derives from the Greek *archi*, a beginning or first instance, and *typos*, a stamp, and denotes the primordial form, the original, of a series of variations. This etymology contributes to a confusion between *archetype* and *stereotype*, a printing term designating the original plate from which subsequent imprints are made and connoting an excessively rigid set of generalizations [my emphases].[16]

Annis Pratt's reminder of the actual implications of any accusation of resorting to 'archetypes' is helpful here in addressing fears of their constrictive presence. In particular, the words emphasized in the above citation facilitate an engagement with archetypes in Esquivel's text that does not imply a signaling of rigid forms, but rather points of reference along a trajectory of development. And so we also need to dispel the myth that looking backwards for influence or inspiration is an inherently conservative act. As we shall see as this chapter progresses, to look to the past in order to uncover now hidden meanings can be an act of empowerment that ultimately undermines the negative implication of tradition in the construction of gender roles and social structures.

Indeed, I would argue that further evidence for this is found in the fact of Esquivel's choosing a historical setting for her story. As a writer clearly interested in the position of women in Mexican society, and in the reasons for their contemporary situation, the decision to set her narrative in the past surely implies both a desire to explore previous sociocultural arenas in order to establish the links between those and the present day, as well as to insert an objective distance between the time in which the text is set and its contemporary readership. It therefore does not make sense to worry that her archetypal cast presents unhelpful models for gendered selfhood. Instead it is much more useful to assume the historical setting and the archetypal dimensions of Tita and her fellow characters are part of a literary strategy designed to reveal both the foundations of gendered identity and the important fact of the legacy of historical versions of womanhood for the lives of her intended readership; for their own *Bildung*.

LOCATING CINDERELLA

Returning to the matter of Tita's birth, there are two main aspects to focus on here: its setting in the domestic realm, and the tears (or, more broadly, water) motif that is first introduced in this scene. To begin with the matter of the kitchen space, this is clearly fundamental to a story whose entire structure is predicated on the activities of that arena. By locating her birth there, Esquivel takes that space as the very foundation of Tita's identity, and thereby pins her narrative to the domestic realm as a foundational context for womanhood. And while the contemporary reader might feel that this offers us, therefore, an antiquated character (in spite of the novel's early twentieth century setting lending historical realism to this), it would be unreasonable to deny that this context continues to inform present-day female identities. Moreover, it is this kitchen setting that enables us to begin tracing the Cinderella intertext in meaningful ways, by linking it to Esquivel's reclaiming of the negativized domestic realm: in a number of interviews the author has affirmed her own belief in the importance of the domestic sphere as a base (not a basis) for the formation of female identity. She has commented that the feminist movements of the sixties and seventies, in which she took part, devalued 'all that was connected to the feminine, with the direct relationship with the earth, with maternity, with emotion, with the home because all of the activities that were carried out within the realm of the homespace had no economic return'.[17] She has also made direct reference to the kitchen as a place which she holds in great regard, 'a sacred place [...] a constant source of knowledge, of pleasure [...] a generating center of life'.[18] In another interview, she describes how the desire for change led to a movement away from the homespace that was, ultimately, fruitless:

> Women didn't go outside the home until my generation. We put our hopes in the public world. We thought the things worth fighting for were outside the home, not inside. We went outside to change that world and we were hoping that a New Man, with a capital M, was going to emerge from that world. But, of course, now we're living in disillusionment because we're realizing that this didn't happen. Now we understand that the system and the progress that we established is, in fact, destroying us. [...] We wanted a New Man who would value things differently, who would value life, who would value every act in the home. We did not want the destruction of the public world, and in reaction to that, we're turning back into the private world. What we're finding is that our private world, our own homes, will remind us where we are from, where we are going, and who we are.[19]

In many ways, then, the focus on the interior as opposed to the exterior realm in her novel appears to be a direct response to what she has experienced as the failures of a particular kind of feminism, and a portrayal of a consequential, necessary, regression inwards towards a zone in which female identity may be grounded, and then rewritten for the better.

At this juncture it is worth taking stock of the kinds of feminist perspectives that can be understood to inform this standpoint, so as to better understand how the reclaiming of the Cinderella paradigm within this specific Latin American context can function as a feminist strategy. *Como agua para chocolate* was written during and published right at the end of 'The Decade of Women', inaugurated in Mexico City in 1975, a period which Asunción Lavrin explains

> forced women of the so-called third-world to reexamine the meaning of feminism as it was then debated by North American and northern European women and to develop a 'position' that would reflect what they perceived to be their distinct cultural traditions and socioeconomic situation.[20]

Thus, at a time when her compatriots across Latin America found themselves struggling for basic civil liberties in a period of widespread military dictatorship, and whose active involvement in a specifically feminist agenda was massively constrained, Esquivel was living in one of the two countries that became a focus for the study of the development of Spanish American feminism (the other being Peru).[21] In light of the varied sociopolitical and national contexts of the region in the decade when Anglo-American and European feminist ideas were reaching those Latin American women in a position to access them, that feminism 'blazed a different trail' in Latin

America is logical,[22] and important to account for in feminist literary criticism, because 'Sharing the ideas of feminist writers in North American and Europe helped to clarify issues, but it did not mean an unquestioned acceptance of their strategies and objectives'.[23] Latin American feminist strategies needed to engage with the conceptualization of gender as it was enacted locally:

> Chief among the contextual factors affecting the specificity of writings on women and gender have been the concepts of *machismo* and its counterpart *marianismo*, a dyad closely connected to the public and private spheres of influence and authority, the private sphere as the site of the home, the public the site of all other social intercourse (Stevens, 1973). *Machismo*, the superevaluation of male qualities, was said to invite and to support the physical and cultural domination of female by male and to color all acts of men outside the home. *Machos* have 'balls' [...] and must prove their masculinity under all circumstances, in their sexual relations as well as in politics, business or work. Accepting their subordination to men in the public sphere, women are assumed to exercise power and authority in the private sphere, even though men are still recognized as the head of the family unit. Moreover, women must display the feminine behavior that counterbalances the masculinity of men [my emphases].[24]

Lavrin's summation of these two key characteristics of gender role formulation in Esquivel's homeland provides especially useful insights into the workings of *Como agua...* It neatly encapsulates the gender-relevant social structures, concepts and ideologies that informed a feminist belief that 'women are as *good* as men but not the *same* as men', so that instead of 'demanding complete equality' women 'advocated strengthening their power and prestige through traditional paradigms of gender, notably motherhood'.[25]

This approach is surely at work in the novel's effective removal of male characters (either through their depiction *in absentia*, or through the weakening of their roles through negative character portrayal), and population with a cast of females the most central of whom is also placed at the center of the homespace—an act now visible as tantamount to the role of women in society being placed at the heart of the narrative. Thus, when the novel does engage with direct comparison of women with men, it does so by signaling the capabilities of women as equally important to those of men but, with the exception of the important narrative thread carried by Gertrudis, the feminized power base of the homestead is portrayed as the location from which women can effect social change. In terms of Anglo-American feminist criticism it might be argued that this approach finds a counterpart in the third of Elaine Showalter's three stages of feminism, outlined in *Towards a Feminist Poetics* (1979); 'The Female Phase' of 1920 onwards in which 'women reject both imitation and protest—two forms of dependency—and turn instead to female experience as the source of an autonomous art'.[26] For this is precisely what the character of Tita achieves.

As further consolidation of this homegrown approach to feminism as an adopted strategy within the novel, Maria Elisa Christie's extremely interesting anthropological reading of *Como agua*... contributes a great deal. Christie establishes connections between the real-life Mexican kitchen spaces in which she has carried out fieldwork—the rites and rituals surrounding them, their relationship with gender roles in Mexican communities—and the story told to us by Esquivel. Her research underlines that it is all too easy to denigrate the kitchen space as a strategy for inciting gender equality if we approach it from only one feminist angle, and is both compelling and comforting in its pragmatism: an important reminder that feminist theories must also be applicable in practice if they are to serve their purpose, whereas at times it becomes difficult to envisage the connections between the complex theorizations of academia and the daily realities of the lives of women for whom such theories purport to speak. Christie references, for example, a series of studies since the 1980s that have demonstrated that food-related topics 'present exceptional opportunities for the investigation of social and cultural transformations', because 'food is an expression of cultural identity and both the kitchen and daily life are spaces in which individuals express their desires and preferences, just as they resist the forces that transform their social environment'.[27] Very usefully, Christie cites Sherry B. Ortner's argument that resistance should be conceived of as much more than straightforward opposition or reaction to domination; it is qualified by 'ambiguousness and ambiguities' that

> emerge from the intricate webs of articulations and disarticulations that always exist between dominant and dominated. For the politics of external domination and the politics within a subordinated group may link up with, as well as repel, one another; the cultures of dominant groups and of subalterns may speak to, even while speaking against, one another; and [...] subordinated selves may retain oppositional authenticity and agency by drawing on aspects of the dominant culture to criticize their own world as well as the situation of domination. In short, one can only appreciate the ways in which resistance can be more than opposition, can be truly creative and transformative, if one appreciates the multiplicity of projects in which social beings are always engaged, and the multiplicity of ways in which those projects feed on and well as collide with one another.[28]

In other words, we do not necessarily have to reject all of what came before in order to transform the present moment—rather, we also have the option of transfiguring the available material or offering up new perspectives on it.

Offering a more purely artistic take on this same idea, María Elena de Valdés echoes Ortner's approach by integrating the notion of reclaiming existing spaces of creativity into a consideration of the literary strategies used in *Como agua...*, writing that

> Women's recuperation of artistic creativity within the confinement of the house, and especially the kitchen and bedroom, is presented by Esquivel not in an ideological argument but rather by means of an intertextual palimpsest which is the hallmark of modern art. I want to conclude with three observations on feminist art in this context. 1) This is not a protest movement; it is a celebration of the space of one's own which may have been hidden from view in the past but is now open to all. 2) At the center of postmodernism there is the vesting of creative weight on the reader, and this makes intertextuality a means of providing an interpretative context [...] 3) The maturity of feminist criticism has moved beyond the need to go headhunting among the misogynist hordes of patriarchy; the challenge today is to celebrate women's creativity in the full domain of the human adventure, from the so-called decorative arts to the fine arts and science'.[29]

What all this means is that even before we begin to consider the underlying, original folk tale, if we are sensitive to the particularities of her milieu we might see the Cinderella paradigm as offering Esquivel a series of contexts, symbols and metaphors that are highly relatable within the Mexican female and/or feminist setting, and that interact with rites of female passage that continue to bear relevance therein even while other feminist perspectives might see these as obsolete.

DECONSTRUCTING CINDERELLA

It is possible to take the Cinderella paradigm as a tool with which to start challenging the disparagement of the domestic realm Esquivel depicts because a consideration of the original narrative, and specifically of the symbolism of the cinders of the hearth from which Cinderella gets her name, requires us to think again about its negative connotations, and to consider the tale in parallel with the arguments made above regarding the subversive possibilities of the kitchen space. In his seminal work *The Uses of Enchantment: The Meaning and Importance of Fairy Tales* (1975), Bruno Bettelheim reminds us of key changes to this motif, undergone as part of the transformation of the oral folk tale into a literary fairy tale, carried out in the late eighteenth century by writers such as Charles Perrault in France, and the Brothers Grimm in Germany. To summarize his key points regarding this, we first need to be aware that 'Long before Perrault gave "Cinderella" the form in which it is now widely known, "having to live among the ashes" was a symbol of being debased in comparison to one's siblings, *irrespective of sex* [my emphases]'.[30] Secondly, where there were gendered associations with the symbolism of the ashes, these were actually positive, not negative, and Bettelheim attributes the shift towards their function as a symbol of debasement to Perrault's patriarchalization of the original, orally transmitted folk tales upon which the French writer's modern texts were based. He then goes on to emphasize the role of ashes in cultural ceremonies of grieving and of ablution because of the association of fire with purification, and says that 'these connotations to purity and to deep mourning' found in the original Italian folktale, for example, have been transformed into their exact opposites, now 'referring to blackness and dirtiness'.[31]

The loss of these more positive characteristics compounds the association of the kitchen space with a life of debasement and drudgery. Again, then, the more ancient associations seem far more fitting to the fictional world created by Esquivel and to her desire to revalue the hearth, and the domestic realm for which it stands as metonym. Bettelheim also then reminds us that 'Cinderella's living among the ashes [...]—from which she derives her name—is a detail of great complexity', for 'in ancient times to be the guardian of the hearth—the duty of the Vestal Virgins—was one of the most prestigious ranks':

> The Vestal Virgins served the sacred hearth and Hera, the mother goddess. With the change to a father god, the old maternal deities were degraded and devalued, as was a place close to the hearth. In this sense Cinderella might also be seen as the degraded mother goddess who at the end of the story is reborn out of the ashes, like the mythical bird phoenix. But these are connections of a historical nature which the average hearer of 'Cinderella' will not readily establish in his [sic] mind.[32]

To hark back to *this* meaning of the name Cinderella and her association with the hearth entirely changes the perspective we might take on Tita's relegation to the kitchen space, and it makes sense, in light of Esquivel's comments above, to assume this more ancient association as part of any reading of her own narrative. Indeed, another compelling addition to this interpretation of Tita's location in the heart of the domestic realm is that the story ends precisely with her cookbook among the only surviving remnants of the great fire that destroys the ranch; her legacy for future generations lying among the now more positivized ashes of its remains, which are said to create immensely fertile land upon which flourished all kinds of life forms and nourishing foodstuffs. The notion that a freer form of womanhood might be nourished by the legacy of Tita's own life is symbolized by her great-niece, whose voice initiates and ends the narrative. The inference of this young woman's voice being our guide through the novel, reading aloud from her aunt's cookbook-cum-diary, gives Esquivel's story an implied orality that harks back to the original nature of the folktales from which the modern fairy tale evolved, as well as invoking and intertwining itself with the oral narrative history of the indigenous cultures of her homeland, and of the women's culture that, according to de Valdés, functions also as a template for this multigenre work: she writes that the novel is a parody of the nineteenth century genre of 'Mexican women's fiction published in monthly installments together with [the] recipes [and] home remedies' of *Como agua...*'s subtitle. 'Cooking, sewing, embroidery, and decoration were the usual creative outlets for these women', she writes, 'and of course [they shared] conversation, storytelling, gossip, and advice', so that 'Writing for other women was quite naturally an extension of this infrahistorical conversation'.[33]

INHERITANCE AND LEGACY

Interestingly, Valdés notes that she has herself inherited a handwritten, hand-sewn nineteenth century Mexican cookbook that closely mirrors the structure of Esquivel's novel, with the 'recipes and home remedies [...] all presented through a running narrative'.[34] And she thereby introduces with a real-life example the question of legacy to which I now wish to turn; the matter of how the life lessons of each generation were transmitted to the next as a positive legacy deeply rooted in the traditionally female realm embraced in the novel as a space of contestation and transformation. The positive legacy that Tita is said to leave for her great-niece and other future generations is central to my location of Esquivel's work in this first stage of the journey of *Bildung* mapped out in this project, just as it is fundamental to the originally intended messages carried within the Cinderella plot. The notion of legacy or inheritance unites the varied archetypal versions of female selfhood that are interwoven into Esquivel's plot and characterization, because it is what they all form a part of for modern versions of womanhood. To read *Como agua...* for this thematic concern throws into relief the varied and numerous ways in which the novel engages the importance of historical archetypes in the construction of individual and social identity categories, as well as that of intergenerational relationships, particularly between mothers and daughters, in sustaining or changing those.

The Cinderella intertext plays a significant role in this because of the modern version's shift of focus away from the matter of sibling rivalry and towards the antagonistic relationship between stepmother and child, and the child's subsequent fight for recognition. Just as in *Como agua...*, the stepmother figure of the fairy tale narrative embodies dominant social values and works to propagate these by ensuring the successful integration of her own daughters into a patriarchal system. As has been explored in depth in critical analyses of the novel, the character of Mamá Elena is the absolute embodiment of the culturally- and historically-specific patriarchy of revolutionary Mexico, the *Porfiriato*, and the legacy that she intends for her daughters is one that sees them adhere to the rules and regulations of that ideological affiliation in ways even she has not been able to—for it is revealed throughout the course of the story that Mamá Elena's own first love was one that transgressed racial boundaries as well as those pertaining to her gender role and social class. Forbidden by her parents to marry the man who was in fact Gertrudis's father, just as she forbids Tita to be with Pedro, she married Juan de la Garza but continued an affair with her own choice of partner. It is said that revelation of this secret induced the heart attack that killed Tita's father and left her a widow, and this subplot complicates a character who would otherwise substantiate the critique leveled at Esquivel's work for being populated with one-dimensional figures. The psychological complexities of a mother who chooses to impose on her own daughters an iron rule akin to that which has so negatively impacted her own life are great. For although Mamá Elena's personal history is not fully revealed until the second half of the story, it is nonetheless a subplot enabling the reader to examine her more meaningfully. She is not the inexplicably nasty stepmother archetype of the traditional Cinderella narrative, but rather a person who has made the bad decision to respond to oppression by becoming the oppressor. Also signaling the matriarch as an example of Esquivel's challenging of gender essentialism, Gaston Lillo and Monique Safarti-Arnaud pertinently highlight that it is she, not a man, who imposes the 'Law of the Father'.[35] Inserted as they are into *Como agua…* these implicit complexities render the Cinderella reference all the more interesting, especially when read through a feminist lens and for the thematic thread of legacy, because they emphasize the role of women in the oppression of women.

Another dimension of intrigue vis-à-vis Mamá Elena's hyperbolic nastiness is the fact that, according to Bettelheim, the good mother and the bad mother are actually the same person. Their division into separate elements responds to the difficulty for the child's mind to handle ambiguity, and thus enables the eventual acceptance of contradictory facets in the same parent; the chastising and the loving figure.[36] Mapped onto the historical archetypal legacies for women offered by the Mexican national imaginary, this Manichean division of good from bad finds a clear parallel in the figures of La virgin de Guadalupe and La Malinche, who embody the virgin/whore dichotomy outlined in Octavio Paz's seminal treatise on Mexican national identity, *The Labyrinth of Solitude* (1950). Through the opposing figures of Mamá Elena and Tita, therefore, we encounter strong inflections of an approach to female *mexicanidad* that echoes Paz's deconstruction of Mexican national identity at large, through a focus on the history of the nation, and in particular of the role of Malinche as *la chingada:*

> Who is the *Chingada*? Above all, she is the mother. Not a mother of flesh and blood but a mythical figure. The *Chingada* is one of the Mexican representations of Maternity, like *La Llorona* or the "long-suffering Mexican mother" we celebrate on the tenth of May. The *Chingada* is the mother who has suffered—metaphorically or

> actually—the corrosive and defaming action implicit in the verb that gives her her name.[37]

In light of this cultural and literary reference, a further challenge to the accusation of over-simplistic characterization is that the good mother figure in Esquivel's text is embodied by the indigenous figure of Nacha, who, when read within the frame of the fairy tale intertext, is a reiteration of the classical Fairy Godmother for Tita's idiosyncratic Cinderella. The creation of this role for Nacha reads, therefore, as a move to rewrite the particular dichotomies of Mexican womanhood as dictated by the figures of the Virgin of Guadalupe and la Malinche—the former 'to make us docile and enduring', the latter 'to make us ashamed of our Indian side', in the words of Chicana writer Gloria Anzaldúa.[38]

Replacing the negative figure of betrayal embedded in the national imaginary, in *Como agua...* the indigenous mother is a figure whose sustained positive influence—and its eventual internalization, as we shall come to explore—is absolutely crucial to the project of self-development embarked upon by the protagonist. Furthermore, this reading challenges the criticism, by some, of the text as failing to meaningfully represent the social structures of postcolonial Mexico, awarding only minor roles to characters that represent the discriminatory racial dimensions of the class system. For example, in her interesting and forceful critique of the novel, Maite Zubiaurre writes that the kitchen space in which Tita and Nacha's relationship is forged is 'unavoidably subjected to a strict hierarchical structure' that is organized around 'the cook and her pupil', but where it is the pupil who has authority over her teacher because, despite everything Nacha teaches Tita, she ultimately remains her servant. 'Of course', Zubiaurre writes, 'all this boils down to the fact that Nacha [is] indigenous, a "destabilizing" circumstance typical of colonized countries and of postcolonialism', and so:

> Tita does not converse democratically with Nacha, nor is the kitchen a site that guaranties absolute solidarity, congeniality, and a sense of community among women. In this case the discrimination and marginalizing of the white affluent woman (Tita) cannot be equated with the much deeper discrimination of the Indian woman (Nacha), even if they cook at the same stove and apparently speak the same culinary language.[39]

While I take her point that discrimination is a nuanced act, it is also possible to argue that the legacy of postcolonialism and in particular of the negative portrayal of the indigenous highlighted in Anzaldúa's above-cited description in *Borderlands/La Frontera: The New Mestiza* (1983) is undercut here, by the deeply positive heritage that Tita gains from Nacha. I do not mean to imply that Esquivel has fully addressed the deeply rooted racial dynamics of postcolonial Mexico—had this been an intention she would surely have written a very different story—but certainly we can say that she has not forcefully propagated these, and find defense for this statement in the continued implication of the Cinderella text in the novel. For as Meacham summarizes, the

> beneficent power that Tita learns from these women of historically oppressed groups offers an alternative to the hierarchical power wielded by Mamá Elena [...] The maternal traditions of love and power are reunited in Tita to provide a reformed image of non-biological nurturing, "based upon a pre-patriarchal knowledge that can be passed from woman to woman in a commitment to fully human values."[40]

If we do take Nacha as a positivized integration of the Malinche archetype into the text via the role of the fairy godmother, it then becomes possible also to recognize other more positive mythical associations and to read her as a wonderful combination of archetypal female figures. For example, María Teresa Martínez Ortiz argues that we can compare Guadalupe and Malinche to the Roman hunter goddess Artemis and goddess of wisdom and handicraft Athena, in line with Shinoda Bolen's reminder that they were 'called virgin goddesses because they represent the independent, self-sufficient qualities in women'.[41] Taking her lead from this, Martínez Ortiz goes on to say that what is

> consistently overlooked by Mexican tradition is the indisputable fact that both Malinche and Guadalupe had attained fame through military and political national and even trans-national enterprises: Malinche as the Indian interpreter in the conquest [...] and Guadalupe since the independence of Mexico all the way to contemporary rallies and protests in defense of undocumented workers in the U.S.[42]

TEARS AND TRANSFORMATIONS

The journey towards such self-sufficiency is connected in both the Cinderella story and *Como agua...* to the tears motif to which we will now turn. Introduced in the birth scene, and continuing to play a role in various key episodes of her life, the motif appears throughout Tita's story, and its importance can be further clarified by reference to premodern versions of the folk tale. There, as Bettelheim tells us, the tears cried by Cinderella as she grieves for her lost good mother nourish a tree that she plants on her mother's grave—a potent symbol of growth and development highly apt to the Bildungsroman and that remains attached to the positive maternal figure.[43] In *Como agua...* this trope is borrowed and reworked as one that the reader comes to associate with Tita's various rites of passage. The second time we read of her crying is when she can no longer refrain from expressing her emotional response to being forced to bake the wedding cake for her sister's marriage to Pedro. Vitally, these tears, as Meacham has also observed, are the initiation of Tita's magical powers:[44] her ability to transmit her feelings to other people is revealed by the wave of sadness and anguish experienced by the guests at the wedding, ruining the party by means of its purgative effects, but allowing her to somehow express her torment. And while the dominant romantic plot encourages a reading of this devastation as wrought, above all, by her frustrated love, the fact is that a more psychologically realist reading would underline also that Tita's distress is directed at her oppressive mother and, by extension, at the patriarchal order that the latter embodies, promotes, defends. And rightly so, for the narrative proves for the reader that even the men in power within that system, like Pedro, are constricted in their movements. It is easy to judge Pedro as a facile character too weak to challenge Mamá Elena's iron will; a Prince without power (and Esquivel gives us no reason to believe that she wants us to see him any other way). But given what his mother-in-law represents, what Pedro is really at a loss to challenge is the system that defines him as male, attributes him qualities accordingly, and regulates his behavior through that artificially imposed role. He is as entrapped by the honor code that Mamá Elena has learned to embody and make work to her benefit as Tita is by the codification of female identity through the framework of *Marianismo* that rewards silent suffering over proactivity.

Reading between the lines in *Como agua…*, therefore, just as Bettelheim and Zipes argue we should examine the modernized versions of the fairy tales in order to uncover and recover their originally intended lessons, it is possible to ascertain a more complex social critique than that belied by the surface plot. And this is continued by the wedding cake episode's functioning as a vital rite of passage. This is the last dish that Tita will be helped to cook in person by her fairy godmother figure. When, that night, Nacha dies of a broken heart, having also finally capitulated to the accumulated sadnesses of her own life (which surely speak metonymically not only of gender-related injustices but also those informed by class and race), Tita's first step into her adult role is taken when she assumes control of the ranch kitchen. And certainly, the chapter that follows the wedding banquet persists in reminding the reader of the foundational role of indigenous cultures in the creation of modern day Mexican culture, because it sustains Nacha's presence as an underlying factor in one of the story's most infamous episodes and the various positive outcomes of those: the 'Quail in Rose Petal Sauce' recipe, whispered to Tita by Nacha's ghost, in which she turns a gift of roses from Pedro into an exquisite meal. One of the most remarked upon parts of the narrative because of its magical realism and because of the hyperbolic romanticism of what occurs, the episode begins when Tita clutches the bouquet of flowers too hard to her chest following Mamá Elena's order to destroy the 'inappropriate' gift, and her blood soaks into the flowers, turning them from white to red. Here, Esquivel imbues the storyline with reappropriated Catholic religious symbolism and heightens Tita's mystical qualities by portraying the originally white petals as a receptacle for her life force—they become a combination of the communion wafer representative of the body of Christ, and the wine meant to symbolize his blood. The dish she creates with those blood-infused flowers emits to all who eat it the passion that she feels for Pedro, and her sister Gertrudis is catalyzed into escaping from the ranch by an overwhelming desire to seek out physical sexual pleasure. In terms of orthodox symbolism, therefore, the purifying and life-giving qualities of the blood of Christ are borrowed from the communion ritual and turned into a ritual of communication; one that motivates Gertrudis herself to seek to bleed—to lose the mark of virginity that, within the social structures embodied by the ranch and its inhabitants, preserves her place within socially acceptable womanhood.

In many ways Gertrudis represents the reclamation of female sexuality as a key stage in feminist endeavors to redress social control of women's bodies, itself in turn a crucial element in achieving gender equality. For later we learn that she has worked as a prostitute not dominantly for economic purposes but in the aim of satisfying the desire initiated in her during the rose petal meal, before going on to join the Revolutionary forces as one of the legendary Mexican *Guerrilleras*—she returns to the ranch as *Generala* of a band of men, thus depicted to have asserted herself within the highly masculinized arena of the Revolution. In terms of the notions of legacy that I have signaled, what this episode means too, then, is that while Tita never liberates herself *per se*, with the help of the positivized indigenous legacy embodied by Nacha, which underpins the reformulation of Catholic symbolism and the ideals that it effects in relation to women's roles, she begins to formulate a legacy of her own by handing to her middle sibling the opportunity to challenge *beyond* the domestic sphere constrictions that she is more quietly unpicking from within the homespace. Thus, from the point of view of my interest in rites of passage, this part of the story encapsulates and transforms a variety of key moments in Mexican female culture: the step into adult life made by Tita's becoming the ranch cook (a position of responsibility and relative autonomy); the Catholic rite of first communion, and first sexual experiences.

MOTHERHOOD AND MADNESS

If we imagine that the love story of the novel had remained straightforward and conventional, the next step in Tita's journey would certainly have been motherhood. And this does become an extremely important feature of her journey of self-development, despite the fact that she never has children: Tita's love and affection for Pedro and Rosaura's son Roberto surpasses the usual aunt-nephew relationship when she effectively becomes his wet nurse. An extension of her role as nourisher of all the ranch inhabitants, and a repetition of sorts of the role that Nacha carried out for her when her own mother was unable to feed her as a child, this occurrence takes on more miraculous proportions when Tita physically produces milk, despite remaining a virgin. Her depiction as a kind of virgin mother is a continuation of the communion theme discussed above, and so further borrowings from archetypal female figures are intertwined in Esquivel's depiction of her protagonist. Then, this multifaceted implication in Tita of the different legacies by which female selfhood is informed, is added to yet again by the description of Tita 'like Ceres personified, the Goddess of plenty'.[45] Now fully realized as a woman when read within the framework of idealized Mexican womanhood, Tita embodies every essential quality: the virginal mother, the guardian of the homespace, the source of sustenance physical and spiritual through which all will survive. As Zubiaurre emphasizes, however, this portrayal might seem to counter the liberation from conservative gender roles that I am arguing Esquivel carries out.[46] The scene therefore leads us back to the conundrum of what Esquivel is trying to do via her depiction of that womanhood: when summed up thusly, it is difficult not to read the text's intended message as the encouragement of a hagiographic vision of a sanctified female identity and correlative social role thoroughly located within the domestic sphere. The protagonist of this novel is certainly not going out into the world and forcefully challenging hegemonic sociocultural orders.

To hold onto my earlier defense of the story's intentions being those of the proper valuing of the centrality of the homespace and all of the work and identities related to that, however, enables a rereading of Tita's unusual engagement with the rite of passage of motherhood in light of the child's death. In the portrayal of that event, the depth of grief that Tita feels precipitates a change in direction for her own future, and this is only made possible by her investment in the role of mother. In other words, it is the legacy of the experience of motherhood that incites Tita's engagement with her future as one in which she can effect change not only for herself but beyond herself. She will do *on purpose* for future generations of women in her family what she only did by accident for Gertrudis, and this is a step towards the consciousness of self and action, of self-knowledge and self-actualization, that is central to this novel's place in the process of *Bildung* explored in this book. It begins when Tita discovers that Roberto has died of malnutrition following Mamá Elena having sent Pedro and Rosaura away, thus to defend the family reputation against any transgressions on the part of her son-in-law and youngest daughter. Agitated by this news into outrightly challenging her mother's authority, and after Elena's violent response, Tita carries herself and a baby pigeon she has been nurturing (a stand-in for her nephew since their separation) up to the enormous ranch dovecote, to take refuge. Mamá Elena orders the ladder removed and abandons her daughter to what she assumes will be a period of reflection on her unacceptable behavior. What instead happens is that Tita refuses to come down even when allowed, and is eventually recovered by the local American doctor, John Brown, who discovers her 'naked, her nose broken, her whole body covered with pigeon droppings. A few feathers [...] clinging to her skin and hair', and running to assume the fetal position when he appears.[47] Archetypally, Tita has become the madwoman in the attic, at the 'impasse confronting those whom cultural conditioning has deprived of the very means of protest or self-affirmation'.[48]

This often overlooked moment in the narrative is fascinating when considered for its intertextual references and possible interpretations within the frame of narratives of self-development. Firstly, Tita's return to the fetal position reads as a symbolic 'reset'—an attempted return to a moment entirely prior to the process of female gender socialization that began as soon as she was born, as is clearly rendered in the birth scene discussed earlier. And in effect this is the closest that Tita comes to fully taking charge of her own self-definition. The grief caused by her adopted son's death instigates a retreat into a space unreachable by Mamá Elena, both physically (she is too afraid of heights to climb up to the dovecote), and psychologically, for this moment of crisis generates a period of mental withdrawal, self-imposed silence and contemplation:

> En lugar de comer prefería pasarse horas enteras viéndose las manos. Como un bebé las analizaba y las reconocía como propias. Las podía mover a su antojo, pero aún no sabía qué hacer con ellas, aparte de tejer. Nunca había tenido tiempo de detenerse a pensar en estas cosas. Al lado de su madre, lo que sus manos tenían que hacer estaba fríamente determinado, no había dudas. Tenía que levantarse, vestirse, prender el fuego en la estufa, preparar el desayuno, alimentar a los animales, lavar los trastes, hacer las camas, preparar la comida, lavar los trastes, planchar la ropa, preparar la cena, lavar los trastes, día tras día, año tras año. Sin detenerse un momento, sin pensar si eso era lo que les correspondía. Al verlas ahora libres de las ordenas de su madre no sabía qué pedirles que hicieran, nunca lo había decidido por sí misma. Podían hacer cualquier cosa o convertirse en cualquier cosa. ¡Si pudieran transformarse en aves y elevarse volando! Le gustaría que la llevaran lejos, lo más lejos posible. Acercándose a la ventana que daba al patio, elevó sus manos al cielo, quería huir de sí misma, no quería pensar en tomar una determinación, no quería volver a hablar. No quería que sus palabras gritaran su dolor.[49]

> Instead of eating she preferred to spend hours on end looking at her hands. She examined them like a baby does, recognizing them as her own. She could move them however she pleased, but she didn't yet know what to do with them, apart from to sew. She had never had the time to stop and think about these things. At her mother's, what she had to do with her hands was strictly determined, no questions asked. She had to get up, get dressed, get the fire going in the stove, make breakfast, feed the animals, wash the dishes, make lunch, wash the dishes, iron the clothes, make dinner, wash the dishes, day after day,

> year after year. Without pausing for a moment, without wondering if this was her hands wanted to be doing. Now, seeing her them no longer at her mother's command, she didn't know what to ask them to do, she had never before decided for herself. They could do anything or become anything. They could turn into birds and fly into the air! She would like them to carry her far away, as far as possible. Walking towards the window facing the patio she raised her hands to the sky; she wanted to escape from herself, didn't want to think about making a choice, didn't want to talk again. She didn't want her words to shriek her pain.

This is the first and only time in *Como agua…* that Tita's work at the ranch is described as drudgery, something that, alone, speaks of the importance of the episode, given the value otherwise placed throughout the novel on all of the activities of the domestic sphere—via their centrality to the structure of the story, the care and details with which they are portrayed, and the creative imperative that they encapsulate. As part of a scene depicting Tita's one opportunity for self-discovery and self-definition, such a contrasting take on that work guides the reader to appreciate the importance of 'choice' that, I believe, informs Esquivel's stance on these key feminist issues. Her novel certainly eulogizes the social and cultural significance of what is traditionally seen as 'woman's work'. However through the inclusion of this episode she gives her protagonist a chance to *choose*; to choose to continue to utilize the skills that are hers; to choose to hand these down as a positive legacy to future generations; to choose to value herself and her contribution; to choose to return to the ranch when she discovers that her mother has been seriously hurt and needs her help. And so, while it is certainly important to ponder how radically different her other options might have been given the historical setting of the story—and, as a corollary, how radically different they would be in a contemporary setting—for the readership to which Esquivel was/is speaking, this factor remains really vital. It creates a space of interrogation and autonomy that was also retained in the Brothers Grimm version of Cinderella, where, Bettelheim emphasizes, Cinderella is not forced to leave the ball by a certain time. Instead, she chooses the time at which she will leave and chooses to avoid the Prince when she does so—by hiding *in a dovecote*.[50] Bettelheim argues that this is legible as a sign of the female protagonist wishing to be chosen based on her true self, and not on the basis of the enhanced version of herself as seen at the palace ball. Obviously in this scene in *Como agua…* the Prince character is not the one from whom Tita wishes to escape, but Mamá Elena and the Prince both embody the same patriarchal order, and the dilemma remains the same in both narratives: conform and compromise one's 'true' self, or seek a space permitting self-assertion.

The avian symbology brought to the fore by this episode has been examined in an extremely thought-provoking take on the novel by Yael

Halevi-Wise, in which she notes the curious range of references to birds throughout the novel, and Tita's frequent connection with them. Departing from recognition of the traditional symbolic roles of birds in literature as signs of liberty or the desire for freedom, Halevi-Wise notes episodes including Tita's being forced to undertake the task of castrating capons for her sister's wedding to Pedro; her conviction that she can hear chicks chirping in the eggs she must crack for the wedding cake;[51] her self-comparison with the quails she has to kill for the March recipe,[52] and the magical realist episode depicting the transference of her frustration and anger onto the ranch hens, who begin to fight, become riled up into a miniature tornado, and eventually self-destruct leaving behind just three plucked, forlorn-looking creatures.[53] Particularly useful to my interests here, is her observation that, despite the novel's many non-realist elements, Tita's imagined flying away does not become a magical reality, because simply escaping her problems is not the path she must take.[54]

Birds, then, are a symbol whose commonality to both novel and fairy tale is condensed in the dovecote episode precisely because of their role in the formulation of autonomy, not as the means to a more permanent escape that we might envisage as the easier solution to Tita's oppression. Moreover, when filtered through the Cinderella intertext, the bird imagery insinuates the presence of the good mother figure, Nacha, as an ever more internalized presence that compels the protagonist towards self-knowledge, self-confidence and subsequently increased autonomy, even as she returns to the site of her effective imprisonment. This reading begins with a return to the symbolism of the hearth. Bettelheim notes in relation to a historical association of the fireside with the mother figure that the idea of ashes therefore may carry positive connotations through memories of warmth and caring, such as those that Nacha provided for Tita. He also notes the connection to ashes as related to grief and mourning, as in the saying 'ashes to ashes'.[55] Focusing on the Brothers Grimm's version of Cinderella, which he presents as more favorable in its depictions of the protagonist, in part because less manipulated by patriarchal ideology than Perrault's *conte* and so more faithful to what he sees as the intended message of the folkloric tale, Bettelheim reminds us that the tree growing on Cinderella's mother's grave is visited by a white bird that grants her wishes, and which is 'easily recognized as the mother's spirit conveyed to her child through the good mothering she gives him [sic]'.[56] Crucially, this spirit is initially instilled in the child herself as 'basic trust', a concept Bettelheim borrows from Erik Erikson's eight stages of psychosocial development (elaborated in *Identity and the Life Cycle* (1959)), and which is given externalized, embodied form in the shape of the helpful animal. Basic trust is both inwardly and outwardly directed if assumed fully—it provides confidence in oneself and in the world around us. 'It is the heritage which the good mother confers on her child which will stay with him [sic], and preserve and sustain him [sic] in direst distress'.[57] The final, fundamental, aspect of this is that even in tales when the animal guardian is killed by the bad mother, that act does not have a negative impact on the Cinderella figure, because by now the protagonist has internalized the strength that is given external form by the animal in question. Thus, although Tita accidentally kills the baby pigeon that she carries up to the dovecote by overfeeding it, we can still read its symbolic presence as indicative of her incipient move towards self-sustenance, because that presence is sustained through the portrayal of Tita with feathers stuck to her body, and in the imagining of her hands transforming into birds: now a neat, double symbol of autonomy and liberty.

As a related aside to these depictions, and in the context of my interest in Esquivel's multilayered intertwining of fairy tale, archetypal and mythical references, it is also difficult to resist the calling to mind by this scene of Tita as a kind of female Icarus figure; one which, in the given context, indicates not the need to curb hubris or to respect the boundaries outlined by parent figures (an act which for the male character would reap rewards but which leaves the female protagonist forever stricken by a repressive patriarchy), but instead the need to challenge accepted truths in order to instigate change—the feminist challenge to rigid social structures. This represents a challenge to one aspect of Bettelheim's analysis that is problematic from a feminist perspective: the 'confidence in the world' implied by the internalization of 'basic trust' must clearly be thought through in terms of its potential consequences for female identities, whereby blind confidence in their social surroundings is a dangerous notion. Instead, it must be more specifically tackled as an issue of confidence in oneself and in one's ability to *impact upon* one's surroundings, akin to Zipes's reminder that the fairy tale genre's quest form functions to 'indicate possible alternative choices' and so the opportunity 'to transform ourselves and the world'.[58]

In fact, the idea of failed ambition is itself restrained here by the safety implied, and self-confidence enabled, by the good mother-figure's now internalized, so now constant, presence. Because, according to Bettelheim, the symbolic dimensions of Cinderella discussed here form part of a narrative thread about the gradual shift in the parent's position as 'all-powerful', and a movement towards Cinderella becoming 'master of her own fate'.[59] For this reason:

> The tree which Cinderella plants on her mother's grave and waters with her tears is one of the most poetically moving and psychologically significant features of the story. It symbolizes that the memory of the idealized mother of infancy, when kept alive as an important part of one's internal experience, can and does support us even in the worst adversity.[60]

And so, in terms of the feminist perspectives and strategies engaged by Esquivel, elucidated earlier in this chapter, these key linkages to the symbolism of the hearth, the earth, and their association with the positive mother figure all connect meaningfully with the story of *Como agua*... As is usually the case in this narrative, the process of reintegration is symbolized by and enacted through food, when Chencha brings Tita a bowl of oxtail soup on a visit to the house where she is staying: 'With the first sip, Nacha appeared there at Tita's side, stroking her hair as she ate [...] How good it was to have a long talk with [her]. Just like old times.'[61]

THE HOLISTIC SELF: THE POSSIBILITY OF DUALISM

This integration of the lessons taught by the good mother figure into the now more positivized self is legible also as part of the equally necessary reintegration of the two opposed parts of the mother figure that, we have seen, are purposefully separated in fairy tale narrative so that they can speak to the child audience's need for clearly defined boundaries. As regards the trajectory of self-development, this is a key stage in the establishment of a self-acceptance and self-confidence that is completely necessary to the eventual establishment of a self-conscious individual; in the sense of one cognizant of the discourses by which she is formed and informed, and who is accepting of her own value. In other words, it is a move towards a holistic view of the self that is able to account for the various interior and exterior, positive and negative forces governing self-formation. According to Bettelheim, this is the ultimate intention of the Cinderella narrative as one which teaches that full self-realization requires both 'good' and 'bad' parents. For this reason, the Ugly Sisters always lose out in the end, despite their lives being made so much easier for them. They do not encounter the adversity that incites the Cinderella character's growth.[62]

That said, as poststructuralist discursive practices have served to make so abundantly clear, as adults we still hold on tight to such dichotomies and apply them as a categorizing strategy enabling us to make sense of the world's complexities. As will be explored in Part Two of this book, the ultimate consequences of such oppositional thought are grave indeed. And as in the works explored therein (*La nave de los locos* by Cristina Peri Rossi and *En breve cárcel* by Sylvia Molloy, in *Como agua...*, postmodernist textual strategies help challenge the limitations of Manichean thinking. As Rosa Fernández-Levin has described it, 'Esquivel juxtaposes seemingly disparate concepts, profane and sacred, by offering a synthesis of pragmatic, mystical, logical, illogical, mundane, extraordinary, rational, and intuitive elements'.[63] These challenging juxtapositions are established via genre-blending, parody, and pastiche, to forward a blurring of boundaries and a quest for spaces of overlap that Manichean thinking does not permit. And it is in line with this that investment in an eventual reintegration within the self of both the 'good' and the 'bad' mother, its depiction as a vital part of the journey of self-formation, bears relevance to a broader postmodernist interrogation of polarized thinking; a move away from 'either/or', and towards the possibility of 'both/and'.

In relation to *Como agua...*'s feminist strategies, this is echoed in the feasibility of a version of female selfhood in which traditionally feminized arenas of activity can be valued for their social contribution and creativity *at the same time* as their imposition as the only valid arena for female activity can be challenged. Women can both love to cook, love to care for others and respond to their maternal instincts if they have them, at the same time as recognizing their socialization towards those roles as connected to a deeply complex gender economy. As regards the text's cultural specificity, the seeking out of dualism finds resonance in the indigenous mythical and archetypal frames of reference already alluded to. Intriguingly, as the main vehicle for this more nuanced approach to womanhood, and although she is clearly intended as our heroine, Tita is not characterized as a purely 'good' girl, either in terms of the patriarchal, middle class moral framework embodied and upheld by Mamá Elena, or in terms of a simplistic feminism that relies on straightforwardly positivized portrayals of female characters. Instead, Esquivel's postmodern text reaches back to premodern Mexican indigenous mythology as a frame of reference in which the embracing of duality was inherent, in particular in relation to the question of gender: I referred above to the arguments regarding the key female figures of La Malinche and La Virgen de Guadalupe as active not passive figures, and their roots, too, can be traced back to the Aztec stories that preceded their modern configuration. John Bierhorst writes in his collection *The Hungry Woman: Myths and Legends of the Aztecs* (1984), that 'Though kings, priests and male deities predominate, Aztec lore is noteworthy for its robust female figures, who are as adventurous as the males and have the power to threaten them'.[64] Defying the Western view of the genders as each other's immediate opposite, these female figures then further embody dualism by being seen as possessors of a variety of conflicting qualities. Presenting an example especially relevant for my interests here, Bierhorst explains that:

> the so-called woman of discord [known also as] Our Grandmother (Toci) [...] belongs to a group of closely related earth spirits that were no doubt worshipped throughout the Aztec realm under one name or another, often simply as Our Mother (Tonantzin). In Mexican lore the goddess typically craves human blood, especially the blood of sacrificed enemy prisoners.
>
> [...]
>
> [However this] earth goddess also had another face. As Snake Woman, who helped Quetzalcoatl ['Feathered Serpent', God of Creation, one of the two most important Aztec male deities] create human life, she could be benevolent; as Snake Skirt (Cihuacoatl), she was the virgin mother of Huitzilopochtli [the other major male deity, the God of War and of the Sun]; and even as the hungry woman with many mouths, she provided grass, forests, pools, springs, and flowers.

Just like the reconciled good and bad mother figures that Bettelheim sees as central to the intended lessons of Cinderella's story, the mythical Aztec mother is also the embodiment of positive and negative characteristics.

What has been established up until now in this chapter is that Tita must hold onto the positive lessons learned with her good mother Nacha in order to consolidate her sense of self, give value to her skills, and recognize her potential. In terms of the episodes from *Como agua...* that I have been discussing, and taking the depiction of her retreat to the dovecote and subsequent time away from the ranch as a key marker in her self-development, it is significant that Tita's duality becomes heightened in the wake of these events. Prior to this, the magical effects of her cooking had been limited to the expression of forbidden emotions—her sadness at the ruined wedding banquet and her sexual desires for Pedro via the quail in rose petal sauce, for example. The slight incursions against authority that she does take in the first half of the text are all fast quelled by the fearful Mamá Elena—for instance, when in January she attempts to offer her own opinion on the family tradition circumscribing her life and is quickly silenced,[65] or when she capitulates, after a brief moment of defiance, to her mother's insistence on the 'right tone' of voice being used to address her.[66]

After the events at the end of the May and in the June chapter, however (and the location of those events at precisely the halfway point of the twelve-chapter book is surely not a chance occurrence), the more self-present Tita begins to enact more direct change on her world by actively *wishing* for certain happenings, which then take place. These acts are an extension and further nuancing of her paralleling, throughout the novel, the qualities of a number of Mexican deities. For example, Fernández-Levin suggests, via Inga Clendinnan's work on Aztec mythology, that when she is able to produce breast milk for baby Roberto Tita is reminiscent of the goddess Mayahuel, represented in Aztec lore as '"She with Four Hundred Breasts" (that is to say innumerable breasts): a dense cluster associated with violence, male potency, dangerous female sexuality and the endless bounty of "sacred milk"'.[67] At that stage in the narrative, those potent qualities remain submerged along with Tita's selfhood. However, after her return to the ranch Tita's powers appear enhanced and, really crucially, the ways in which she can exercise them has shifted from a secret (even to her) communication of hoped-for change via her creative cooking skills, to the strength of her spoken word. This now clearly enunciated 'I' engenders direct change according to her wishes because, Tina Escaja observes, Tita's words take on 'a certain demiurgic function'.[68] Hence, the wishes she makes before placing the traditional porcelain doll in the Three Kings' day bread almost all become true (tradition actually says that the person who receives the doll in their slice of bread can make a wish, not the person placing the doll in the bread)—that her mother's ghost would stop haunting her, that her niece Esperanza would be allowed to marry, that her sister Gertrudis would come home.[69] More powerful still is the alignment between her angry reflections on her sister's attempted imposition on Esperanza of the same family tradition that has trapped Tita, and what eventually happens to Rosaura:

> ¡Ojalá que a Rosaura la boca se le hiciera chicharrón! Y que nunca hubiera dejado escapar esas repugnantes, malolientes, incoherentes, pestilentes, indecentes y repelentes palabras. Más valía que se las hubiera tragado y guardado en el fondo de sus entrañas hasta que se le pudrieran y agusanaran. Y ojalá que ella viviera lo suficiente como para impedir que su hermana llevara a cabo tan nefastas intenciones.[70]
>
> If only Rosaura had burnt her mouth to a crisp! And never let those foul, filthy, frightful, repulsive, revolting, unreasonable words escape from her mouth. They would have been better swallowed and kept deep in her bowels until they were putrid and worm-eaten. And if only she would live long enough to prevent her sister from carrying out such terrible intentions.

The lack of insight into the reasons behind Rosaura's weak-willed and unquestioning capitulation to patriarchal family tradition and structure, and her subsequent, deeply unfavorable comparison with Gertrudis and Tita as women of the same generation who choose to defy, each in their way, the antiquated social mores that she and her mother unquestioningly follow, mean that the elder sister is ultimately more vilified even than Mamá Elena. And she dies a horrible death, bloated and stinking, her insides rotted by digestive ailments, in much the way described by her sister here.

THE GOOD, THE BAD AND THE AMBIGUOUS

It seems, then, that by the end of Tita's journey—and unlike all of the other texts studied in *Gender and the Self...* the end of the novel really is the end of her life because she dies along with Pedro in the final scenes—she has succeeded in drawing together the nuances of her being, and the result is an empowered woman finally in charge of her own destiny. I should acknowledge that one of the persistent points of discussion about *Como agua...*'s achievements that would challenge this interpretation questions the value of Tita as a role model for women when her primary driving force remains the pursuit of a very orthodox romantic love for a man whose positive qualities are never actually presented to the reader. I have not wanted to dwell on the romantic plotline here because my interests lie instead in the ways in which Esquivel's character development can be mapped onto the concerns of the narrative of self-development, and I feel that what is made abundantly clear by means of this approach is that this is not simply an unproblematized heterosexual love story that leaves its female character in the same passive role from beginning to end. Nonetheless, and despite my confidence in the many positive achievements of Esquivel's portrayal of this *Bildungsheldin*, it remains important to address the limitations of the story's portrayal of that selfhood. For while it is certain that Tita's powers strengthen and she becomes more self-sufficient, her influence remains in the main an accidental one. Although she moves from transmitting unvocalized emotions to being able to vocalize desires that then become true, she is never absolutely cognizant of her powers and this does take away from her qualities as a potential role model despite the pragmatic and valuable recuperation of the real-world space of the kitchen via Esquivel's feminism. Tita is both kind and cunning, yes, but not intentionally so. She incites change, yes, but more often as a magical counter-product of her desires, not as a direct result of her proactivity. For these reasons, her story sits perfectly at the start of the journey towards self-knowing selfhood that I explore in this study. Tita is an initiator of a longer project, and it is not *her* self-articulation that becomes the ultimate product of this narrative. But I do not, at all, wish to imply that this is a bad thing, because feminism is a communal activity, and as Maite Zubiaurre has so succinctly put it, 'Tita opens [many] doors, even if she does not dare to walk through them'.[71]

In the end, while some critics see the inclusion in *Como agua para chocolate* of fairy tale and other stock characters as prescriptive, I find this enormously revelatory, if perhaps not radical. This novel is populated by archetypes because it is *about* archetypes. In unearthing and borrowing from earlier versions of the Cinderella tale, its symbolisms and motifs, and by inferring or referring to other significant archetypal female figures mythical, folkloric and religious, Esquivel successfully undermines the critique leveled at her for relying on romanticized and essentialist ideals of the homespace as the 'feminine' realm; a facet of her work that also entails a revisionist approach to the denigration of that realm even by feminism itself. It is her revelation of legacy and her creation of a different heritage that matters. In Tita, the author has created a palimpsest through which are made visible the multiple figures that have been given a role to play in the formulation of the female selfhood whose depiction, questioning and gradual reconstruction is explored in this study. We can trace in her a female lineage from the vestal virgins and the goddess Hera, to Malinche and the Virgin Mary, to Cinderella, to the Madwoman in the Attic; and beyond her in Esperanza, the narrator of her story, whose dominance of the spoken and written word are thanks to the foundations laid by her great aunt, and on to the reader who will make her/his own decisions about the good, the bad and the ambiguous qualities Esquivel has presented to us. Legible as both a recuperation of the positive female archetypes of the mythical and folkloric worlds, and as a portrayal of the manipulation of those figures by patriarchal and Manichean ideologies, when read as a story that speaks of the phase of *construction* of gendered identities, Esquivel's novel is especially useful.

NOTES

1. Debra Castillo cited by Elizabeth Moore Willingham, 'An Introduction to Esquivel Criticism', in Elizabeth Moore Willingham (ed.), *Laura Esquivel's Mexican Fictions* (Eastbourne, UK: Sussex Academic Press, 2010), pp. 4–48, p. 5.
2. Antonio Marquet, 'Cómo escribir un best-seller? La receta de Laura Esquivel', *Plural: Revista Cultural de Excélsior* 237 (June 1991), 58–67.
3. Marquet, 'Cómo escribir...', p. 58. 'un mundo plano, observado desde un ángulo—injustificadamente favorable para la protagonista—en que sólo existe blanco y negro, sin matiz alguno'.
4. Diane Long Hoeveler, 'Like Words for Pain/Like Water for Chocolate: Mouths, Wombs, and the Mexican Woman's Novel', in Diane Long Hoeveler and Janet K. Boles (eds.), *Women of Color: Defining the Issues, Hearing the Voices* (Westport, CT: Greenwood Press, 2001), pp. 121–132, 125–126.
5. Long Hoeveler, 'Like Words for Pain', p. 126.
6. Tony Spanos, 'The Paradoxical Metaphors of the Kitchen in Laura Esquivel's *Like Water for* Chocolate, *Letras Femeninas*, 21.1/2 (Primavera-Otoño 1995), 29–36, p. 30.
7. María Teresa Martínez-Ortiz, 'National Myths and Archetypal Imagery in Laura Esquivel's *Like Water for Chocolate*', in Eric Skipper (ed.), *Recipe for Discourse: Perspectives on Like Water for Chocolate* (Amsterdam: Rodopi, 2010), pp. 174–188, p. 174.
8. Moore Willingham, 'An Introduction to Esquivel Criticism', p. 35.
9. Esther Kleinbord Labovitz, *The Myth of the Heroine: The Female Bildungsroman in the Twentieth Century: Dorothy Richardson, Simone de Beauvoir, Doris Lessing, Christa Wolf* (New York: Peter Lang, 1986), p. 2.
10. Laura Esquivel, *Como agua para chocolate: Novela de entregas mensuales con recetas, amores y remedies caseros* (New York: Anchor Books, 1992), p. 4. All subsequent references are taken from this edition and all translations are my own.
11. Cherie Meacham, '*Como agua para chocolate*: Cinderella and the Revolution' in Eric Skipper, *Recipe for Discourse: Perspectives on Like Water for Chocolate* (Amsterdam: Rodopi, 2010), pp. 101–113, p. 102.
12. Meacham, 'Cinderella and the Revolution', p. 102.
13. Donald Haase, *Fairytales and Feminism: New Approaches* (Detroit: Wayne State University Press, 2004), p. 7.
14. Jack Zipes, *Fairytales and the Art of Subversion* (1983) (London; New York: Routledge, 2006; 2012), pp. ix–x.
15. Zipes, *Fairytales*, p. xi.
16. Annis Pratt, *Archetypal Patterns in Women's Fiction* (Bloomington: Indiana University Press, 1982), p. 3.
17. Interview by Anabel Campo, 'Laura Esquivel: el sabor dulce de la vida' cited in Kathleen Johnson '*Como agua para chocolate*: Tita, una nueva imagen de la mujer latinoamericana', *The South Carolina Modern Language Review*, 1.1, 2002, 29–43, p. 36. 'todo lo que tenía que ver con lo femenino, con la relación directa con la tierra, con la maternidad, con la emoción, con el hogar porque todas las actividades que se realizaban dentro del ámbito de la casa no tenían retribución económica'.

18. Cited in Spanos, 'Paradoxical Metaphors', p. 5.
19. Interview by Claudia Lowenstein, 'Revolución interior al exterior: an interview with Laura Esquivel (author of *Como agua para chocolate*)', Anne M. Wiseman (trans.), *Southwest Review* 79.4 (1994), 592–607, p. 600.
20. Asunción Lavrin, 'Unfolding Feminism: Spanish-American Women's Writing, 1970–1990', in Domna C. Stanton and Abigail J. Stewart (eds.), *Feminisms in the Academy* (Ann Arbor: University of Michigan Press, 1995), pp. 248–273, p. 248.
21. Lavrin, 'Unfolding Feminism', p. 248.
22. Kathleen Legg, 'Latin American Feminism and Women's Suffrage', in Marsha E. Ackermann et al. (eds.), *Encyclopaedia of World History: Crisis and Achievement, 1900–1950*, Vol. 5 (New York: Facts on File, Inc., 2008), page 1 of 2.
23. Lavrin, 'Unfolding Feminism', p. 249.
24. Lavrin, 'Unfolding Feminism', p. 249. Referencing Evelyn P. Stevens, 'Marianismo: The Other Face of Machismo in Latin America', in Ann Pescatello (ed.), *Female and Male in Latin America* (Pittsburgh: University of Pittsburg Press, 1973).
25. Legg, 'Latin American Feminism', page 1 of 2.
26. Elaine Showalter, 'Towards a Feminist Poetics', in Mary Jacobus, *Women Writing About Women* (London: Croom Helm, Barnes & Noble, 1979), pp. 22–41, p. 36.
27. Maria Elisa Christie, 'Naturaleza y Sociedad desde la perspectiva de la cocina tradicional mexicana: Género, Adaptación y Resistencia, *Journal of Latin American Geography*, 1.1 (2002), p. 22.
28. Sherry B. Ortner, 'Resistance and the Problem of Ethnographic Refusal', *Comparative Studies in Society and History*, 37.1 (January 1995), 173–193, pp. 190–191.
29. María Elena de Valdés, 'Verbal and Visual Representations of Women: *Como agua para chocolate/Like Water for Chocolate*, *World Literature Today*, 69.1, Postmodernism/Postcolonialism (Winter 1995), 78–82, p. 82.
30. Bruno Bettelheim, *The Uses of Enchantment: The Meaning and Importance of Fairy Tales* (London: Penguin, 1975), p. 236. Bettelheim notes that 'In Germany, for example, there were stories in which such an ash-boy later becomes king, which parallels Cinderella's fate'. The title of the Brothers Grimm version, *Aschenputtel*, refers to 'a lowly, dirty kitchenmaid who must tend to the fireplace ashes', and was instrumental in shifting the implied meaning of the ashes motif.
31. Bettelheim, *The Uses of Enchantment*, fn., pp. 254–255.
32. Bettelheim, *The Uses of Enchantment*, p. 254.
33. de Valdés, 'Verbal and Visual Representations', p. 78.
34. de Valdés, 'Verbal and Visual Representations', p. 82, endnote 1.
35. Gastón Lillo and Monique Safarti-Arnaud, '*Como agua para chocolate*: Determinaciones de la lectura en el contexto posmoderno', *Revista Canadiense de Estudios Hispánicos*, 18.3 (Primavera 1994), 479–490, p. 487.
36. Bettelheim, *The Uses of Enchantment*, p. 67.
37. Octavio Paz, *The Labyrinth of Solitude* (1950), Lysander Kemp (trans.), (New York: Grove Press, 1985), p. 75.
38. Gloria Anzaldúa, *Borderlands/La Frontera: The New Mestiza* (San Francisco, CA: Spinsters/Aunt Lute, 1987), p. 31.
39. Maite Zubiaurre, 'Culinary Eros in Contemporary Hispanic Female Fiction: From Kitchen Tales to Table Narratives', *College Literature*, 33.3 (Summer 2006), 29–51, p. 46.
40. Meacham, 'Cinderella and the Revolution', p. 107.

41. María Teresa Martínez Ortiz, 'National Myths and Archetypal Imagery in Laura Esquivel's *Like Water for Chocolate*', in Eric Skipper (ed.), *Recipe for Discourse: Perspectives on Like Water for Chocolate* (Amsterdam: Rodopi, 2010), pp. 167–181, p. 172.
42. Martínez Ortiz, 'National Myths and Archetypal Imagery', pp. 172–173.
43. Bettelheim, *The Uses of Enchantment*, p. 257.
44. Meacham, 'Cinderella and the Revolution', p. 105.
45. Esquivel, *Como agua...*, p. 77. 'Ceres personificada, la diosa de la alimentación en pleno'.
46. Zubiaurre, 'Culinary Eros in Contemporary Hispanic Female Fiction: From Kitchen Tales to Table Narratives', *College Literature,* 33.3 (Summer 2006), 29–51, pp. 44–45.
47. Esquivel, *Como agua...*, p. 101.
48. Phyllis Chesler, *Women and Madness* (New York: Avon Books, 1973), p. 7.
49. Esquivel, *Como agua...*, p. 109.
50. Bettelheim, *The Uses of Enchantment*, p. 263.
51. Esquivel, *Como agua...*, p. 26.
52. Esquivel, *Como agua...*, p. 47.
53. Esquivel, *Como agua...*, pp. 217–218.
54. Yael Halevi-Wise, 'Simbología en *Como agua para chocolate*: Las aves y el fuego', *Revista Hispánica Moderna*, 52.2 (December 1999), 513–522, p. 513. 'a pesar de que esta novela sí contiene muchos elementos de carácter mágico, aquí las manos de Tita permanecen inmóviles. No es volando como ella lograría librarse del terrible destino a que su madre la ha condenado'.
55. Bettelheim, *The Uses of Enchantment*, fn., p. 254.
56. Bettelheim, *The Uses of Enchantment,* p. 259.
57. Bettelheim, *The Uses of Enchantment,* p. 258.
58. Jack Zipes, *Fairytales and the Art of Subversion* (1983), 2nd edn. (London; New York: Routledge, 2012), p. xiii.
59. Bettelheim, *The Uses of Enchantment*, p. 257.
60. Bettelheim, *The Uses of Enchantment*, p. 257.
61. Esquivel, *Como agua...*, p. 124. 'Cuando dio el primer sorbo Nacha llegó a su lado y le acarició la cabeza mientras comía [...] Qué bien le hizo platicar largo rato con Nacha. Igual que en los viejos tiempos...'.
62. Bettelheim, *The Uses of Enchantment,* p. 274.
63. Rosa Fernández-Levin, 'Ritual and 'Sacred Space' in Laura Esquivel's *Like Water for Chocolate*', *Confluencia*, 12.1 (Fall 1996), 106–120, p. 107.
64. John Bierhorst, *The Hungry Woman: Myths and Legends of the Aztecs* (New York: William Morrow and Company, 1984), p. 9.
65. Esquivel, *Como agua...*, p. 9.
66. Esquivel, *Como agua...*, p. 11.
67. Inga Clendinnen, *Aztecs: An Interpretation* (Cambridge: Cambridge University Press, 1991), cited by Fernández-Levin, 'Ritual and Sacred Space in Laura Esquivel's *Like Water for Chocolate*', *Confluencia*, 2.1 (Fall 1996), 106–120, p. 114.
68. Tina Escaja, 'Women, Alterity and Mexican Identity in *Como agua para chocolate*, in Eric Skipper (ed.), *Recipe for Discourse: Perspectives on Like Water for Chocolate* (Amsterdam: Rodopi, 2010), pp. 3–27, p. 11.
69. Esquivel, *Como agua...*, pp. 175–176.
70. Esquivel, *Como agua...*, pp. 150–151.
71. Zubiaurre, 'Culinary Eros', p. 47.

BIBLIOGRAPHY

Ackermann Marsha, E., et al. (eds.), *Encyclopaedia of World History: Crisis and Achievement, 1900–1950*, Vol. 5 (New York: Facts on File, Inc., 2008).

Anzaldúa, Gloria, *Borderlands/La Frontera: The New Mestiza* (San Francisco, CA: Spinsters/Aunt Lute, 1987).

Bettelheim, Bruno, *The Uses of Enchantment: The Meaning and Importance of Fairy Tales* (London: Penguin, 1975).

Bierhorst, John, *The Hungry Woman: Myths and Legends of the Aztecs* (New York: William Morrow and Company, 1984).

Chesler, Phyllis, *Women and Madness* (New York: Avon Books, 1973).

Christie, Maria Elisa, 'Naturaleza y Sociedad desde la perspectiva de la cocina tradicional mexicana: Género, Adaptación y Resistencia, *Journal of Latin American Geography*, 1.1 (2002), 17–42.

de Valdés, María Elena, 'Verbal and Visual Representations of Women: *Como agua para chocolate/Like Water for Chocolate*', *World Literature Today*, 69.1, Postmodernism/Postcolonialism (Winter 1995), 78–82.

Escaja, Tina, 'Women, Alterity and Mexican Identity in *Como agua para chocolate*, in Eric Skipper (ed.) *Recipe for Discourse: Perspective on Like Water for Chocolate* (Amsterdam: Rodopi, 2010), pp. 3–27.

Esquivel, Laura, *Como agua para chocolate: Novela de entregas mensuales con recetas, amores y remedies caseros* (1989) (New York: Anchor Books, 1992).

Fernández-Levin, Rosa, 'Ritual and 'Sacred Space' in Laura Esquivel's *Like Water for Chocolate*', *Confluencia*, 12.1 (Fall 1996), 106–120.

Haase, Donald, *Fairytales and Feminism: New Approaches* (Detroit: Wayne State University Press, 2004).

Halevi-Wise, Yael, 'Simbología en *Como agua para chocolate*: Las aves y el fuego', *Revista Hispánica Moderna*, 52.2 (December 1999), 513–522.

Johnson, Kathleen, 'Como agua para chocolate: Tita, una nueva imagen de la mujer latinoamericana', *The South Carolina Modern Language Review*, 1.1 (2002), 29–43.

Kleinbord Labovitz, Esther, *The Myth of the Heroine: The Female Bildungsroman in the Twentieth Century: Dorothy Richardson, Simone de Beauvoir, Doris Lessing, Christa Wolf* (New York: Peter Lang, 1986).

Lavrin, Asunción, 'Unfolding Feminism: Spanish-American Women's Writing, 1970–1990', in Domna C. Stanton and Abigail J. Stewart (eds.), *Feminisms in the Academy* (Ann Arbor: University of Michigan Press, 1995), pp. 248–273.

Legg, Kathleen, 'Latin American Feminism and Women's Suffrage', Marsha E. Ackermann et al. (eds.), *Encyclopaedia of World History: Crisis and Achievement, 1900–1950*, Vol. 5 (New York: Facts on File, Inc., 2008), page 1 of 2.

Lillo, Gastón, and Safarti-Arnaud, Monique, 'Como agua para chocolate: Determinaciones de la lectura en el contexto posmoderno', *Revista Canadiense de Estudios Hispánicos*, 18.3 (Primavera 1994), 479–490.

Long Hoeveler, Diane, 'Like Words for Pain/Like Water for Chocolate: Mouths, Wombs, and the Mexican Woman's Novel', in Diane Long Hoeveler and Janet K. Boles (eds.), *Women of Color: Defining the Issues, Hearing the Voices* (Westport, CT: Greenwood Press, 2001), pp. 121–132.

Long Hoeveler, Diane, and Boles, Janet K. (eds.), *Women of Color: Defining the Issues, Hearing the Voices* (Westport, CT: Greenwood *Press*, 2001).

Lowenstein, Claudia, 'Revolución interior al exterior: An Interview with Laura Esquivel (author of *Como agua para chocolate*)', Anne M. Wiseman (trans.), *Southwest Review* 79.4 (1994), 592–607.

Marquet, Antonio, 'Cómo escribir un best-seller? La receta de Laura Esquivel', *Plural: Revista Cultural de Excélsior* 237 (June 1991).

Martínez Ortiz, María Teresa, 'National Myths and Archetypal Imagery in Laura Esquivel's *Like Water for Chocolate*', in Eric Skipper (ed.), *Recipe for Discourse: Perspective on Like Water for Chocolate* (Amsterdam: Rodopi, 2010), pp. 167–188.

Meacham, Cherie, '*Como agua para chocolate*: Cinderella and the Revolution' in Eric Skipper (ed.), *Recipe for Discourse: Perspective on Like Water for Chocolate* (Amsterdam: Rodopi, 2010), pp. 101–113.

Moore Willingham, Elizabeth, 'An Introduction to Esquivel Criticism', in Elizabeth Moore Willingham (ed.), *Laura Esquivel's Mexican Fictions* (Eastbourne, UK: Sussex Academic Press, 2010).

Ortner, Sherry B., 'Resistance and the Problem of Ethnographic Refusal', *Comparative Studies in Society and History*, 37.1 (January 1995), 173–193.

Paz, Octavio, *The Labyrinth of Solitude and Other Writings* (New York: Grove Press, 1985).

Pratt, Annis, *Archetypal Patterns in Women's Fiction* (Bloomington: Indiana University Press, 1982).

Showalter, Elaine, 'Towards a Feminist Poetics', in Mary Jacobus, *Women Writing About Women* (London: Croom Helm, Barnes & Noble, 1979), pp. 22–41.

Skipper, Eric (ed.), *Recipe for Discourse: Perspectives on Like Water for Chocolate* (Amsterdam: Rodopi, 2010).

Spanos, Tony, 'The Paradoxical Metaphors of the Kitchen in Laura Esquivel's Like Water for Chocolate, *Letras Femeninas*, 21.1/2 (Primavera-Otoño, 1995), 29–36.

Stanton, Domna C., and Stewart, Abigail J. (eds.), *Feminisms in the Academy* (Ann Arbor: University of Michigan Press, 1995).

Zipes, Jack, *Fairytales and the Art of Subversion* (1983), 2nd edn. (London; New York: Routledge, 2012).

Zubiaurre, Maite, 'Culinary Eros in Contemporary Hispanic Female Fiction: From Kitchen Tales to Table Narratives', *College Literature*, 33.3 (Summer 2006), 29–51.

2 Eva Luna *by Isabel Allende* (1987)

Isabel Allende is one of the writers most associated with the Post-Boom and *Eva Luna*, her third novel, contains many of the common elements of that wave of Spanish American literature as it was described in the Introduction. In this take on the Bildungsroman, Allende narrates the development of the eponymous protagonist across a time span very comparable to that of Laura Esquivel's *Como agua para chocolate*, discussed in the previous chapter, so that we learn about the events surrounding her birth, and about her life up until the age of around thirty years old. This time the scene is set in Venezuela, the country that became Allende's adopted home following the establishment, in 1973, of the Pinochet regime in her native Chile. Although the country is never directly mentioned in the story, critics have outlined the narrative's broad mapping onto the sociopolitical history of that nation from around 1908 until circa 1969, spanning periods of dictatorship, the discovery of national oil wealth, and the development of the guerrilla movement of the 1960s. Still, Allende does not tie her narrative down to a strictly chronological timeline, thus to 'liberate [herself] from the tyranny of facts' and gain 'freedom of movement within the world that she creates and recreates',[1] in the words of José Otero. The subsequent nebulousness of its setting, the archetypal characters by which it is populated, and the requirement made of the reader to suspend disbelief in order to fully embrace its intratextual milieu, all conspire in Allende's folkloric narrative, where the heroes and villains of the fairy tale realm are reembodied in the archetypal figures of her Latin American context. This chapter explores Allende's work for its thematic interest in, and deployment of, tropes borrowed from relevant mythical and fairy tale narratives, again examining their role in relation to matters of the construction of gendered identities, and as part of the broader examination of the gender critique presented in Spanish American narratives of selfhood that is elucidated throughout *Gender and the Self in Latin American Literature*.

Much like her fellow Post-Boom author Esquivel, Allende's literature, and in particular her perspectives on gender, have generated debate among those exploring her textual universe. Beth E. Jorgensen's 2002 article '"Un puñado de críticos": Navigating the Critical Readings of Isabel Allende's work', does an excellent job of summing up the varied modes and motivations informing an oscillation between criticism and appreciation of her literary output, and in particular encapsulates concerns with the 'ideological value' of her texts that are of relevance to my interests in the novel as a narrative of female development:

> No one disputes Allende's abilities as a story teller, no one denies her creation of [a] feminocentric fictional world, and no one argues with her success in adapting popular literary genres to new uses, but opinion is deeply divided on the relative liberalism or conservatism of her novel's politics.[2]

As part of her summary of this dimension of Allende criticism, Jorgensen refers to Gabriela Mora's well-known 1985 critique of the author's first two novels and their portrayal of women in society, and to her identification of elements that are 'objectionable' from a feminist perspective: 'the feminine affinity for magic and nature, the passivity of subaltern characters'; their prioritization of 'acts of individual forgiveness and solitary recuperation over a continuing struggle for justice'; 'characters built upon essentialized and stereotypical qualities, the emphasis on predestined events, the recurrence of love as a motive for social action, and the overblown egotism of the characters toward whom the reader is made to feel sympathetic'.[3] Jorgensen's summary of Donald Shaw's discussion of Allende in *The Post-Boom in Spanish American Fiction* (1998) is also useful: 'he invites readers to draw their own conclusions about such issues as the role of determinism, the melodramatic polarization of good and evil and its strong emotionalism, the idealization of the oppressed classes, and the privileging of love over activism and individual initiative over collective action'.[4] In sum, Shaw has labelled Allende the Post-Boom writer who is 'the most "reconciled to the system", which may help to account for her popular appeal, but does not enhance her credentials as a feminist and social progressive'.[5]

Allende clearly self-identifies as a feminist, though, quipping that in fact she was of that mindset even before the term had come into use in Chile, so 'nobody knew what the heck was wrong with me'.[6] Hers is a feminism that seems to move between the liberal humanist and culturalist points on the spectrum, so that she is by no means as radical in her approach to gender critique as, we will see, Cristina Peri Rossi, or Sylvia Molloy, the writers whose work is explored in Part Two—either in terms of the formal experimentation that she has openly said she has no interest in, or in terms of her ideological agenda.[7] She 'embraces instead a vision of the complementarity of male and female [...] which proposes cooperation between men and women for the changing of societal values';[8] a perspective that appears to be embedded in the very structure of *Eva Luna*, where chapters focused on Eva's life story and on that of her eventual partner, Rolf Carlé, are alternately recounted until the two meet and their stories become intertwined. Allende also seems, in line with Shaw's comment above, very comfortable with the understanding of certain qualities as being 'male' and 'female', in quite essentialist terms:

> Women working together—linked, informed and educated—can bring peace and prosperity to this forsaken planet [...] I think that the time is ripe to make fundamental changes in our civilization. But for real change, we need feminine energy in the management of the world. We need a critical number of women in positions of power, and we need to nurture the feminine energy in men.[9]

What Allende does not accept, however, is the assumption that power should be predicated on sexual difference. So whereas she says she is not afraid of being accused of writing kitsch or sentimental literature,[10] 'What I fear most is power with impunity. I fear abuse of power, and the power to abuse... I'm fed up with the power that a few exert over the many through gender, income, race, and class'.[11]

This confident recognition of things 'as they are', while opening itself up to accusations of essentialist understandings of gender, is nonetheless fruitful when considered in connection with my interest in a notional phase of identity construction, for Allende's approach is, even in light of what might be seen as its failings, revelatory of existing structures and the versions of gendered selfhood that are possible within that established framework. There is room for Allende's kind of feminism in this project precisely for that reason: her work serves to outline the issues in question here pertaining to the development of ossified gendered identities. And whether that is achieved purposefully or through what might be deemed as a failure to dig deeper into gender categories, such outlining is a necessary first step towards the confrontation of hegemonic discourses.

Her own response to the kind of criticism described above has been to acknowledge her limitations but to insist on the validity of personal perspectives in the depiction of the world by emphasizing that one should write about what one knows: 'first-hand testimony seems fundamental to me'.[12] From this we can infer that Allende's feminism, too, responds to the world as she experiences it *as a woman*, and such a notion is substantiated in relation to *Eva Luna* in particular, given her comments on the connections between the story she wrote, Eva as its protagonist, and the progress of her own *Bildung* up until the time she created this novel:

> *Eva Luna* had a wonderful, positive feeling. That was the discovery that finally I liked being a woman; for forty years I wanted to be a man; I thought that it was much better to be a man. When I was in my forties, I discovered that I had done all the things that men do and many more, that I had succeeded in my life. I was okay. And that's what the story is about; it's about storytelling and about being a woman.

These feelings on the part of the author do seem to validate critical concerns regarding her attitude towards the patriarchal social order. But whereas they are problematic from more radical feminist perspectives they also explain the optimism by which *Eva Luna* is characterized; a positive tone that is of pertinence to my interests in the story as one of female self-development and that is connected in important ways to the use of the fairy tale genre within the framework of what Stephen Hart has termed her 'popular feminism'.[13]

RENEGOTIATED REALITIES AND FAIRY TALE FEMINISM

This 'popular' feminism is matched in the thematic interests and stylistic qualities of Allende's literature because, as part of her Post-Boom identity, she has embraced the inclusion of popular culture in her writing as the culture of the masses, speaking against the elitism with which the Boom text came be to associated. The subversive qualities of this cross-genre approach are widely recognized and, as part of her postmodern, neo-realist narrative style, highly relevant to my approach to *Eva Luna*, for a major facet of the genre-blending for which she has come to be known is her use of magical realism; a form that has been theorized as pertinent to the goal of challenging hegemonic structures. Inciting its reader to assume the possibility of numerous, coexistent, and possibly contradictory 'realities'—i.e., assumed truths—magical realism facilitates the possibility of not just textual play at the level of challenges to generic categories, but also with regards to 'the metanarratives or ideologies that these conventions uphold',[14] as Theo L. D'haen has argued. As such, magical realism obviously shares a number of qualities with the fairy tale genre, and the extent of this commonality is made clear in Marina Warner's description of fairy tales themselves in *The Beast to the Blond: On Fairy Tales and their Tellers* (1994):

> all the wonders that create the atmosphere of the fairy tale disrupt the apprehensible world in order to open spaces for dreaming alternatives. The verb 'to wonder' communicates the receptive state of marveling as well as the active desire to know, to inquire, and as such it defines very well at least two characteristics of the traditional fairy tale: pleasure in the fantastic, curiosity about the real. The dimension of wonder creates a huge theatre of possibility in the stories: anything can happen.[15]

The 'theatre of possibility' of which Warner speaks is very visible in Allende's writing, and is seen in this novel in particular via the intertwining of mythical and fairytale narratives and their respective archetypal figures. Specifically, I will examine here the author's textual interaction with Eva as a rewriting of the biblical character of Eve, her well-documented connection to the literary figure Scheherazade, and her relationship with the mother and godmother figures that accompany her as, like Esquivel's Tita, a Post-Boom version of Cinderella.

The postmodern genre-blending and intertextuality that draw these tropes into her literature stem from the fact of Allende's belonging to the Post-Boom 'mainstream', whose writers 'practice a return to modified mimesis, to a certain optimism, and to a certain confidence in their ability to understand how things are'.[16] It is also the result, it seems clear, of her greater self-confidence at the time of writing *Eva Luna*, which appears to have lent itself to the creation of a world less deterministic than those of her first two novels. And that creative task finds in the respective frameworks of the Bildungsroman and the fairy tale helpful allies in moving away from what has been deemed a problematic portrayal of events as predestined or predetermined in those earlier works, mentioned in the overview of criticism of her writing above. As part of her engagement with the new historical novel genre in *La Casa de los Espíritus* (1982) (*The House of the Spirits*, 1985) and *De Amor y de Sombra* (1985) (*Of Love and Shadows*, 1987), that textual strategy inflected a continuation of the 'pessimism and emphasis on the unintelligibility of time and causality' of Boom literature.[17] But in *Eva Luna*, the retrospective narrative through which Eva's *Bildung* is traced is key to undermining the sense of the protagonist's life being predestined, and it means that Allende's characteristic use of prolepsis takes on a different role here: contrary to what Stephen Hart has argued—'that it suggests the text has a premonition about the future, and encourages a sense of mystery about life'—in this novel the technique serves to reclaim some of the narrative control that it implies when used in a traditionally Realist mode.[18] Eva can make such statements because she is writing in hindsight, with a knowledge of what has been and of how she has come to be where, and who, she is. Hence, even when reference is made to 'destiny' this does not tie the protagonist to finite consequences, but simply reflects the shape her journey has *already* taken. Moreover, as we shall see in relation to both the original good mother figure, and the fairy godmother trope in the novel through the role of the characters that I read as Eva's 'Post-Boom godmothers', what is depicted is not a sense of having been manipulated by some greater force, but of having 'beaten the system' by means of benevolent intervention on the part of a cast of supportive individuals; of having escaped an imposed destiny by being encouraged to work at the development of individual talents and to gain knowledge of the world and of the self—the task residing at the heart of the female Bildungsroman.

These ideas also underpin my reading of *Eva Luna* as a Bildungsroman much more than as a Picaresque novel, as some critics have argued, although there are elements of both genres at play in the text. I concur, in this sense, with Claudette Williams, who says that 'unlike the picaresque author, Allende does not intend merely to disturb or depress the reader', thus depicting 'a victim of the system who nevertheless exploits the system through resourcefulness and unprincipled pragmatism'.[19] For where in the picaresque the question of survival is celebrated, in Allende's text importance is placed on

> Eva actively seek[ing] to learn something positively useful from each bad experience. The author does not dwell on the obstacles that stand in the way of women's liberation and progress. She opposes the reality of deprivation and oppression with the will to transcend misfortune that characterizes her protagonist.[20]

And it is in this way that Eva embodies Allende's professed belief that 'we advance in an ascending spiral. Sometimes it seems that we are walking in circles without moving from one level to the next, but it isn't like that. We progress, we grow, we learn'.[21] My examination of her work from this point on maintains an interest in this sense of self-definition as an act not constrained by destiny but as a journey of reimaginings of the material at hand for reference and inspiration in that task, embarked upon via the remolding of the archetypal figures presented in the text.

LIBERATING LEGACIES: UNDOING BIBLICAL *BILDUNG*

Eva's folktale-esque fictionalization of her own life, her central and forceful belief that she can tell her reality as she would like it to be and accordingly become the person she wishes to be, finds its roots in her relationship with her mother, who, as will be discussed later on, encouraged her imaginative drive, and whose own beginnings are relayed by Eva to the reader at the very beginning of her own story, and in the magical, mythological tone that characterizes the whole text. This beginning also serves to introduce the protagonist's coming-to-be as the text's central narrative thread, and is carefully deployed to underline the removal of determinism from Eva's story from its very beginning:

> Me llamo Eva, que quiere decir vida, según un libro que mi madre consultó para escoger mi nombre. Nací en el último cuarto de una casa sombría y crecí entre muebles antiguos, libros en latín y momias humanas, *pero eso no logró hacerme melancólica, porque vine al mundo con un soplo de selva en la memoria.* Mi padre, un indio de ojos amarillos, provenía del lugar donde se juntan cien ríos, olía a bosque y nunca miraba al cielo de frente, porque se había criado bajo la cúpula de los árboles y la luz le parecía indecente. Consuelo, mi madre, pasó la infancia en una región encantada, donde por siglos los aventureros han buscado la ciudad de oro puro que vieron los conquistadores cuando se asomaron a los abismos de su propia ambición. Quedó marcada por el paisaje y de algún modo se las arregló para traspasarme esa huella. [Emphases mine.][22]

> My name is Eva, which means life according to a book my mother consulted in order to choose my name. I was born in the back room of a somber house and grew up among old furniture, books in Latin

> and human mummies, *but that didn't make me melancholy, because I came into the world with a breath of the jungle in my memory.* My father was an Indian with yellow eyes who came from the place where one hundred rivers meet, smelled like the rainforest and never looked directly at the sky because he had grown up under the canopy of the trees and light seemed indecent to him. Consuelo, my mother, spent her childhood in that enchanted region, where for centuries adventurers have looked for the city of gold that the conquistadors saw when they peered into the abyss of their own ambition. She was marked by that landscape and somehow managed to pass that sign onto me. [Emphases mine.]

Many aspects of this beginning passage evoke the fairy tale, and by extension the genre's mythical roots. To begin with, as an introduction to the narrator-protagonist's own identity, it is a creation story of sorts. It is also purposefully imbued with the mark of mythology through references to the 'ancient'—the furniture that is described in this way, and the cultures that are called to mind through the mention of the books in Latin and the mummies. Allende then also draws on references to a more specifically Spanish American world of mystery; the jungle and the indigenous tribes that inhabit such mysterious places as those that seduced the conquistadors and whose depiction without geographical specificity borrows directly from the fairy tale mode—where 'the hundred rivers meet' and where the world is dominated by the uncontrollable power of nature. Finally, Consuelo, whose lack of clear origin immediately shrouds her in mystery and who will later be described as having a 'lash' of red hair that contrasts greatly with the green of the jungle,[23] is portrayed to seem as enchanted as the region in which she grows up; as a kind of mystical forest creature who will hand her powers on to her daughter.

The passing down of this personal mythology from mother to daughter is a reflection of the oral rather than textual origins of both myths and folk tales, and bears further cultural contextual relevance through the central importance of the spoken narrative to the indigenous cultures of Spanish America. This orality is then further reflected in the first person narrative perspective of the novel, which positions the reader in the liminal space between objectivity and subjectivity: the story can be engaged with both as if being read *to* us, and/or as if we are the teller of the tale. Interestingly, this narrative perspective therefore echoes the traditional audience involvement of the folktale, as well as the proactivity that the postmodern text requires of its reader.

Furthering the archetypal mystique surrounding the figure of Consuelo, Eva's matrilineal origins are then described as follows:

> Los misioneros recogieron a Consuelo cuando todavía no aprendía a caminar, era solo una cachorra desnuda y cubierta de barro y

> excremento, que entró arrastrándose por el puente del embarcadero como un diminuto Jonás vomitado por alguna ballena de agua dulce.[24]
>
> The missionaries took Consuelo in before she had even begun to learn to walk. She was just a naked babe covered in mud and excrement who dragged herself up onto the jetty like a diminutive Jonas spat out by a fresh water whale.

The explicit connection made here between Consuelo and the bible via the story of Jonah initiates her framing within the discourse of Catholicism upon arrival at the missionary camp. Yet her experience of the other, immensely different world that surrounds that enclave saves her from further inculcation by religious discourse by providing her with contrasting perspectives on the world, which will later enable her to retain an objective distance from the education imposed upon her at the convent to which she is eventually sent—as is implied by her persistent conviction 'that the meagre sun shining in the patio could not be the same one that beat down on the jungle home she had left behind'.[25] Already accustomed to a world of different signs, symbols and sounds, Consuelo is simply not as porous to the religious ideology that underpins gender roles in the Spanish American context as she might otherwise have been.

And her questioning of their implication in attributing meaning to lived experiences is a vital element of the legacy she hands to her daughter, one that is interwoven into the story of Eva's own creation in the unusual circumstances surrounding her conception: she is the result of her mother's amorous affair with the South American Indian gardener who works with them at the house of the eccentric Professor Jones. The affair begins on the day the gardener is bitten by a snake and Consuelo, wishing to save the man from the fate of being mummified by the Professor, hides him and cares for him, eventually deciding to 'live up to her name' and console him by making love to him.[26] Her erotic medicinal measure cures the gardener, and thus the story of Eva's conception becomes a retelling of the biblical story whose role in establishing and legitimizing male domination in western cultures has been profound: Consuelo and the Indian reintepret the roles of Adam and Eve in the Garden of Eden. In Robert Segal's view, this is one of two creation stories from the Bible (the other that of Noah and the Ark) that can be qualified as myths, in line with the folklorist approach to myth as stories 'above all [...] about the creation of the world'.[27] But here, the garden, the deadly snake, and a man and woman both of mysterious origins, become inextricably linked in the creation of a girl whose name 'means *life*',[28] not the beginning of death and the moral decay of the human race.

Also examining this episode Linda Gould Levine perceives the further integration of folktale and myth in the image of the snake because of the folklore of the Guajiro tribe native to parts of Venezuela, in which the snake is a 'representation of sickness, death and danger', but for whom this negative significance can be changed when the snake is 'killed and water, the "principle of life," is extracted from it'—something Gould Levine sees symbolically completed here via the sexual act.[29] Further to this, she associates the creature with the myth of Apollo's shrine, in which a sacred snake was fed by a virgin, and comments that

> [i]t is fascinating to see how Allende interweaves these different symbolic meanings into her newly transformed myth of her protagonist's creation [...] Eva, the offspring of this hybrid combination of mythological symbols [...] is born with a legacy of life bearing forces, femininity and renewal suggested by *luna* or moon.[30]

In Allende's rehearsal of the Christian grand narrative then, and through its interweaving with other belief systems and their creation myths, rather than responsible for the downfall of mankind, woman (represented by both Consuelo and Eva) is recast as the life-giving savior. Moreover, this is achieved by an act of carnal love outside of wedlock that transgresses a number of further doctrinal boundaries. And yet, nonetheless, as Eva acknowledges,

> [l]as circunstancias algo extrañas de mi concepción tuvieron consecuencias más bien benéficas: me dieron una salud inalterable y *esa rebeldía que tardó un poco en manifestarse, pero finalmente me salvó de la vida de humillaciones a la cual estaba destinada*. De mi padre heredé la sangre firme [...] A mi madre debo todo lo demás. [Emphases mine.][31]

> the somewhat strange circumstances of my conception were above all of positive consequence: they gave me immutable health and *the rebelliousness that took a while to manifest itself but in the end saved me from the life of humiliation for which I was destined*. From my father I inherited strong blood [...] I owe all the rest to my mother. [Emphases mine.]

Divine punishment for Consuelo's 'sin' never comes. Instead, the 'breath of jungle' left in Eva's memory seems, in the end, to symbolize her mother's memories of the jungle as a world free of the imposition of hegemonic discourses upon the female gendered identity; an idea that here informs the recuperation of the Garden of Eden and begins Eva's freeing from an imposed destiny by infusing her with rebellion—with the will to *act* against assumed truths and rigid ideologies. In thus rewriting the story of Adam and Eve, Allende/Consuelo figuratively free Eva from the restraints of a mythical bequest that has for millennia been foundational to the construction of gender roles. Furthermore, in the context of this study (especially because we will see this foundational narrative reappear and be challenged again in Part Two, in Cristina Peri Rossi's *La nave de los locos*) it is worth recognizing that the story of Adam and Eve, the story of mankind's movement from innocence (childhood), to knowledge (maturity), and the everlasting repercussions of this coming into consciousness, can perhaps be seen as the original Bildungsroman.

Whereas perhaps problematic in terms of poststructuralist notions of the discursively created subject to which no 'prior' moment applies, within the frame of Allende's Post-Boom optimism and particular feminism, the possibility of this 'happy beginning' is very powerful in its way. And that power is advanced via rewritings of other archetypal associations. For example, in the lunar references of Eva's surname we again find ourselves in the territory of essentializing associations, clearly based upon physiological cycles specific to the female body, of woman/the feminine with the moon. But Allende's already evident desire to challenge archetypes as well as to redeploy them via their positivization is evident in how she has one aspect of Eva's personal, bodily experience destabilize the symbolic gendered associations that her surname draws over her: as Gould Levine too goes on to note, 'Allende provides an interesting twist consistent with the ambiguities of the text' when she has Eva stop menstruating between the ages of seventeen and twenty seven. A detail that becomes a metaphor for her liberation from a specifically biological determinism,[32] but that enables the retention of the more positive associations that come with the connection between Eva, life, and Luna, moon, such as the force of renewal that Eva recognizes as part of herself and of her story: 'I had the sense of having lived several lives, of having transformed into smoke each night and of having been reborn in the morning'.[33] As a consequence of this, although we might query Allende's choice of archetypal reference points and their failure to move beyond the conflation of sex and gender, this story is simultaneously legible as a Bildungsroman 'that reflects the individual's ability to use adverse social conditions to prosper rather than to be defeated',[34] with regard not just to material conditions, but symbolic ones too.

In the end through the portrayal of Eva's physical coming-to-be, Allende rewrites a spoiled utopia in order to be able to expose its negative implications as a point of departure, but also to reclaim it as an end goal: the access to knowledge refused to humankind in the story of Genesis is the ultimate aim of the Post-Boom female Bildungsroman, because it entails the self-knowledge and social agency towards which the *Bildungsheldin* must move. Figuratively enabled to start afresh, without the baggage of original sin and its limiting implications for womanhood, Eva can function as the vehicle for moving towards a newly configured utopia that Allende clearly envisages as a necessary, motivating force for change. For she has articulated just this notion in relation to the idea of the project of a regional Latin American identity, one aim of which we can surely assume would be female liberation, in light of comments such as those cited at the start of this chapter: 'Of course [such an identity] is a utopia', she has said, 'but I believe it is necessary to start by dreaming of it'.[35]

REVERSIONING CINDERELLA

This subversive approach to the archetypes and stories informing female selfhood is continued by Allende's recourse to contemporary rereadings and rewritings of fairy tales via the act described by John Stephens and Robyn McCallum as 'not so much a retelling as a *re-version*, a narrative which has taken apart its pre-texts and reassembled them as a version which is a new textual and ideological configuration'.[36] Thus, another point in common with Esquivel's *Como agua para chocolate* is her use of the Cinderella tale in particular as exemplary of the genre's interconnection with the same interrelated processes of socialization and personal growth as the Bildungsroman, and which shares with both that genre and the Post-Boom writer a didactic investment in a socially—and individually—useful experience of that process. As narratives that enable psychosocial development in the early years of life, fairy tales are extremely apt to the study of gender as cultural and discursive construct, as has been made evident by the numerous feminist reworkings of such narratives worldwide—including in Latin America, as has been discussed, for example, in Patricia Anne Odber de Baubeta's useful overview of the fairy tale intertext in women's writing from the Hispanic world.[37] As explored in the previous chapter, the reworking of key fairytale archetypes and plotlines has been a vital aspect of the literary challenge to gender-formative discourses, and whereas Allende is not included in Odber de Baubeta's overview, in light of *Eva Luna* she is most certainly one of those writers who have 'ironically' made use of a narrative form that has been 'frequently blamed for the infantilization of women [but which] has now become an important tool in the task of "writing back" against patriarchal social structures'.[38]

If this generic dimension of Allende's writing has been infrequently considered it is presumably because any consideration of her work in terms of the magical aspects that would signify fairy tale or mythical intertexts is focalized through an interest in magical realism. But that element of the Allendian style is much less present in *Eva Luna* than in the first two novels that served to inform critics' characterization of her writing, and its more subtle manifestation is one of the reasons why the narrative calls to mind the fairy tale realm, instead of inciting immediate recourse to magical realism as analytical frame. What subversive approaches to fairy tale analysis and/or rewriting and magical realism have in common at the ideological level is encapsulated in D'haen's words, cited above: the desire to problematize the assumed democracy of the realist illusion and to provoke questions in the reader regarding the nature and representability of social realities. And as I have begun to explore, in Allende's work such a challenge is informed also by a kind of optimism deeply reminiscent of the fairy tale genre. In the tales, Warner relates this to their being neither 'passive or active; their mood is optative—announcing what might be'. 'The genre', she writes, 'is characterized by a 'heroic optimism', as if to say, 'one day, we might be happy, even if it won't last'.[39] Intriguingly, these words could just as easily have been put to use in describing the much-remarked-upon ending of *Eva Luna*, which presents the reader with two options for the romance thread of the narrative: the first a more pessimistic one in which Eva and Rolf are only happy together for a time, the second evoking the fairy tale 'happily ever after'. The reader is thus left with the enigma of which would be true, and the refusal of closure only leaves as certain the fact that happiness will be theirs 'for a time'. Very cleverly, this means that if we want it to be more, then we have to follow in Allende's footsteps and decide on the more optimistic version, hence performing in our own act of reading the politics of hope for which she argues, and which she sees as central to the Post-Boom mindset: 'We are more hopeful people', she has said. 'This is an important element of what has defined our wave'.[40]

Thus, while we know that this idealism is one of the reasons for which Allende has been accused of writing oversentimental books, and of the oversimplification of political complexities as a corollary, reading her work in the light of the fairy tale genre reveals a place for such optimism that not only further affirms the tales' openness to adaptation, but also taps into a deeply human psychological need. It returns us, thereby, to the notions of utopia implicit in Allende's reversion of Genesis: for whereas the happy ending that is the ultimate culmination of such narrative optimism might be deemed facile in the postmodern context, it is psychologically profound in its representation of, Jack Zipes tells us by citing Freud, '"unfulfilled but *possible* futures to which we still like to cling in fantasy" [italics mine]'.[41] He continues:

> Obviously, Freud would not condone clinging to our fantasies in reality. Yet [German Marxist philosopher] Ernst Bloch would argue that some are important to cultivate and defend because *they represent our radical or revolutionary urge to restructure society* so that we can finally achieve home. [Emphases mine.][42]

Yet more resounding is Zipes further summary of Bloch's ideas regarding 'the projected fantasy and action of fairy tales' in words that, for the way in which they capture sentiments that she frequently expresses, could have been spoken by Allende herself about her own literary project:

> [The] projected fantasy and action of fairy tales [has] a forward and liberating look: human beings in an upright posture who strive for autonomous existence and a nonalienating setting that allows for democratic cooperation and humane consideration. Real history that involves independent human self-determination cannot begin as long as there is exploitation and enslavement of humans by other humans. The active struggle against unjust and barbaric conditions in the world lead to home, or utopia, a place nobody has known but that represents human kind coming into its own.[43]

Zipes's discussion begins with his interest in the 'quest for home' that he sees as embedded in the fairy tale, and which is also extremely relevant to the project of the *Bildungsheldin*, indicating as it does 'a socialization process and acquisition of values for participation in society where the protagonist has more power of determination' and which can be '*regressive* or *progressive* depending on the narrator's stance vis-à-vis society [emphasis in the original]'. This is fascinating when read in light of one of the most well-known summaries of the classical, male Bildungsroman narrative trajectory and, as shall be seen, that of *Eva Luna*:

> A child of some sensibility grows up in the country or in a provincial town, where he finds constraints, social and intellectual, placed upon the free imagination. His family, especially his father, proves doggedly hostile to his creative instincts or flights of fancy, antagonistic to his ambitions, and quite impervious to the new ideas he has gained from unprescribed reading. His first schooling, even if not totally inadequate, may be frustrating insofar as it may suggest options not available to him in his present setting. He therefore, sometimes at quite an early age, leaves the repressive atmosphere of home (and also the relative innocence), to make his way independently in the city [...] There his real 'education' begins, not only his preparation for a career but also—and often more importantly—his direct experience of urban life. The latter involves at least two love affairs or sexual encounters, one debasing, one exalting, and demands that in this respect and others the hero reappraise his values. By the time he has decided, after painful soul-searching, the sort of accommodation to the modern world he can honestly make, he has left his adolescence behind and entered upon his maturity.[44]

It is intriguing how Jerome Buckley's synopsis, put forward in *Season of Youth: The Bildungsroman from Dickens to Golding* (1974), maps onto the basic plot of Cinderella, for if we exchange just a few elements of the archetypal Bildungsroman plot for some of the most well-known components of that fairy tale, there is a revelation also of the extent to which that story in its modern form (informed above all by the version published by Charles Perrault) encapsulates the traditional course of *Bildung* for women: Cinderella, too, is constrained in her activities, but by the wicked stepmother, not (visibly) by her father. She, too, is frustrated by the limits of her setting, although because they limit her access to the necessary romantic denouement that will enable her to reach the accepted pinnacle of womanhood—becoming a wife. Her 'real education' is not related to a career, then, but to learning what she must do in order to become 'appropriately' female, and it is only after then that sexual experiences will become relevant to her life—loss of her virginity will equate to *her* maturity.

The concept of home/utopia is relevant here because that home is synonymous with the happy 'accommodation' into society that is the main objective of the classical *Bildungsheld*'s journey, and because 'home' for the *Bildungsheldin* is so differently qualified. It lacks in the sense of autonomy of the male version, meaning that feminist versions of either narrative must rearticulate what home/utopia might stand for—just as Allende has begun to do via her description of Eva's conception. And in this sense Allende reworks both the Bildungsroman and the Cinderella narrative in *Eva Luna* by continuing to highlight and invert the traditionalized gendering of spaces in parallel with their respective relation to power: her protagonist actually reverses the direction of the male journey towards selfhood, leaving the big city for the backwaters of Venezuela and finding there the first place that will be home-like for her, in the house of Riad Halabí. In fact, in this Eva reminds us of the depiction of the typified female Bildungsroman narrative as described by Elizabeth Abel et al., who discuss how, while

> the young hero roams through the city, the young heroine strolls down the country lane. Her object is not to learn how to take care of herself, but to find a place where she can be protected, often in return for taking care of others.[45]

In the localized vocabulary of her Spanish American context, this geographical shift in the narrative can be read as depiction of the 'two Venezuelas'—the nation's dichotomous division into center and margins—which Otero perceives as a statement by Allende on the political marginalization of citizens who live beyond the boundaries of the capital or major cities; a divide that has contributed to uneven development and, subsequently, inequality of opportunity and participation in the national arena.[46] And to some degree Eva evinces this dichotomy, in the sense that she takes on yet another domestic role in this new household, continuing the life of the *muchacha* into which she was born. However, positives are brought by the kindly Turkish immigrant, who treats her well and, most vitally, provides her with a formal education that gives her access to the written language that will become her means of gaining independence on all levels, arranging for her to have lessons with the Schoolteacher Inés. It is thus that Riad Halabí becomes a positive father figure—he gives her access to the power of the written word, and in doing so undermines the male domination of logos. Moreover, and in the typically dualistic Post-Boom style that will always blur the boundaries of archetypal figures, he also becomes her first lover, and thus informs her sexual education in meaningful ways, too:

> Riad Halabí era sabio y tierno y esa noche me dio tanto placer, que habrían de pasar muchos años y varios hombres por mi vida antes de que volviera a sentirme tan plena. Me enseñó las múltiples posibilidades de la feminidad para que nunca me transara por menos. Recibí agradecida el espléndido regalo de mi propia sensualidad, conocí mi cuerpo, supe que había nacido para ese goce.[47]

> Riad Halabí was wise and tender and that night he gave me so much pleasure that many years and several men would have to pass through my life before I once again felt so fulfilled. He taught me the possibilities of femininity so that I would never settle for less. I gratefully accepted the splendid gift of my own sensuality, I got to know my body, and I knew I had been born in order to experience such enjoyment.

This positive interchange between man and woman is fitting to Allende's feminism: Eva gives Riad a level of acceptance that his facial disfiguration from a harelip has never allowed him to experience, and he gives her an extremely positive start on the journey of self-knowledge at the level of her sexuality—a key aspect to any feminist interest in experiences of self-definition. It is also important to recognize that there is no abuse of power depicted here, so even if read through orthodox gendered symbolisms, the retreat into a 'feminized' space brings happy rewards in terms of female self-development. And Eva's experiences there again present a challenge to the 'destiny' implied by the fixity of the oppositional characterization of male and female, and depict instead the possibilities for more harmonious relationships that can be envisaged from Allende's feminist stance. In the end, then, it is possible to view Eva's journey away from the nation's 'centre' to the marginalized, sleepy jungle town of Agua Santa, as a journey back to a novelistic conceptualization of Eden, wherein she will recuperate the word (knowledge) denied to women by the Genesis narrative and depart afresh, armed with a means by which to change her world for the better.

WRITE OF PASSAGE

In terms of my continued interest in challenging determinism in relation to gendered identity, Eva's access to education in Agua Santa is absolutely fundamental. It is through her studies that she initially embarks on the journey of exploration that takes place as a physical journey for the male *Bildungsheld*, as, 'Availing myself of an encyclopedia and of the knowledge of my teacher I travelled the world'.[48] But her primary interest is the exploration of the linguistic realm and the opportunities for creative self-expression it has to offer. An avid storyteller since early childhood, now for the first time she discovers what it means to be able to record all of the experiences that have thus far contributed to the development of her selfhood, her worldview, and her narratives; something that Susan de Caravalho links to the thematic concerns of the Bildungsroman by, very rightly, suggesting that this 'growth process towards literature is the primary focus' of the novel.[49] For, given what it provides Eva with, the taking up of the pen is a major rite of passage for this *Bildungsheldin*. In fact, in view of Allende's fervent belief in the importance of women's writing as a form of liberation, having Eva make this discovery is tantamount to her transformation into a meaningful feminist figure, as she enacts through it a defiance of what her author has described as 'the first rule' of patriarchal societies: the idea 'women [...] have to stay in their house and be quiet'. Her female characters, Allende has affirmed, are feminists because they 'defy the rule of silence, and they write'.[50]

Enabled to remove herself of the yoke of illiteracy, so clearly paralleled with the absence of a social voice and, within the context of female *Bildung*, the self-articulated 'I' that drives a number of the novels examined in this book, what Eva discovers in the power of narrative is a means by which to mold reality, to manipulate and improve upon it:

> Sospechaba que nada existía verdaderamente, la realidad era una material imprecisa y gelatinosa que mis sentidos captaban a medias. No había pruebas de que todos percibieran del mismo modo [...] Si así fuera, cada uno vive en soledad absoluta. Ese pensamiento me aterraba. Me consolaba la idea de que yo podía tomar esa gelatina y moldearla para crear lo que deseara, no una parodia de la realidad [...] sino un mundo propio [...] donde yo imponía las normas y las cambiaba a mi antojo.[51]

> I suspected that nothing really existed, that reality was an undefined and gelatinous material that my senses only grasped to a certain extent. There was no proof that we all see the world the same [...] If that were the case, we each live in absolute solitude. That thought terrified me. What consoled me was the idea that I could take that gelatinous mass and mold it in order to create what I wanted, not a parody of reality [...] but a world of my own [...] where I set out the norms and changed them according to my desires.

This perspective on the creative possibilities of language is the most important aspect of her mother's bequest to her; the gift of imagination fed by the idea that reality 'also has a magical dimension' and that it is 'legitimate to exaggerate that dimension and add color to it thereby make our journey through life less boring'.[52] For this reason it can be seen to intertwine key notions related to the matter of female archetypes and their legacies for future generations of women in the novel. To begin with, the spinning of tales as generative of her own life, both in the sense of her individual psychological or emotional development and in the sense of it enabling her physical survival by providing for material needs, exists simultaneously in Eva with the desire to create stories to save others, too—like those she tells Rolf to free him from the nightmares of his past, or to Elvira to keep her company when they are to be separated.[53] She even gives the gift of another language to Riad's wife Zulema, teaching her Spanish by means of storytelling.[54]

As is well recognized, in this the character of Eva is built upon the foundation provided by the female storyteller from the *Thousand and One*

Tales of the Arabian Nights—a text which Allende has explained was an enormous source of inspiration for her,[55] and which she has Eva discover at around the same age as she did (about fifteen, so at a crucial stage on the journey towards adulthood). Although critics such as Stephen Gregory have underlined the conservative nature of the original tales, which functioned to uphold and not to subvert the traditional Islamic social structure that they depict, he also acknowledges 'the feminist radicalization of the figure of Scheherazade' that saw her adopted as a 'figurehead for Latin American women writers'.[56] Evincing this by reference to Helena Araújo's well-known piece 'La Scheherazade criolla' (1980), Gregory explains the main thrust of the Colombian critic's argument was that 'the acquisition by women of an authentic narrative voice will lead to their liberation from male-imposed restraints'.[57] In terms of the generic motifs of the Bildungsroman this legacy provides the special talent that the protagonist must develop in order to find her place in the world. And of course, for the female protagonist, that gift is the tool with which she must challenge the order of that world before she can meaningfully take up a place within it; accept it as 'home'.

POST-BOOM MOTHERS AND GODMOTHERS

This idea is central to the broad context of this study's interest in the role of women's writing in the definition of Spanish American female selfhood, and is clearly central, also, to Allende's own perspectives on what storytelling can achieve. The inheritance of the vision of writing as an empowering force made possible by the 'radicalization' of literary archetypes like Scheherazade is carefully interwoven into the portrayal not only of Eva, but, first of all, that of her mother. It thus also sustains Allende's investment in familial relationships between women as key to both storytelling and selfhood. The deeply autobiographical connections between herself and Eva resonate here once again in that Allende always writes, she says, for the same assumed reader: for her mother.[58] This way she continues 'the oral tradition of storytelling that I was brought up in', which she credits for the frequent comparison of her stories with folk tales: 'maybe that is the voice of my mother, my grandmother, the maids at home, these women telling stories'.[59]

The cast of female characters that appear as varied reconfigurations of the archetypal fairy godmother, watching over Eva once she is orphaned, might be understood, therefore, to embody those familiar female voices in the text; each one pertinent to her self-development in some way, some of Eva's 'godmothers' are more fairy-like than others, but all four conform to the cycle of departure and return characteristic of these kinds of guardians, and which always ensures that the girl is never completely abandoned. I count Consuelo herself as the first of these, for she returns in spirit form whenever Eva needs, her as is paradigmatic of such figures. Secondly comes

Eva's actual *Madrina*, bestowed the title by Consuelo before her death. Ironically, however, she is the least nurturing of all of these figures, and in fact is responsible for setting Eva to work as a domestic servant at the age of seven, following the death of the eccentric Professor Jones. She thus becomes a kind of hybrid between the wicked stepmother who forces Cinderella into a form of domestic slavery, and the godmother who would usually ensure the protagonist's ultimate reward for her hard work and enable her to progress to a better life. The woman for whom Eva is first sent to work by her *Madrina* is also described in such a way as to make her reminiscent of the archetypal wicked stepmother:

> la doña había pasado buena parte de su vida en una notaría, escribiendo en silencio y juntando las ganas de gritar que sólo ahora, jubilada y en su casa podía satisfacer. Todo el día daba órdenes en su afán de hostigamiento, enojada con el mundo y con ella misma.[60]

> the Doña had spent much of her life working as a notary, writing in silence and accumulating the desire to scream that only now, retired and in her own home, she was able to satisfy. All day she gave orders in her zeal for harassment, angry with the world and with herself.

It is meaningful, though, that Allende, like Esquivel, takes the time to provide some back story for a character that would otherwise remain without nuance. Although the detail is not great, there is enough of a sense of a woman downtrodden by the patriarchal world in which she has survived—further symbolized and epitomized by her lazy, alcoholic brother who sleeps and gambles while she runs the household—and within which she has not been able to develop the most socially apt of identities: unmarried and childless, *la Doña*, has failed to integrate herself into the realms of admired womanhood. Like Mamá Elena in Esquivel's narrative, her bitterness can be understood in the context of broader issues, not just as a simplistic nastiness of the type that Eva will discover via the radio soap operas to which she begins listening while working at this house. Through this minor character, Allende makes clear that which the traditional fairy tale does not: that this kind of bitterness is a social malady generated by unequal power relations and gender roles and which, if allowed to persist, risks becoming the legacy of the young heroine.

The third of Eva's 'godmothers' is Elvira who, although lacking in the magical qualities of the more traditional one, nourishes and nurtures Eva during their time together at the house of the *solterona*. Despite the more routine role she has to play in Eva's life, Elvira's function is just that which might be expected of a Post-Boom fairy godmother: hidden in her otherwise ostensibly conventional nature, and in stark contrast to her apparently ungrudging acceptance of her own life situation, is a political awareness that she passes on to Eva, who writes: 'I was not of an age to be interested in politics, but Elvira filled my mind with subversive ideas about how to disobey our employers'.[61] Given what the Spinster and her brother represent—the conservative oligarchy—Elvira's inclination to incite Eva's dormant rebelliousness is not only crucial to her politicization, but to that of the novel overall. Following Eva's first truly rebellious act, when she is slapped for being insolent and retaliates by pulling her *patrona's* 'hair' from her head (it turns out to be a wig) before running away, Elvira welcomes her with open arms when she is eventually returned by her less-than-sympathetic *madrina* and tells Eva something that the protagonist later recognizes as 'the best advice I have ever received in my life': 'that's good, little bird… you have to put up a fight. No one dares to touch rabid dogs, but the docile ones get kicked. You must always fight'.[62]

By openly encouraging Eva *not* to remain passive in life, Elvira differs from the more traditional fairy godmother, for although she is supportive, she does not proactively encourage Eva's self-alignment with the patriarchal order. Instead, she offers the wisdom she has earned from experience, and in doing so directly discourages passivity in her *pajarito*. In line with this, it is also intriguing that the nickname Allende has Elvira choose for her adopted goddaughter is that of 'little bird'—for it calls to mind the avian symbolism discussed in relation to Esquivel's narrative and the transformation, in some versions of Cinderella, of the lost mother figure's spirit into helpful animal companions, one example of which is the bird. As discussed in Chapter One of the this book, the death of such animal figures has no negative bearing on the protagonist, thereby demonstrating her internalization of the positive forces represented by the mother. By having Elvira name Eva *pajarito*, Allende might be seen to be reinscribing this symbolism thereby to, early on, imbue Eva with the self-reliance that it connotes.

Somewhat paradoxically, however, another key role this kindly woman plays in Eva's life is that of introducing her to the radio soap-opera world in which 'the patient always triumphed and the villains were punished accordingly',[63] and which was the beginning of the *telenovela* genre later set to work in Allende's hybrid text. Both of these melodramatic forms are structured around the same binaries of good and evil as the modernized folktale, and can themselves be understood as contemporary takes on that form, reflecting as they do the social mores, attitudes, and beliefs of their contemporary contexts. Typically of the equivocal nature of these Post-Boom godmothers, Elvira's recognition of the need for rebellion in life is contrasted by her uncritical enjoyment of these products of popular culture. She complains to Eva: 'Listen, little bird, why does no one ever get married in your stories?'[64] She may be aware of the corruption inherent to their patriarchal context on other levels, but remains critically unaware of the profoundly important interrelationship between institutions such as that of marriage—its historical mediation of the gender roles upon which patriarchal society is structured—and the broader spectrum of politics by which her country is governed. Elvira finds Eva's stories pessimistic in contrast to those of the radio dramas, and unfulfilling as a result. In this, her character reflects an important point made by Zipes about the role of 'need' in the production of fairy tale narratives, and the influence of this on the variety of versions of individual tales that can be found. He contends:

> the tales are reflections of the social order in a given historical epoch and, as such, they symbolize the aspirations, needs, dreams, and wishes of the people, either affirming the dominant social values and norms or revealing the necessity to change them. According to the evidence we have, gifted narrators told the tales to audiences who actively participated in their transmission by posing questions, suggesting changes and circulating the tales among themselves.[65]

Unlike in the oral tradition, the narrative of a written text clearly cannot incorporate suggestions from its audience; however, it can be reworked to reflect the needs perceived by the author. Elvira, by reflecting the continued desire for a representation of the world constructed with Manichean simplicity, reminds us of one of the features of fairy tales that contribute to their usefulness and popularity: their capacity to break the world down and make sense of its complexities. But Eva, in her more ambiguous approach to storytelling, makes a step towards deconstructing frameworks of meaning structured around the dichotomies whose constituent parts remain implicitly gendered.

In her encouragement of Eva's creative capacities, Elvira combines forces with Eva's final godmother figure, Mimí—a character clearly intended to challenge the polarized formulation of gender identities. Eva first meets Mimí when she is Melecio, a schoolteacher who works at night in a male Drag cabaret and who is portrayed as suffering from gender dysphoria. In her role as Post-Boom godmother, it is Mimí who is eventually most instrumental in convincing Eva to start writing down her stories, in particular by bringing her a typewriter on which to work.[66] The typewriter is imbued with magical qualities through the 'fantastical' packaging in which it has been wrapped by Mimí, and by her own characterization via descriptions of her as a 'mythical creature'[67] and as a 'creature of fiction'.[68] It is through such portrayals that, more clearly and more directly than the other three figures discussed above, Mimí is attributed the magical status of the traditional fairy godmother paradigm, and her function as a guide for Eva in the journey towards what is undoubtedly portrayed as her 'true calling' in life also further links her with the archetype.

Most significant in terms of the impact that this character has on the representation of gender within the story is the fact that by this point Mimí is a transsexual actress and thus a character that functions to evince the performative nature of gendered identities in a number of ways. In the *telenovela* in which she stars, she plays the villainous Alejandra,[69] an iniquitous woman demonstrative of the similarities between the unambiguous characters of the fairy tale and those of the world of the *telenovela*, so that

Allende marries together various kinds of popular culture of pertinence to her social milieu. Conversely to her clear-cut soap character, however, Mimí's androgyny—she never has the operation that would complete her process of gender realignment—means that while playing a character formulated within the polarized symbolic order of the melodrama, she concurrently problematizes that binary system. Ultimately accepted, in fact adored by the public, Mimí is a character through which Allende promotes boundary crossing in a number of ways, playing with the configuration of generic and gender conventions by constructing a distinctly unpolarized character and then placing him/her in a neatly polarized performative role within the intertext that functions to give the novel its metatextual quality.

That said, critics have also highlighted this character as exemplary of the limitations of Allende's feminism. For example, Catherine R. Perricone makes the pertinent observation that 'Allende's figuration results in a man transformed into the type of woman demanded by a patriarchal society',[70] whereas Wolfgang Karrer emphasizes how while Melecio's 'transgression seriously challenges traditional views of gender, [it] fails to do the same for the power relations between the sexes', causing the 'retention of revised but clear gender roles [that] mark the underlying political unconscious of the novel'.[71] In the end, as far as her role as a contemporary reimagining of the mothering guardian goes, Mimí both successfully responds to type and incites change. For what is crucial is that the 'destiny' towards which this unorthodox character has helped guide Eva is a vocation, not an imposed social role as wife, mother, with agency in the domestic sphere only, if at all. Eva's written creation, her own *telenovela*, will have tangible political impact even though it is subjected to censorship at the hands of the military leaders against whom the guerrilla revolt in which she takes part and about which she writes takes place:[72] even while within the fictional world she is not able to tell the whole story, the novel *Eva Luna does* include a full account of those events and their challenge to the established sociopolitical system. Moreover, the fact of its censorship will also be revealed, permitting a double exposure of the realities of corrupt, male-dominated politics. In view of these elements, whereas comments by critics expressing concern about Allende's 'subordination of political concerns to [matters of] narrative craft' do have some validity,[73] it is also the case that, through the climactic events of the story, Allende shines a light on the nature and role of mythmaking in the context of twentieth century Spanish American politics. Through her reworking of the fairy tale as a kind of story that, as Warner reminds us, has long been feminized—'definitely girly [...] taste for them reveal[ing] lack of intellectual—and possibly even moral—fibre',[74] she at once renders visible and inverts the normalization of a male dominated world view and the subsequent historical accounts that can be manipulated into damaging grand narratives.

Overall, what Allende explores and exemplifies in *Eva Luna* is that social change requires and can be achieved by means of reengagement and rewriting of the foundational or grand narratives by which that same reality is (in)formed. Both this kind of reconfiguration, and any questions about the level of success with which it is achieved, thus become spaces of critique within which the impact of the 'original' story is exposed. Where the 'stories' in question are, as here, those told about, involved in, and formative to, the construction of orthodox gendered identities, such spaces becomes vital to the revelation of the problems that must be addressed, facilitating consideration of the impact of long-established patriarchal gender constructs on contemporary gendered identities. And so, whereas the structural and thematic implication of biblical, literary and fairy tale archetypes in *Eva Luna* might lend themselves to criticism for their failure to be radically forward-projecting in the sense of creating new identities as frameworks for reference, the optimism Allende's work engages on behalf of feminism, and the glimpses of utopia that it provides, remain extremely valuable.

It is therefore, I would argue, viable to move away from the kind of negative response that focuses on the limitations of Allende's feminism, and to focus instead on what can be derived from the work in terms of a greater understanding of the trappings of gender, its role and its norms. We can thus attribute a double edge to Allende's own vision of her work as 'uncovering a deeper reality, instead of projecting a different one',[75] by understanding her work to achieve an aim that Warner has attributed to the fairy tales from which she borrows: their 'boundlessness [...] serves [...] precisely to teach where boundaries lie. The dreaming gives pleasure in its own right, but it also represents a practical dimension to the imagination, an aspect of the faculty of thought, and can unlock social and public possibilities'.[76]

NOTES

1. José Otero, 'La historia como ficción en *Eva Luna* de Isabel Allende, *Confluencia*, 4.1 (Fall 1988), 61–67, p. 61.
2. Beth E. Jorgensen, '"Un Puñado de Críticos": Navigating the Critical Readings of Isabel Allende's work', *Latin American Literary Review*, 30.60, Isabel Allende Today (July–December 2002), 128–146, p. 133.
3. Jorgensen, 'Un Puñado de Críticos', p. 134.
4. Jorgensen, 'Un Puñado de Críticos', p. 134.
5. Jorgensen, 'Un Puñado de Críticos', p. 135.
6. Isabel Allende, TED Talk: 'Tales of Passion' (March, 2007), <http://www.ted.com/talks/isabel_allende_tells_tales_of_passion?language=en> [Accessed 07/04/2015].
7. John Rodden and Isabel Allende, 'The Responsibility to Tell You', in John Rodden (ed.), *Conversations with Isabel Allende* (Austin: University of Texas Press, 1999), pp. 223–236, p. 228.
8. Claudette Williams 'Isabel Allende's *Eva Luna*: In Search of an Affirmative Feminist Discourse', *Revista Interamericana de Bibliografía*, 48.2 (1998), 437–452, p. 448.
9. Allende, TED Talk: 'Tales of Passion'.

10. Rodden and Allende, 'The Responsibility to Tell You', p. 229.
11. Allende, TED Talk: 'Tales of Passion'.
12. Quoted in Donald Shaw, *The Post-Boom in Spanish American Fiction* (Albany, NY: State University of New York Press, 1998), p. 11. 'El testimonio de primera mano me parece fundamental'.
13. Stephen Hart, *Isabel Allende: Eva Luna and Cuentos de Eva Luna* (London: Grant & Cutler, 2003), p. 76.
14. Theo L. D'haen, 'Magical Realism and Postmodernism: Decentring Privileged Centres', in Lois Parkinson Zamora and Wendy B. Faris (eds.), *Magical Realism: Theory, History, Community* (Durham, NC: Duke University Press, 1995), pp. 191–208, p. 201.
15. Marina Warner, *The Beast to the Blonde: On Fairy Tales and their Tellers* (London: Vintage, 1994), p. xvi.
16. Shaw, *The Post-Boom*, p. 56.
17. Shaw, *The Post-Boom*, p. 55.
18. Hart, *Isabel Allende*, p. 46.
19. Williams, 'Isabel Allende's *Eva Luna*', p. 443.
20. Williams, 'Isabel Allende's *Eva Luna*', p. 443.
21. Cited in Shaw, *The Post-Boom*, p. 56. 'Creo que avanzamos en una espiral ascendente, a veces parece que andáramos en círculos sin movernos del mismo nivel, pero no es así. Progresamos, crecemos, aprendemos'.
22. Isabel Allende, *Eva Luna* (1987) (Barcelona: Random House Mondadori S.A., 2003), p.9. All subsequent references are taken from this edition and all translations are my own. Claudette Williams also notes that 'the opening sentences of the novel [...] preclude determinism'.
23. Allende, *Eva Luna*, p. 10.
24. Allende, *Eva Luna*, p. 9.
25. Allende, *Eva Luna*, p. 14.
26. Allende, *Eva Luna*, p. 24.
27. Robert A. Segal, *Myth: A Very Short Introduction* (Oxford: Oxford University Press, 2004), p. 5.
28. Allende, *Eva Luna*, p. 9.
29. Linda Gould Levine, *Isabel Allende* (New York: Twayne Publishers, 2002), p. 60.
30. Gould Levine, *Isabel Allende*, p. 61.
31. Allende, *Eva Luna*, p. 37.
32. Gould Levine, *Isabel Allende,* p. 61.
33. Allende, *Eva Luna*, p. 268. 'tenía la impresión de haber vivido varias vidas, de haberme vuelto humo cada noche y haber renacido por las mañanas'.
34. Gould Levine, *Isabel Allende*, p. 62.
35. Verónica Cortínez, 'Polifonía: Entrevista a Isabel Allende y Antonio Skármeta', *Revista Chilena de Literatura*, 32 (November 1988), p. 86. 'Por supuesto que es una utopía [...] pero yo creo que hay que empezar por soñarlo'.
36. John Stephens and Robyn McCullum, *Retelling Stories, Framing Culture: Traditional Story and Metanarratives in Children's Literature* (London; New York: Garland Publishing, Inc, 1998), p. 4.
37. Patricia Anne Odber de Baubeta, 'The Fairy-Tale Intertext in Iberian and Latin American Women's Writing', in Donald Haase (ed.), *Fairy Tales and Feminism: New Approaches* (Detroit: Wayne State University Press, 2004), pp. 129–147.
38. Odber de Baubeta, 'The Fairy-Tale Intertext', p. 144.

39. Warner, *From the Beast to the Blonde*, p. xvi.
40. Cited in Shaw, *The Post-Boom*, p. 10. 'Somos gente más esperanzada [...] Este es un punto bien importante de lo que ha marcado a nuestra ola'.
41. Jack Zipes, *Fairy Tales and the Art of Subversion* (London; New York: Routledge, 1983; 2012), p. 173.
42. Zipes, *Fairy Tales*, p. 173.
43. Zipes, *Fairy Tales*, p. 173.
44. Jerome Buckley, *Season of Youth: The Bildungsroman from Dickens to Golding* (Cambridge, Mass.: Harvard University Press, 1974), p. 17.
45. Elizabeth Abel, Marianne Hirsch, Elizabeth Langland (eds.), 'Introduction', *The Voyage In: Fictions of Female Development* (Hanover, NH; London: University Press of New England, 1983), p. 8.
46. Otero, 'La historia como ficción', p. 64.
47. Allende, *Eva Luna*, pp. 189–190.
48. Allende, *Eva Luna*, p. 176. 'Valiéndome de una enciclopedia y de los conocimientos de mi maestra, yo viajaba por el mundo'.
49. Susan de Caravalho, 'Escrituras y Escrituras: The Artist Protagonists of Isabel Allende', in *Discurso Literario* 10.1 (1992), p. 60.
50. Inés Dölz-Blackburn, George McMurray, Paul Rea, Alfonso Rodríguez and Isabel Allende, 'Interview with Isabel Allende', *Confluencia*, 6.1 (Fall 1990), 93–103, p. 101.
51. Allende, *Eva Luna*, p. 177.
52. Allende, *Eva Luna*, p. 28. 'también tenía una dimensión mágica y [...] es legítimo exagerarla y ponerle color para que el tránsito por esta vida no resulte tan aburrido'.
53. Allende, *Eva Luna*, p. 102; pp. 242–243.
54. Allende, *Eva Luna*, p. 146.
55. See for example, Alvin P. Sanoff, 'Modern Politics, Modern Fables' and Juan Andrés Piña, 'The "Uncontrollable" Rebel', both in Rodden (ed.), *Conversations with Isabel Allende*.
56. Stephen Gregory, 'Scheherazade and Eva Luna: Problems in Isabel Allende's Storytelling', *Bulletin of Spanish Studies*, LXXX.1, 2003, 81–101, p. 84.
57. Gregory, 'Scheherazade and Eva Luna', p. 85.
58. Elyse Crystall, Jill Kuhnheim, Mary Layoun and Isabel Allende, 'An Interview with Isabel Allende', *Contemporary Literature*, 33.4 (Winter 1992), 585–600, p. 589.
59. Crystall et al., 'An Interview', p. 596.
60. Allende, *Eva Luna*, p. 57.
61. Allende, *Eva Luna*, p. 74. 'Yo no estaba de edad de interesarme por la política, pero Elvira me llenaba la mente de ideas subversivas para llevar la contra a los patrones'.
62. Allende, *Eva Luna*, p. 69. 'Fue el mejor consejo que he recibido en mi vida'; 'Así está bien pajarito—me animaba Elvira –. Hay que dar bastante guerra. Con los perros rabiosos nadie se atreve, en cambio a los mansos los patean. Hay que pelear siempre'.
63. Allende, *Eva Luna*, p. 73. 'Siempre triunfaban los pacientes y los malvados recibían su castigo'.
64. Allende, *Eva Luna*, p. 73. 'Oye, pajarito, ¿por qué en tus cuentos nadie se casa?'.
65. Jack Zipes, *Breaking the Magic Spell: Radical Theories of Folk and Fairy Tales* (1979), 2nd edn. (Lexington: University of Kentucky Press, 2002), p. 7.

66. Allende, *Eva Luna*, p. 234.
67. Allende, *Eva Luna*, p. 236.
68. Allende, *Eva Luna*, p. 238. 'criatura mitológica'; 'criatura de ficción'.
69. Allende, *Eva Luna*, p. 233.
70. Catherine R. Perricone, 'Allende and Valenzuela: Dissecting the Patriarchy', *South Atlantic Review*, 67.4, Spanish American Fiction in the 1990s (Autumn 2002), 80–105, p. 99.
71. Wolfgang Karrer, 'Transformation and Transvestism in *Eva Luna*', in Sonia Riquelme Rojas and Edna Aguirre Rehbein (eds.), *Critical Approaches to Isabel Allende's Novels* (New York: Peter Lang, 1991), pp. 151–163, p. 160.
72. Allende, *Eva Luna*, pp. 279–280.
73. Gould Levine, *Isabel Allende*, p. 71.
74. Warner, *From the Beast to the Blonde*, p. xiii.
75. Crystall et al., 'An Interview', p. 590.
76. Warner, p. xvi.

BIBLIOGRAPHY

Abel, Elizabeth, Hirsch, Marianne, Langland, Elizabeth (eds.), 'Introduction', *The Voyage In: Fictions of Female Development* (Hanover, NH; London: University Press of New England, 1983).

Allende, Isabel, *Eva Luna* (1987) (Barcelona: Random House Mondadori S.A., 2003).

Allende, Isabel, TED Talk: 'Tales of Passion', http://www.ted.com/talks/isabel_allende_tells_tales_of_passion?language=en [Last accessed 07/04/2015].

Buckley, Jerome, *Season of Youth: The Bildungsroman from Dickens to Golding* (Cambridge, MA: Harvard University Press, 1974).

Castillo, Debra A., *Talking Back: Towards a Latin American Feminist Criticism* (Ithaca, NY; London: Cornell University Press, 1992).

Cortínez, Verónica, 'Polifonía: Entrevista a Isabel Allende y Antonio Skármeta', *Revista Chilena de Literatura*, 32 (November 1988), 79–89.

Crystall, Elyse, Kuhnheim, Jill, Layoun, Mary, and Allende, Isabel, 'An Interview with Isabel Allende', *Contemporary Literature*, 33.4 (Winter 1992), 585–600.

de Caravalho, Susan, 'Escrituras y Escrituras: The Artist Protagonists of Isabel Allende', *Discurso Literario* 10.1 (1992).

D'haen, Theo, 'Magical Realism and Postmodernism: Decentring Privileged Centres', in Lois Parkinson Zamora and Wendy B. Faris (eds.), *Magical Realism: Theory, History, Community* (Durham, NC: Duke University Press, 1995), pp. 191–208.

Dölz-Blackburn, Inés, McMurray, George, Rea, Paul, Rodríguez, Alfonso, and Allende, Isabel, 'Interview with Isabel Allende', *Confluencia*, 6.1 (Fall 1990), 93–103.

Gould Levine, Linda, *Isabel Allende* (New York: Twayne Publishers, 2002).

Gregory, Stephen, 'Scheherazade and Eva Luna: Problems in Isabel Allende's Storytelling', *Bulletin of Spanish Studies*, LXXX.1 (2003), 81–101.

Jorgensen, Beth E., '"Un Puñado de Críticos": Navigating the Critical Readings of Isabel Allende's work', *Latin American Literary Review*, 30.60, Isabel Allende Today (July- December, 2002), 128–146.

Karrer, Wolfgang, 'Transformation and Transvestism in Eva Luna', in Sonia Riquelme Rojas and Edna Aguirre Rehbein (eds.), *Critical Approaches to Isabel Allende's Novels* (New York: Peter Lang, 1991), pp. 151–163.

Luthi, Max, *Once Upon a Time: On the Nature of Fairy Tales* (Bloomington, IN: Indiana University Press, 1976).

Mackintosh, Fiona, 'Twentieth-Century Argentine Women's Writing', in Donald Haase (ed.), *Fairy Tales and Feminism: New Approaches* (Detroit: Wayne State University Press, 2004).

Odber de Baubeta, Patricia Anne, 'The Fairy-Tale Intertext in Iberian and Latin American Women's Writing', in Donald Haase (ed.), *Fairy Tales and Feminism: New Approaches* (Detroit: Wayne State University Press, 2004), pp. 129–147.

Otero, José, 'La historia como ficción en *Eva Luna* de Isabel Allende, *Confluencia*, 4.1 (Fall 1988), 61–67.

Perricone, Catherine R., 'Allende and Valenzuela: Dissecting the Patriarchy', *South Atlantic Review*, 67.4, Spanish American Fiction in the 1990s (Autumn 2002), 80–105.

Rodden, John, and Allende, Isabel, 'The Responsibility to Tell You', in John Rodden (ed.), *Conversations with Isabel Allende* (Austin: University of Texas Press, 1999), pp. 223–236.

Rosendo González, Pablo, 'Isabel Allende: Secretos de mujer', *3 Puntos,* 4.203 (May 17, 2001), 61–70.

Segal, Robert A., *Myth: A Very Short Introduction* (Oxford: Oxford University Press, 2004).

Shaw, Donald, *The Post-Boom in Spanish American Fiction* (Albany, NY: State University of New York Press, 1998).

Stephens, John, and McCullum, Robyn, *Retelling Stories, Framing Culture: Traditional Story and Metanarratives in Children's Literature* (London; New York: Garland Publishing, Inc, 1998).

Warner, Marina, *The Beast to the Blonde: On Fairy Tales and their Tellers* (London: Vintage, 1994).

Williams, Claudette, 'Isabel Allende's *Eva Luna*: In Search of an Affirmative Feminist Discourse', *Revista Interamericana de Bibliografía*, 48.2 (1998), 437–452.

Zipes, Jack, *Breaking the Magic Spell: Radical Theories of Folk and Fairy Tales* (1979), 2nd edn. (Lexington: University of Kentucky Press, 2002).

Zipes, Jack, *Fairy Tales and the Art of Subversion* (1983), 2nd edn. (London; New York: Routledge, 2012).

Part II

Deconstruction

Exile and Gender

3 La nave de los locos/ The Ship of Fools *by Cristina Peri Rossi* (1984)

> Writers first appear in the courts of the pharaohs who appoint scribes with two missions: to record reality and to prophesy the future. Art fulfils a premonitory role not because art has the capacity to foretell the future but because art is a reading of reality. I believe that the future is inscribed in our present reality if, of course, we know how to read.
>
> Cristina Peri Rossi[1]

The theme of exile has been described by Roberto Gonzalez Echevarría as a 'founding literary myth in Latin America'.[2] The harsh sociopolitical realities of the 1970s that were the historical prelude to the literature of the Post-Boom period stimulated the prevalence of exile as a thematic concern in novels written during and after the years of dictatorships and *desaparecidos*, as Spanish American writers tried to account for the traumas of life under authoritarian rule. It is also, however, a topic whose recurrent motifs and metaphorical dimensions make it dovetail on a number of levels with my particular focus on the question of gendered identities and their discursive development. For exile and the *Bildung* of gender with which this study is concerned are connected via the notion of the journey, and so the works read in this second phase of my triadic framework are examined for the exilic experiences they depict, and for the ways in which the ventures portrayed—very different in nature, as we shall see—contribute to the critique of normative gendered identities by discovering in exile a deconstructive space that provides critical distance from ideologically—induced and institutionally—upheld markers of gender and sexuality.

I begin this deconstructive stage with Uruguayan writer Cristina Peri Rossi's postmodern novel *La nave de los locos*, a text informed by various personal experiences of exile. A well-established and prize-winning author and teacher of comparative literature, the openly left-wing and lesbian Peri Rossi was forced to flee her homeland as a result of the Uruguayan civic-military dictatorship of 1973–1985. The year prior to the coup d'état that initiated the eight-year-long regime, she fled Uruguay for Barcelona, where she has remained ever since (aside from a short time in France during 1974 as a result of being targeted by the Francoist authorities).[3] During the Uruguayan regime, her physical exile was reinforced by the authorities' figurative disappearing of her; her works and any mention of her name in print completely forbidden.[4]

This decision to eradicate her from the national canon, however, seems only to have institutionalized a cultural lacuna of which Peri Rossi was very aware from a young age, for she tells in a 1998 interview that even as a young child she was a voracious reader, working her way through an uncle's library of some thousand works by the age of twelve, at which point he asked what observations she had made on the number of women writers there were in his library. She replied that she had read the works and biographies of the British writer Virginia Woolf, American Sylvia Plath and Argentine Alfonsina Storchi, and her uncle asked if she could recall their endings. When she responded that yes, they all died, he told her: 'Yes, women do not write, and when they write they commit suicide'.[5]

Peri Rossi goes on to explain in the interview that she immediately recognized how this extremely negative attitude to women's writing encapsulated far more widespread limitations founded upon the polarization of gender roles in her social arena:

> Evidentemente me di cuenta de que [el mundo de la literatura] era un mundo difícil para las mujeres, porque implica una gran independencia, pero eso ya lo había comprobado en otros órdenes de la vida. No sólo para ser escritora se necesitaba ser independiente, sino para hacer cualquier cosa que no fuera ama de casa [...] Se necesitaba ser muy independiente para fumar, se necesitaba ser muy independiente para usar pantalones, se necesitaba ser muy independiente para silbar. Recuerdo que cuando era chica, veía a mis amiguitos silbar, y un día yo me puse a intentar silbar. Me llamó mi abuela y me dijo: ¡Las niñas no silban! Eso es de varones.[6]

> Obviously I realized that [the world of literature] was a difficult world for women, because it implied great independence, but that was something I had already seen in other areas of life. A woman didn't only need independence in order to be a writer, but in order to be anything other than a housewife [...] A woman required much independence in order to smoke, much independence in order to wear trousers, much independence in order to whistle. I remember when I was a young girl and I saw my male friends whistling, and one day I tried whistling. My grandmother called me over and said to me: 'Girls don't whistle! That's for boys'.

The gender-based prejudices and roles that this author has experienced, then, existed prior to and outlived the civic-military regime. It is thus of no surprise that Peri Rossi's novel, as we shall see, openly participates in a key dimension of the Latin American feminist response to authoritarianism: its outlining as the ultimate, extreme consequence of the deeply ingrained prejudices of patriarchy.[7] It is also understandable that the theme of exile for Peri Rossi is not one confined to the question of politically enforced physical expulsion, but rather one to be explored in a variety of guises, drawing together experiences of marginalization catalyzed by an array of sociopolitical forces, and revealing for the reader the interconnectedness of those.[8]

A defined understanding of the traumatic, identity-effacing experience of exile and the development of a critical vocabulary that enables its analysis is central to exile studies, and the move towards defining the impact of exile has led to the setting-up of what have become, as Sophia A. McClennan sums up, two camps, whose polarized approaches lead them to examine exile literature 'according to a binary logic, where exile either produces creative freedom or it traps the writer in restrictive nostalgia'.[9] Given the nature of Peri Rossi's text, only the latter approach can be seen as relevant here, for she has clearly sought out more productive than pessimistic ways of reading the characteristics and impact of exile. Indeed, she stated in a 1993 interview that she did not wish to publish in full her collection of poems *Estado de exilio* (only eventually published in a bilingual edition as *State of Exile*, in 2008) because she felt its tone was one of complaint; the usual 'sobbing of exile'. Instead of contributing to the 'ceremony of pain, as if it were the only thing that could be said about exile', she wanted to acknowledge that there are other things to be said about it, too.[10] In this, Peri Rossi partakes in what Parizad Dejbord has described as an approach to exile in literature that, by establishing connections between it and questions of identity, moves away from the task of defining the essence of exile and towards that of 'questioning and demystifying the very idea of cohesive identity'.[11] As I do, Dejbord recognizes Peri Rossi's exilic universe as one whose exploration is a 'positive, liberating experience, nourished by the idea of ambiguity'.[12]

The disparate cast she has created as a vehicle for this aim centers around protagonist Equis (the letter X in Spanish), a political exile on a seemingly directionless journey around the globe. But he is accompanied along the way by his friend Vercingétorix, a man temporarily disappeared by an unnamed authoritarian regime and whose sexual mores (a fascination for dwarves and children) continue to problematize his social integration once freed;[13] by Morris, an outcast for his general eccentricity and rejection of dominant ideologies; Graciela, marginalized in the deeply patriarchal world depicted in the novel by her female identity, feminist ideologies, and subsequent choice to live an unorthodox life rather than capitulate to social norms; Gordon, an ex-astronaut who has fallen in love with the moon and cannot return to it; and Lucía, a woman he meets on a bus full of women going to have illegal abortions in London, and then later again when she performs in a drag porn show. It is Lucía's story and the feelings she engenders in him that finally enable Equis to solve the riddle whose solution becomes the drive behind the latter part of his own tale, and the major message of the novel itself.

For reasons that will become clear, the female cast of the novel and their interactions with Equis will be paid particular attention in my discussion of the novel, but for now it is important to note that Peri Rossi's combined depiction of exile both in its most empirical sense and as synonym for social marginalization—indeed even for straightforward loneliness in the face of lost or unrequited love, as in the case of Gordon and the moon, for example—underscores her approach to exile as a universal condition made inevitable by the failure of our categories of identification to account for the nuances of subjectivity. For it is this aspect of her work that the analytical framework of this book, its interest in the remapping of trajectories and unpicking of the rites of passage of self-development, reveals in particular: the exile narrative and the Bildungsroman are connected by their shared investment in the notion of the journey, and in their grasp of that journey as an experience that shapes selfhood. Structurally, stories of geographical exile mirror the outward movement of the journey into the social arena that is one of the most significant aspects of the novel of development. In the classical Bildungsroman, it would be this venture away from home and what are, at that moment of departure, seen as its constrictions, that initiates the formative adventure of the *Bildungsheld*.

We should recall, though, that feminist revisions of the genre have underscored the fact of this journey outwards being historically denied to women—just as Peri Rossi's childhood experiences make abundantly clear. And herein is found an important similarity between the protagonists of exile narratives and that forbidden female journey of discovery: both are defined as transgressive within the terms of the patriarchal economy. Regarding comparisons of the exile narrative and the Bildungsroman, therefore, a key distinction must be made between the naive prototypical *Bildungsheld*'s exploratory adventure to find himself, and the heightened level of self-awareness of the exile. Whereas the young protagonist of the novel of formation embodies a process of development recognizable only in hindsight, the exiled individual is fully cognizant of his or her enforced expulsion. In terms of identity, therefore, we encounter a contrast between the *Bildungsheld*'s identity in the *process of becoming*, and the exile's identity as one in the *process of being undone*.

In no sense a normative Bildungsroman, then, Peri Rossi's work is one I feel can usefully be described as an 'Anti-Bildungsroman': a postmodern take on the journey of formation that reframes the Bildungsroman's central dialogue between self and society in a dystopic world that quickly reveals the exclusionary practices of hegemonic power systems. Leading on from the revelations about the constructedness of gendered selfhoods carried out by Allende's and Esquivel's works and examined in Part One, Peri Rossi's novel further unmasks the ideological frameworks (whose literary parallels, I have underlined in the Introduction, are found in proscriptive approaches to genre) that enable the setting up of the center/margin dichotomy and its many corollaries. Adopting poststructuralist discourses and postmodern representational strategies, she seeks to dismantle orthodox notions of gendered selfhood by drawing parallels between the fundamental role of gender in the Manichean world view of authoritarian dictatorships, and the hegemonic order at large.

THE DUALISMS OF EXILE: IDENTITY AND LOCATION

As I have stated above, it is the journey motif shared by the exile narrative and the Bildungsroman's central, interrelated tenets of self-development and social integration that are my dominant interests in this chapter. Given this, the question of location both physical and ideological/metaphorical, also becomes central to an informed reading of *La nave de los locos* within the terms of my framework. Indeed, that this is true is surely encapsulated in the very title of the novel; a reference to the medieval practice, discussed by Michel Foucault in *Madness and Civilization: A History of Insanity in the Age of Reason* (1961; 1964) and recounted by Equis in chapter eight, of shipping those deemed too mad to live in mainstream society out to sea and leaving them to perish on an abandoned boat; ideologically defined as outsiders and forced into a physical space designated 'outside', as a result. And thusly summed up, the practice of the Ship of Fools recalls Hélène Cixous's meaningful interrogation, set out in *La jeune née* (1975), of the exclusionary processes of binary thinking:

> Where is she?
> Activity/Passivity
> Sun/Moon
> Culture/Nature
> Day/Night
> Father/Mother
> Head/Heart
> Intelligible/Palpable
> Logos/Pathos
> Form, convex, step, advance, semen, progress
> Matter, concave, ground- where steps are taken, holding-and dumping-ground
> Man
> Woman[14]

Extremely useful in rendering clear the mutually informative relationship between the patterns of binary thinking and the formulation of orthodox notions of gendered identities, as Toril Moi has underlined, Cixous's illustration demonstrates how 'it doesn't matter which 'couple' one chooses to highlight: the hidden male/female opposition with its inevitable positive/negative evaluation can always be traced as the underlying paradigm'.[15] Further still, the ultimate consequences of the signs, symbols and metaphors of the patriarchal economy are neatly encapsulated by the *mise en page* of the final pair, with 'woman' *under* 'man', Cixous thereby highlighting the crucial fact that dualistic thinking not only defies equality, but pushes inequality to its full conclusion: an ideological standpoint from which one half of each opposition is considered dominant over its counterpart. Effectively, she was emphasizing, not only are all binary pairs gendered, but so is the imbalance that resides within them, and in the terms of the current hegemonic framework it is the feminized element that is always forced out from the powerful center, and into the margins: in other words, into exile.

Hence, it is actually within the workings of binary thought that the first connections between gender and exile are to be found, and this stresses the fact that the double meaning of the term exile, which is both identity *and* location, can also be applied to gender. When Cixous asks *where* woman is to be found in this system, she shows her to be *in exile*: in the marginalized element of each divided pair that is set up and maintained by the prioritizations of binary logic. Comparably, Julia Kristeva writes in 'La femme' (1974) that she understands 'by "woman" that which cannot be represented, that which is not spoken, that which remains *outside* naming and ideologies' [my emphases].[16] This is a perception of female identity whose obvious parallels with exile are summarized by Moi when she writes that if, as Cixous has shown,

> femininity is defined as lack, negativity, absence of meaning, irrationality, chaos, darkness,—in short as non-Being—Kristeva's emphasis on marginality allows us to view this repression of the feminine in terms of *positionality* rather than essences. What is perceived as marginal at any given time depends on the position one occupies. [Emphasis in the original.][17]

In other words, where Cixous successfully highlights the position of women in binary thought, Kristeva emphasizes that the absence of any real female/feminine essence undermines the patriarchal symbolic order's attempts to naturalize the suppression of the female/feminine within its structure. This 'relational "definition"' of femininity as nothing more than 'that which is marginalized by the patriarchal order', is one 'as shifting as the various forms of patriarchy itself', and enables Kristeva to make the key point that 'men can also be constructed as marginal by the symbolic order'.[18] Her comment, then, points towards a need to interrogate the genderedness of exile in all its guises (as location, experience and identity) because, as Margaret R. Higonnet has put it, 'allusions to territories, margins, outsiders, or one's place should not be slightly dismissed'; are not 'just metaphors, but names of actual spatial devices that maintain hierarchies of power and privilege', and the realm of the marginal, of exile, is undeniably feminizing and feminized.[19]

THE GENDERING/GENDERED SPACES OF EXILE

Kristeva's definition of the feminine as positional or locational is highly pertinent to the study of gender that I wish to carry out here, for in Peri Rossi's text it is precisely the feminization of a male protagonist by placing him in exile, and the new perspectives that this affords him, that mean he can become a vehicle for the kind of deconstruction of dualistic thinking and its gendered consequences carried out in the novel. The ambiguity created by means of combining *that* protagonist with *this* setting is absolutely necessary to the story she tells: the lessons that Equis learns along his way would to a female protagonist be reiterations or clarifications of known problems. They would not represent, as they do for him, a journey of realizations with the potential to radically rearrange the social order. She thus makes of exile a space of critical distance that enables the challenging of the very discourses by which it is created, providing thereby the context for Equis's journey towards a greater self-consciousness and social conscience.

It is with this objective in mind, I believe, that the feminization of the exilic realm and its related symbologies are fully embraced in the novel, in an unabashed confrontation with the language of the patriarchy whose destabilization is the text's ultimate goal. Peri Rossi purposefully engages the gendered associations at play, reworking and undercutting the traditional female tropes and paradigms used by the symbolic order to maintain and justify its oppression of the feminine. In other words, in *La nave de los locos* Peri Rossi echoes Kristeva's location of 'the negativity and refusal pertaining to the marginal in "woman", in order to undermine the phallocentric order that defines woman as marginal in the first place'.[20]

Peri Rossi has explained that for her, the protagonist of her exile narrative could only be male, because 'for the collective unconscious the [politically] exiled individual is always male [...] the figure of the revolutionary continues to be masculine'.[21] Contrastingly, to seek out the feminine in the vocabulary of exile studies is quickly to come to the notion of the homespace; the point of origin that, standing as opposition to exile, is precisely what makes exile possible, and which woman is 'invested with [...] the responsibility of representing, and even reproducing'.[22] In other words, as is now well recognized and just as Peri Rossi acknowledges above, gender roles as traditionally determined by the rule of patriarchal heterosexuality masculinize the public and political spheres and link the homespace, the private and the domestic with the feminine:

> Extranjero. Ex. Extrañamiento. Fuera de las entrañas de la tierra. Desentrañado: vuelto a parir.[23]
>
> Stranger. Ex. Estrangement. Out of the depths of the earth. Eviscerated: given birth to once more.

Here, then, the kind of archetypal associations of woman with the earth explored in Part One, and notions of birth with uprooting come into play to reinforce an understanding of woman as place of origin. She is the initial site of expulsion, of rejection, of a forceful and painful separation, and the experience of exile is expressed in the above citation from the very beginning of the novel as a repetition of all of these.

It logically follows, therefore (rightly or wrongly), that the consequence of these symbolic associations is a differing relationship between the two genders and the home space itself that will also transfer into differing experiences of exile. If the discourses of gendered identity teach 'woman' to associate herself with 'home' and all that the term implicitly carries, both what she leaves behind and what she carries with her will distinguish her experience of expulsion from that of her male counterpart. This interpretation of the relationship between exile and heterosexual gendered identities is supported by Amy Kaminsky:

> The rupture that causes anguish in the male exile originates in the vital connection between the citizen (by definition male) and his country, which is severed in the condition of exile. Integrity for the male exile is possible only if he returns home, or if [...] he reproduces 'home' in place of exile [...] The female exile, who was never completely at one with her country, experiences a different sort of split. It would be both cruel and naïve to suggest that women do not suffer in exile, but they may also have something to gain from exile as women, free of the oppressive sexism of the home culture. The rupture a woman experiences is not a rending from an always-nourishing home, but a mitosis, a split not from within but within the self, into two distinct beings—the self and the double—that can enable transcendence.[24]

In this account, woman, already '[e]xiled within patriarchy and within the *patria*',[25] paradoxically central to yet marginalized from a national space she is given the task of symbolizing but denied full political agency in, can feasibly be understood to find opportunities for the freer exploration of her identity in exile, whereas the male gendered exile finds his identity problematized by that rupture. Yet because, within the terms of the heterosexual matrix, woman remains an object of desire despite the painful experiences with which she is associated, and because within the world of exile the return home is also desired, woman is paradoxically also made the embodiment of a positivized homespace:

> La mejor manera que tiene un extranjero de conocer una ciudad es enamorándose de una de sus mujeres, muy dadas a la ternura que inspira un hombre sin patria, es decir, sin madre [...] Ella construirá una ruta que no figura en los mapas y nos hablará en una lengua que nunca olvidaremos.[26]

> The best way for a foreigner to get to know a new city is to fall in love with one of its women, very given to tenderness and inspiring for a man without a nation, that is to say, without a mother [...] She will build a route that does not appear on maps and will talk to us in a language that we will never forget.

In this footnote, one of the many interjections that the author makes into her highly metafictional narrative, Peri Rossi deploys feminized notions of home that evince Kaminsky's assertion that exile narratives with male protagonists portray a character 'lost, confused, alienated, and in search of himself via a reconciliation with his past and a connection with the feminine'.[27] Homeland and motherhood are clearly aligned here, when Peri Rossi equates a lack of national identity with the lack of a mother figure. And the suggestion that to know a woman from a particular country is to know the country itself collapses the categories of female gender and nation further into one another; a symbolic move that, left unchallenged, has important and restrictive implications for the female identity. As Kaminsky points out in her study *After Exile* (1999), however,

> Peri Rossi's stark identification of homeland with mother, her bland implication that the exile is always male, her apparently neutral observation of European women's eroticization of the racial other, and her presumption of universal heterosexuality, all encased in the language of sentimental romance, indicate that this advice be read ironically.[28]

Peri Rossi's male protagonist might seem the quintessential exile, and his depiction engages many of the gendered symbolisms that can be associated with exile and the spaces in which it is played out, but an ironic attitude such as the one visible here reminds the reader to question typical associations.

The dissolving of assumed connections and resultant problematization of the social order is then furthered by the fact that Equis's real origins are never revealed to the reader; a feature of the narrative introduced as a conscious decision on the part of the narrator:

> Haré notar, por último, que a diferencia de *Don Quijote de la Mancha*, obra en la cual el autor tampoco quiso nombrar el lugar donde su protagonista había nacido, es casi imposible trazar un mapa de los viajes de Equis por el mundo.[29]

> I will note, lastly, that unlike in *Don Quijote de la Mancha*, a work whose author also did not wish to name the place in which his protagonist was born, it is almost impossible to trace the map of Equis's travels throughout the world.

This obfuscation of his origins equals a severing of the ties that bind the individual to the cultural and ideological spaces of both home as the affective/female point of origin, and nation as the political/male sphere, imbuing Equis instead with an ambiguous, in effect androgynous, quality. This, of course, is most forcibly compounded by the protagonist's self-selected, minimalist name, and also lack of the surnames that in Hispanic cultures allow a tracing of both matrilineal and patrilineal heritage, although always through the paternal line. This self-naming initiates a symbolic chain reaction that decouples Equis from an association with the masculine and liberates him from the inheritance of all that might be associated with 'the name of the father' (both culturally and in the Lacanian sense), thus imbuing him with dissentient qualities and implying he does not wish to participate in the continuation of the existing social order, as Raúl Rodríquez-Hernández has also suggested.[30] What is more, Equis's name openly challenges the oppositional and gendered foundations of that social order by recalling the 'XX/XY' chromosomal markers, but engaging only the element shared by both sexes, forgetting the part that would decide his gender and define his selfhood.

Instead, he remains both ambiguous and androgynous—a quality compounded by another vital facet of his characterization, revealed in the novel's latter stages (although subtly hinted at throughout): Equis is impotent. Peri Rossi's castrated male X, then, does not 'mark the spot' at all, but instead embodies unfixity of place, of self, and embodies thereby the possible deconstruction of hegemonic systems of categorization and organization. Peri Rossi has commented that 'Freud said that the self is a despot that wishes to eliminate contradictions', but 'to eliminate our contradictions is to eliminate a very important part of ourselves',[31] and it is precisely this acknowledgment for which Equis appears to be the vehicle. Set up as a dualistic character who is feminized and made Other by his exilic condition, yet still informed and influenced by his preordained access to hegemonic discourses, Equis is a postmodern *Bildungsheld* because his itinerant journey will teach him to see clearly—to face seeing clearly—the damage wrought by the hegemonic discourses that organize his social surroundings.

THE GENDERED/GENDERING LANGUAGE OF EXILE

Equis is not, then, a character completely free from the very start of his story of the orthodox language, associations and frames of reference of the patriarchal symbolic economy. In the third chapter of the novel we encounter Equis in the role of male beholder of the female form as he whiles away his time in exile watching repeated, subsequent showings of Donald Cammell's 1977 film *Demon Seed,* starring Julie Christie, in which she is brutalized and eventually impregnated by a robot that has developed higher consciousness. In an interesting article that underscores the reach of Peri Rossi's text by arguing that this scene in the novel is an 'indictment of gender victimization perpetrated by the film industry', Leah Fonder-Solano applies Laura Mulvey's seminal ideas on the male gaze to highlight that as 'a male spectator, [Equis] feels compelled toward an implicit identification with the machine's omnipotent masculine force'—as clearly exemplified by the following passage from the text:[32]

> Solo y anhelante, a la espera (una espera que se prolonga demasiado, multiplicando morbosamente los detalles, con un regodeo oscuro que

invita a la complacencia) de la maquina implacable que se lanzará sobre la bella Julia Christie [...] Solo y anhelante, escuchando su propia respiración amplificada por el resuello de la maquina excitada; solo con el temor de que sus propias fantasías aparezcan ahora en la pantalla, y dividido entre el amor de Julie Christie, el deseo de salvarla y la secreta, maligna complacencia con lo que va a ocurrir...[33]

Alone and eager, waiting (too long a wait that gruesomely multiplies the details, with a dark, perverse pleasure that invites satisfaction) for the implacable machine that will throw itself upon the beautiful Julie Christie [...] Alone and eager, listening to his breath amplified by the rasping breath of the excited machine; alone with the fear that his own fantasies might appear now on screen, and torn between his love for Julie Christie, the desire to save her and the secret, malign satisfaction in the face of what is about to happen...

Vercingétorix, who is with him at the cinema, draws a parallel between the savage robot and the dictators heading the regimes that they have both escaped, and so Equis's self-alignment with the sexual powers of the robot make him representative, although he is clearly not entirely at ease with his responses, of the extreme masculinity upon which such authoritarian regimes are founded.

Holding on to the sense of Equis as the kind of protagonist and narrative vehicle established above, it is possible to examine in detail some of the ways in which Peri Rossi embraces the gendering language of the hegemony as a tactic by which to expose its power structures, and also to challenge the gendered associations and resultant inequities of dichotomous thinking. In particular, this is achieved through the use of a descriptive vocabulary that engages orthodox paradigms of woman/the feminine in the creation of what might be termed a female symbolic order: Equis's ambiguous portrayal and the dual perspectives it affords is continued by Peri Rossi's giving Equis a descriptive vocabulary by which to engage with the world around him, and that becomes a means of positivizing the feminine tropes it knowingly deploys. She challenges the extremes of patriarchy through her text by wholly embracing feminized tropes and by placing this vocabulary in the mouth of a male exile on a journey of development, thereby making of it a language of contestation.

As particularly interesting examples of this inversion of the hegemonic language of gender stand the tropes of liquidity, encapsulated in a variety of ways by references to the sea and other forms of water, for which Peri Rossi notes a personal predilection.[34] This liminal space is a traditionally female paradigm that plays an important role in her depictions of exilic experiences. Embraced as a fluid space in which/a force by which the binary logic of the phallocentric order can be undermined, it enables exploration of an important reversal of generic norms in this novel via the pivotal role that female characters play in Equis's journey and the lessons he learns along the way—even through relatively minor characters. This is not to suggest that the male characters are not interesting or significant, but nor would I say that they make as much of a contribution to Equis's personal development and eventually radical shift in worldview as the women he encounters.

Symbolically, the connection of water to exile and to notions of the feminine begin in the movement that is the cause and consequence of exile, when the deviant individual, seen to have gone beyond the established norms of one's social context, is forced to turn that ideological step outside into a geographical migration. Metaphors of excess and overflow are therefore apt for the description of the exile's situation, and these also play upon paradigmatic understandings of woman as the embodiment of excess (ideas that will be pertinent again in the discussion of the female body undertaken in Part Three). This vocabulary is invoked even in the descriptions of the first woman we see Equis encounter in the novel. At the start of the narrative, Equis is traveling by boat (an obvious parallel with the 'Ship of Fools' of the title), and on that part of his journey he interacts with a woman character identified only as 'the Beautiful Passenger'. She is intriguingly described as having 'green eyes and wide sea, swinging hips and plunging necklines',[35] so that his view of her (the novel is written in the third person but focalized through Equis) evokes a heterosexual male gaze of desire, drawing on conventional associations of the female body with the natural world and sexualizing its shapes and movements.

A second key episode exemplifying feminized visions of excess depicts another of Equis's unconventional and brief love affairs, this time with a woman much older than he, who is described in great physical detail and, again, by use of liquid tropes to heighten the sense of the character's femininity. Through Equis's admiring gaze the reader sees the woman's 'celestial, water-blue eyes', and also noteworthy is the description of the couple as 'a solicitous son accompanying an ancient mother',[36] which normalizes their soon-to-become unorthodox relationship. As a consequence of this initial description, the change in their relationship that the reader by now awaits, but remains tentative of, appears as yet more transgressive than it might have done without the shadow of such traditional interpretations of male-female and age relationships. This excess, carrying with it the trace of the feminized trope of liquidity, is reflected in the body of the lady and fully appreciated by Equis:

> Equis se inclinó y hundió su mano bajo el vestido. Rozando fantásticas moles de carne blanda y tersa que parecían deshacerse—tibiamente—entre sus dedos, avanzando por nubes de algodón que al tocarlas mostraban pozos negros, como la luna, Equis llegó hasta el borde mismo del calzón.
>
> [...]
>
> En cuanto al corpiño, que era de una tela firme y compacta, Equis lo desabrochó enseguida, satisfecho de escuchar el tic del cierre, al abrirse, y lo hizo descender por el arco de los hombros, dejando que

la múltiple, láctea y mullida carne blanca se desparramara, escapándoselo de las manos, en abundantes pliegues.[37]

Equis leaned and slid his hand under her dress. Stroking fantastic rolls of soft, smooth flesh which seemed to melt warmly between his fingers, crossing clouds of cotton that, upon being touched, revealed dark craters like on the moon, Equis arrived at the waistband of her panties.

[...]

When it came to her bodice, which was of a sturdy, compact fabric, Equis undid that straight away, satisfied by the clicking sound of the fastener as it opened, and he slipped it down over the arch of her shoulders, allowing the abundance of milky white flesh to spill through his fingers in ample folds.

Finally, the use of this paradigmatic vocabulary is continued when Equis meets Graciela, who will play a pivotal role in both the reader's understanding of Equis and of the aims of the text by furthering his own understanding of himself and his sociocultural context. Compounding the role in the formulation of the narrative of a feminized metaphorical language, her first appearances in the story are also told through the adoption of this symbolism, giving her a primordial aspect:

siempre parecía recién salida de una inmersión en el mar, con residuos acuáticos en el pelo, en los brazos, en las piernas. Las gotas transparentes de agua se fijaban en los poros de la piel, se aferraban allí, como diminutas lentes. Como aquellas bolas de ópalo en cuyo interior hay menudas piedras de colores, filamentos vegetales, trozos de vidrio y pequeñas cuentas, dispuestas de manera irregular y cuyo conjunto [...] nos fascina como el fondo del mar o la investigación de los cielos.[38]

She always looked as if she had just risen from the sea, with droplets of water in her hair, on her arms, on her legs. Those transparent droplets stuck to the pores of her skin, they clung there, like miniature lenses. Like those round opals inside which there are tiny coloured stones, filaments, fragments of glass and small beads, arranged in an irregular manner and whose combination [...] fascinates us like the bottom of the sea or the study of the skies.

Graciela, just like the Beautiful Passenger and Equis's elderly lover, is thus steeped in orthodox femininity. Despite the fact that no actual mention of that specific term is made, the imagery with which she is surrounded certainly enhances our sense of her gendered identity, demonstrating the informative power that such gendered tropes can have.

What is crucial about the use of this language, as mentioned above, is that it is deployed by Equis as a male character made ambiguous by his exilic status, which has begun to afford him a more pluralistic view of the geographic and sociopolitical spaces in which he finds himself. Therefore, this language is not to be taken at face value, but interpreted in line with his own simultaneous inside/outside status: it deploys stereotypes but at the same time challenges them, and this is communicated via Equis's responses to the women in these scenarios: the Beautiful Passenger is objectified by his gaze but nonetheless portrayed as an active, not as a passive figure, so that she might further be understood to serve as a depiction of precisely the kind of female behavior feared by the patriarchal social order. For example, when she beats Equis in a game of chess she is depicted in that act in ways that point towards her characterization as a castrating female:

> como un cirujano corta, abre la piel de un solo movimiento, ella hundía el alfil en la casilla vacía y extirpaba el peligro, avanzando, siempre avanzando.[39]

> in the manner in which a surgeon cuts open skin in a single movement, she plunged her bishop into the empty square and removed the threat to her pieces, advancing, always advancing.

Unsurprisingly, then, she is also the one who initiates what the reader is left to assume, when first reading the novel, is a sexual encounter between herself and Equis, and even the brief portrayal of this scene is carried out in terms that imbue her with a sense of dominance:

> ella cerró la puerta y comenzó a quitarse el vestido, sin haberse despojado antes de los zapatos.[40]

> she closed the door and began to take off her dress, without having removed her shoes first.

Particularly valuable to my readings here is Equis's still being 'ready to follow her to her cabin' even after her defeat of him, because when reading with hindsight we know that Equis's impotence meant that penetrative sex will not take place.[41] As a result, this is an undoing of expected scenarios in which the male ego will be recovered by his conquering of the female body and the restoration of the active/passive binary. Instead, Equis seems not to have feared adopting a more passive role, and this is indicative of a deconstructive potential that increases steadily throughout the novel, in light of the various formative experiences afforded to him by, in particular, encounters with female characters.

In terms of his brief romance with the older lady, many of the words chosen, such as the verb 'hundir' with its other possible meaning of 'to submerge', and the references to 'warm' and 'milky' flesh, all evoke traditionalized perceptions of femininity that do concretize her role for him as a mother figure, and contribute to the novel's patterns of portrayal of the 'feminine' as characterized by all of these qualities. But we cannot ignore that Equis takes pleasure in a body that defies norms of beauty and of age in relation to the female gendered identity; a body potentially seen as excessive/transgressive on a number of levels.

Lastly, Equis begins to associate Graciela with the exploration of sea and sky; of unknown worlds that remain outside of the organizational systems of his own environment—the environment from which he finds himself constantly on the run, but can never really escape. Also significant about his encounter with Graciela, described by him as 'in the splendor of youth; in that moment of radiance in which beauty, more than a quality of facial features or physique, is the result of passage into maturity',[42] is that it gives the first real hint at the impotence so fundamental to his characterization and potential as the vehicle for Peri Rossi's deconstructive message. When Graciela interrogates him on his encounter with the elderly woman, and asks 'Would you do it with me too?'[43] his response is intriguing:

> Equis se sobresaltó, como cuando su madre abría de improviso la puerta y lo sorprendió en el cándido entretenimiento de clasificar sellos; de alguna manera, entonces—y ahora—tenía la certeza de estar decepcionando, en parte, a alguien.[44]

> Equis jumped, like when his mother unexpectedly opened the door and surprised him in the innocent act of classifying stamps; somehow, then and now, he felt certain of having somehow disappointed someone.

The humorous construction of this flashback to his past, which invites the reader to expect a scenario in which a mother intrudes on her adolescent son masturbating, signals the fact of Equis's sexual impotence and symbolic castration. The full significance of his sexual dilemma will be discussed further below, when it comes to play a more direct role in the denouement of the story, but for now it is informative to reading the imagery in which he cloaks Graciela: sensitized to the suffering that can be caused by the imposition of gender and sexuality norms on the individual, in hindsight it is clear that Equis's language does not imply a fear of the unknown that woman so often comes to represent within hegemonic discourses, but nor does he suppress that fear by envisaging Graciela as passive, a territory ripe for his explorations, because he cannot interact with her in the manner implied by that characterization. Therefore, despite the contradictions at work here, rather than hold down the female gendered identity, forcing it to remain in the realm of the 'outside', as an outsider himself, Equis's association of Graciela with the sea depicts Graciela/woman as absorbed into 'the largest global mass' in such a way as to transform her into 'an uncontrollable force of nature, mocking the constraints of the social arrangements that would seem to have defeated [her]'.[45] This is a reversal of normalized gendered associations with the journey motif that have also informed debates around the validity of the female Bildungsroman, where the normative male 'sets out to win, conquest and dominate' and where 'no-one, or at least few, would expect a woman to discover, conquest or explore new territories'.[46] Instead, straight after this conversation Graciela leads Equis off to explore a hard-to-reach cave once used by women to defend the island from attack when the men were away at sea.[47]

If Equis were a different kind of male protagonist, the portrayal offered through his eyes to the reader of Graciela, and indeed of the sixty-eight-year-old woman, could be interpreted as a reductive and essentialist vision of woman as nothing more than the object of desire, but by now the reader is fully aware of his unconventionality at the levels of gendered and sexual identities. By presenting the reader with challenging scenarios embracing notions of the castrating female and gerontophilic sexual preferences, as well as invoking the threat of 'the feminine' as constituted by a lack of rigidity, control and classification, Peri Rossi furthers Equis's transgressive nature and heightens the reader's sense of his role as seeker of new social orders. And these aspects of the novel render clear its position within the broader context of Latin American feminist practice which, according to Rodríguez-Hernández, 'centers, amongst other things, on an interrogation of and defiance towards traditional representations of women in patriarchal societies' and 'brackets off the absolute notion of the Self as a singular masculine entity, a phallic entity, that cancels out and suppresses any other form of representation'.[48]

The events discussed so far occur in the first third of the novel, by which time Equis has found himself in another rendering of the ship of fools, the mystically named *Pueblo de Dios* God's Town on an island in the country of M., a place inhabited by exiles of all kinds who, just like Equis, 'seem to emerge from some distant horizon, or to have been born of themselves'.[49] In this environment, a truly ambiguous place thanks to its isolated location and hodgepodge of inhabitants, who cannot cohere under the banner of a given national identity, or religious, political or cultural discourse, Equis's sensitivity to the role of language in formulating a Manichean worldview whose fulcrum is the setting up of gendered binaries, is heightened:

> En casi todas las lenguas [...] entre las más antiguas [palabras] está la palabra Sol. No es difícil explicar por qué. ¿Macho o hembra? Según enseña Borges, por el cual Equis experimenta un ambiguo afecto, los idiomas germánicos que tienen género gramatical, dicen *la sol*. También los guaraníes y—curiosamente—la antigua cosmogonía del Japón habla de una diosa sol, hembra.[50]
>
> In almost all languages [...] amongst the oldest [words] is the word Sun. It is not difficult to explain why. Male or female? According to Borges, for whom Equis feels an ambiguous fondness, those Germanic languages that are grammatically gendered render this word female. As do the Guaraní tribe and—strangely—the ancient cosmology of Japan also speaks of a sun goddess.

I find this pondering noteworthy because it is one of a series of subtle indications appearing throughout the novel of an increasingly profound grasp on the part of Equis of the more pervasive, more insidious aspects of gender oppression. Moreover, in its reaching back in time to search out the moments at which gender became such a central factor of our organizational systems, it feeds into Graciela's later revelations to both Equis and the reader of the fundamental role of the first Western exile narrative in the formulation of gender inequity: a feminist activist, she begins a project of interviewing schoolchildren in order to gauge their perceptions of gender roles in light of the story of Adam and Eve in the Garden of Eden. To cite just one of the responses she gets (from a young girl):

> Dios había creado a Adán y lo había rodeado de plantas de aves y de peces, pero necesitaba un semejante. Entonces Dios lo acostó, lo hizo dormir y de una costilla de su costado, creó a Eva. Y Adán se regocijó. Los problemas empezaron porque ella era un poco curiosa y le hizo caso a la serpiente. Por culpa de Eva las mujeres tenemos mala fama en este mundo.[51]

> God had created Adam and surrounded him with plants, birds and fish, but he needed a companion. So God put him to sleep and created Eve out of a rib from his chest. Adam was pleased. The problems started because she was a bit curious and began listening to the serpent. Because of Eve women have a got a bad reputation in this world.

Encapsulating the impact of the weight of the blame for humankind's expulsion from paradise, this answer emphasizes that, from a female perspective, the impossibility of a return to paradise is in fact the impossibility of a return to an identity not symbolically marked by the actions of Eve, or to a symbolic realm whose language will not invoke that transgression. From the moment the apple was picked from the tree, difference was inserted into the relationship between man and woman so that, as Kristeva has put it, 'between the two sexes a cleavage or abyss open[ed] up.'[52]

In light of this, Peri Rossi's paradoxical use of that language is also revealed as a vital strategy by which to undermine the prejudices of the symbolic economy, for it is the abyss between the sexes that is bridged by Equis's ambiguous, eventually androgynous qualities. If the female characters discussed in this section are central to Equis's journey of self-development, it is because his interactions with the opposite sex are informed by heterosexual patriarchal values and categorizations of women, and rendered in the vocabulary of that order, yet simultaneously embracing of the feminized exilic metaphors of fluidity (liquidity) and excess (the challenging of boundaries physical and ideological). Equis is enabled by the fact that he is already 'outside', by the fact of his access to the realm of phallic power being cut off, by his exposure to a world that is extremely feminized as counter to the extreme masculinity of the patriarchal system, to rid himself of the fear of the feminine that he is incited to as a male in patriarchal society, and as evinced in the cinema scene.

DREAMS AND ENIGMAS

In the end, Equis is enabled by this dislocation from the rigidity of the hegemonic order and relocation in the structurelessness of exile to interact more meaningfully with the realms of human experience otherwise cut off to him by their feared association with loss of control, the subliminal and the subconscious—namely the dreams whose role in the text will now be examined, and which are vital to the continuation of Equis's paradigm-shifting journey of self-development. This analytical shift is also facilitated by the fact that the author herself has noted that 'the world of dreams is very similar to that of language. There are no words [in it] but it is organized as a world of symbols. It seems to me that the process by which a dream is formed and that of language are very similar'.[53]

That Graciela and Equis meet on an island primarily inhabited by fellow exiles, all of whom now live on the margins of the world, in an ex-centric place of non-belonging, recalls Equis's identity as a man with no origin, just as the above description of Graciela as a kind of enigmatic sea creature of mysterious origin underpins the reader's sense of her rootlessness, also. Together, the two characters thus represent a lack of origin that, placed in relation to the generic constraints of the traditional Bildungsroman, leave them untethered from the social roots to which a classical *Bildungsheld* would eventually return and accept, at least to some degree. In defiance of such generic patterns and social integration, the characters of Peri Rossi's novel, whilst not depicted as relishing their itinerant existence, seem clear about its comparative positivity given the alternative options they faced, so that acceptance of the norm is never a possibility, and they will remain as outsiders.

As a reflection of this irremediable ex-centricity, the structure of Peri Rossi's text, which does not need to attempt to relocate its protagonists within an established framework, takes on a form that echoes the non-orthodox nature of the characters by which it is populated. The leitmotif of the tapestry that hangs in the Cathedral of Gerona, depicting the divine creation of the world—the moment of origin as explained by the Judeo-Christian grand narrative—functions at once as a scaffold around which the story of Equis's meanderings is structured and as a cause of fragmentation of the text (thereby highlighting the constructed nature of all narratives), which interrupts Equis's story and emphasizes its lack of clear trajectory. The asterisked footnote that informs the reader of the location and nature of the artwork also points out what is, for Equis, its disconcertingly harmonious depiction:

> Se trata de *El tapiz de la creación*, de la catedral de Gerona. En alguno de sus viajes, Equis vio este tapiz. Y se conmovió. A diferencia de la

tapicería gótica, que combina elementos paganos y corteses con símbolos cristianos, el de la creación es mucho más austero, corresponde a esa religiosidad medieval capaz de construir un mundo perfectamente concéntrico y ordenado. Pero cualquier armonía supone la destrucción de los elementos reales que se le oponen, por eso es casi siempre simbólica. Equis contempló el tapiz como una vieja leyenda cuyo ritmo nos fascina, pero que no provoca nostalgia.[54]

This is the *Tapestry of the Creation*, in the Cathedral of Gerona. On one of his journeys, Equis saw this tapestry. And he was moved [/shaken]. Unlike in gothic tapestry, which combines pagan and courtly elements with Christian symbols, this one is much more austere, corresponding to that medieval religiosity capable of constructing a perfectly concentric and ordered world. But any kind of harmony supposes the destruction of the elements that oppose it, and for that reason it is almost always symbolic. Equis contemplates the tapestry like it were an old legend whose story fascinates but provokes no nostalgia.

The protagonist's reaction to the tapestry is equivocally described using a verb, *conmover*, which means at once to be emotionally moved by something, but also to be shaken or unsettled by it. Given Equis's complex relationship with the ideological structures of the world, it is arguably the latter meaning that is most implied here. This is enhanced by its description as of a 'medieval religiosity', which locates the tapestry in a historical moment far away from the postmodern one of Equis's existential crisis and makes it representative of a past whose structural impositions have no place in the world as he experiences it. Rather, it embodies a problematic and constrictive world that can only be produced through the subordination of its unwanted elements. Equis's total lack of nostalgia in the face of this vision confirms that, regardless of the difficulties of the structureless world of exile in which he lives, he does not suffer from the desire to return that is endemic to exiled individuals. Instead, his seemingly directionless journey is one dedicated to the undoing of the oppressive effects of binary thought via the unpicking of the exilic processes by which it functions.

Mary Beth Tierney-Tello connects the tapestry motif to the use of allegory in Peri Rossi's novel, in which 'various characters act as virtual mouthpieces for expounding on ideas about the meaning of sexual and national identity and the nature of exile' so that 'the narrative often seems to suggest its own interpretation'.[55] She conjectures that this self-explanation is a typical feature of allegorical narratives, but also considers the particular trajectory of Equis's journey and the tapestry motif as further layers of the text's allegory. In line with my understanding of the tapestry, this critic also reads it as an image 'that strives to represent the origin of man' in such a way as to offer coherence in the face of chaos. She posits that

> the allegorical mode used by Peri Rossi draws attention to [...] a crisis of representation: due to the sociopolitical and literary contexts, the authority of the 'world picture', indeed the very possibility of representing our world at all, has been cast into doubt. The nature of this crisis is brought into focus through the juxtaposition of the allegorical tapestry of the Creation, which depicts a fixed, closed representational order, and the counter-allegory woven by the series of tableaux of [Equis's] journey through our imperfect, fragmented, violence-tom contemporary society, which undoes the authority of the divinely 'authorized' representation.[56]

Despite his lack of outright nostalgia for the old order, however, Equis is not portrayed as immune to the trauma that the loss of structure can cause, nor to the identity crises that can be engendered by the removal of limits potentially experienced as comforting at the same time as restraining; his journey is still taking place. Moreover, this ambiguous relationship with order, its necessity and the necessity of its rejection, is evoked through the portrayal of dreams which, as Timothy Foster has put it, 'beg for interpretation and, in a Freudian sense, conceptualize instinctual drives, repressions and sociocultural prohibitions'.[57] The narrator explains that:

> Cuando [Equis] despierta de malhumor, es que oscuramente sabe que ha tenido una revelación en el sueño; una clase de revelación tan poderosa e insoportable que ha sido preferible olvidarla. [...] El sentimiento de culpa que nace de esa traición a la enseñanza oculta de los sueños le provoca mal humor.[58]

> When Equis wakes up feeling sullen, it is because on some level he knows that he has had a revelation whilst asleep; a kind of revelation so powerful and unbearable that it has been preferable to forget about it. [...] The feeling of guilt that is generated by this betrayal of the hidden teachings of dreams puts him in a bad mood.

The example of his dreams that immediately follows, however, is a recurring one that Equis does remember, and he is left with feelings of pleasure at its end, suggesting, then, an ability to read its meaning. This, I argue, implies a shift in Equis's development; a growing ability to confront the realities of his/the world, however harsh they are revealed to be by his subconscious.

That the dream and its meaning are significant for Equis means they are for the reader's understanding of Peri Rossi's tale, too, so that we are incited to work to understand them. This encouragement of active approaches to reading is derived of the postmodern and allegorical qualities of the narrative but also further imbues *La nave de los locos* with aspects of the Bildungsroman genre, because it promotes the education of the reader as a corollary to the learning experienced by the protagonist. The dreamscape recounted here, which I will quote at length given its importance to my arguments, appears to continue the symbolic thread of water imagery that has been linked to notions of the feminine throughout the novel, and thereby further reveal Equis's paradoxically orthodox and non-orthodox relationship with women (and with the gendered underpinnings of the social order):

> Como se trata de un sueño repetitivo, Equis sabe perfectamente que al final de la playa hay una casa alta, de piedra gris, con un balcón sobre el mar y que los días en que la marea sube es muy difícil llegar hasta la casa, ya que el camino de acceso está invadido por las aguas, él no sabe nadar y las olas alcanzan grandes dimensiones. Como siempre la pesca se demora en virtud de las dificultades con los aparejos, a la hora de ir a la casa el mar ha crecido y emprende el camino con una sensación inminente de riesgo y peligro. Inevitablemente, Equis descubre que las aguas han trepado hasta el balcón y las olas acorralan contra el muro; no puede regresar, porque el mar, hacia atrás, ha invadido toda la costa; no puede avanzar, porque las aguas no se lo permiten. En el único lugar donde todavía hace pie (un pequeño borde de piedra, contra el muro), las aguas son muy azules, muy densas. En esa situación tan angustiante, siente, además, que le pesan los aparejos y los implementos de pesca, pero no puede desprenderse de ellos, pues están atrapados en la roca.
>
> A pesar de todo, despierta con la sensación de que el paseo y la pesca han sido agradables. Tanto placer le hace sospechar que, en realidad, no se trataba de pesca, sino de otra cosa.[59]
>
> As this is a recurring dream, Equis knows perfectly well that at the end of the beach there is a tall house, of grey stone, with a balcony overlooking the sea, and that on days when the tide comes in it is very difficult to reach the house, because the path to it is overcome by water. He does not know how to swim and the waves become big. As always, fishing takes a long time in light of difficulties handling the equipment, and by the time comes to go home the sea is encroaching and he starts out on the path with a sense of imminent danger. Inevitably, Equis discovers that the water has reached as far as the balcony and the waves are crashing against the walls; he cannot turn back, for the sea has covered everything behind him; he cannot go forward because the water blocks his route. At the only place where he can still stand (a little stone ledge against the wall), the water is very blue, very dense. In that very upsetting situation, he feels that his fishing equipment is weighing him down, but he cannot let go of it, because it is caught in the rocks.
>
> In spite of everything, he awakens with a feeling that the trip and the fishing were enjoyable. And such a sense of pleasure makes him

> suspect that, in fact, the dream was not about fishing, but about something else.

Given the presentation of water imagery in the novel as a feminized motif, discussed earlier, it is possible to follow Equis's suggestion that this dream is not really about fishing but about something else, and to reapply feminized readings of water imagery, and the connections between woman, water and exile, in a reinterpretation of this dream sequence. One such possible reading envisages the grey house at the end of the beach that Equis cannot reach as the homespace to which he, as an exile, no longer has access. The water that surrounds him keeps him from the edifice whose balcony, given the background against which this novel was written, is highly suggestive of authority and power, and especially of political discourse, recalling the television footage of the leaders of Latin American dictatorships standing tall over the nation and announcing the installation of their regime. (It also similarly calls to mind the depiction of the fascist aesthetic of the cement factory to which Vercingétorix is disappeared.[60]) The house, therefore, may symbolize the nation as homespace too. The fishing equipment that bears down on him and gets stuck in the rocks can be understood to represent that which he carries in real life, not materially speaking, but ideologically so; that which is the cause of his ejection from the realm of power symbolized by the grey edifice—it is a crude phallic symbol that brings his problematized masculinity into play as a quality contributing to his exclusion and to his remaining in the zone of danger, rather than within the safety of the hegemony symbolized by the house to which he would usually, as a man, have unchallenged access.

The question remains, however, what symbolic role the water in this dream can come to have in this interpretation. If still to be understood as feminized, representative of femaleness, it may compound, as it gradually makes difficult his entrance into the house, the idea that it is Equis's inability to deploy the phallic power with which he was born that is at the root of his exile. If this is the case, the fact that Equis feels such pleasure when he wakes from the dream becomes highly intriguing. Yet more tellingly, the water in this dream poses no real threat to Equis, for he says at the beginning:

> Las aguas son transparentes y se puede contemplar en toda su extensión el tránsito de los peces. Pero además, Equis puede sumergirse en ellas hasta quedar tapado por las aguas, sin necesidad de nadar, sin mojarse, sin ahogarse, como si, en realidad, se tratara de aire.[61]
>
> The water is transparent and the movements of the fish can clearly be seen. But what is more, Equis can submerge himself in it until completely covered, and he does not need to swim, does not get wet, does not drown, as if it was, in fact, air.

Thus I would argue the dream should indeed be understood to 'be about something else' (or perhaps even something Other). It provides one more positivized representation of exile from the patriarchal hegemonic order by deploying the metaphor of water in the representation of that exile as a space facilitating new possibilities and experiences. What is more, the authoritative norms symbolized by the house proverbially 'built on sand' are portrayed as unstable, as we wonder how long, in any case, such a house will last at all. Subsequently, if womankind—and the other Others with which she is aligned in Peri Rossi's novel—is found present here in the symbolism of water, the dream may also be seen to include insinuations that, eventually, the weight and inflexibility of patriarchy will allow for its undoing, as its weak foundations are pulled out from underneath it by that female force—one clearly represented by the female characters of the novel. The illogical world of dreams is hence portrayed as one filled with meaningful revelations, with the capacity to undermine the rigidity and logic of the dominant social and symbolic orders, and with very positive effects for the exiled individuals who are at once within and outside that order: outside, because they are no longer allowed access it, and simultaneously inside, because they continue, even in their absence, to be defined by the requirements that it imposes upon their identities.

This illogical world can be read in gendered terms as a feminine space whose excess, free flow and alterity stand in opposition to the logic and definition of patriarchy, never better encapsulated than by the solid grey of the building in the dreamscape. As a whole I read this dream as one about confrontation with difference, and the acceptance of difference as unproblematic. This interpretation relies upon the reading of water as a symbol of the womanhood (assisted by the noun 'agua' being gendered female in Spanish) that opposes Equis's assumed male identity, and into which he is able to submerge himself without any negative consequences for his own selfhood. The dream serves as a space of excess in which the subconscious can engage with the upsurge of real concerns, and where the fear of the feminine as a threat to the dominant order is brought under control.

In this way the episode contributes to the overall thrust of the narrative of *La nave de los locos*, throughout which Equis makes a gradual progression towards an unquestioning acceptance of otherness, and especially gendered otherness, and which also entails a greater level of self-acceptance on his part. Indeed, the themes of exile, gender, dreams and the refutation of binary logic are ones that encircle the narrative of this novel by serving as its point of departure and the medium through which its conclusion is expressed. On the very first page of the text the reader is recounted in the first person a dream that begins with the receipt of an order: 'The city at which you arrive, describe it'.[62] The narrator of the dream says: 'Obediently, I asked: "How should I distinguish between what is significant and what is not?"'[63] Suggestively, no answer is given, and instead the scene switches to one where the owner of the narrative voice is in a field, working at the task of separating wheat from chaff:

> Trabajaba en silencio, hasta que ella llegó. Inclinada sobre el campo, tuvo piedad de una hierba y yo, por complacerla, la mezclé con el grano. Luego, hizo lo mismo con una piedra. Más tarde, suplicó por un ratón. Cuando se fue, quedé confuso. La paja me parecía más bella y los granos, torvos. La duda me ganó.
>
> Desistí de mi trabajo. Desde entonces, la paja y el grano están mezclados.[64]

> I was working in silence, until she arrived. Bending over the ground, she took pity on a blade of grass and I, to please her, mixed it with the grain. Then she did the same with a stone. Later, she pleaded for the inclusion of a mouse. When she left, I was left confused. The chaff seemed more beautiful and the grain unyielding. Doubt overcame me.
>
> I stopped working. Since then, chaff and grain have remained mixed.

The activity undertaken in this dream acts out the binary logic critiqued by Peri Rossi's novel, and its refusal of this divisive process is encapsulated in the character's decision to allow wheat and chaff to stay mixed. Moreover, the intervention of the woman has added a blade of grass and a small mouse to the original mixture. Borrowing a phrase from Luce Irigaray's deconstructive interpretation of the Freudian account of femininity, Tierney-Tello uses

> the notion of "an old dream of symmetry" to refer here to what Peri Rossi denounces as oppressive, patriarchal logic whereby representation and identity are founded upon binary systems that exclude and marginalize the other, unable to account for difference in any inclusive, pluralistic way.[65]

Her ensuing interpretation of the dream is succinct and highly valid, where she reads it as

> an oneiric reelaboration of the Fall of Man, which can be read, in this postmodern context, as the fall from the kingdom of the illusion of innocent and unproblematic representation, from the prelapsarian realm where the realization of the master narrative still seemed possible.[66]

Through its highly fragmented and metafictional plot and prose, right from the start the novel presents a series of interlinked *petit récits* that counter the grand narrative whose undoing is begun here specifically by 'the insertion of an active feminine element ("she") into the scene of representation' that means, for Equis, 'it becomes impossible to make the decisions regarding inclusion and exclusion with the same surety as before'.[67]

Furthermore, the difficulty of continuing to envisage the world in oppositional terms eventually translates into the events of the denouement of the novel—and there can be said to be one despite its lack of clear linear plot, as its interpretation as a postmodern take on the Bildungsroman makes clear. The nineteenth tableaux, named 'London', begins with a dream narrative in which Equis is posed a question:

> una pregunta que flotaba como un enigma, como aquellos acertijos que los reyes, enamorados de sus hijas, proponían a los pretendientes.
>
> Príncipes, caballeros degollados en el insensato afán de resolver la oscura adivinanza que conservaba a las hijas para los padres. En el sueño, Equis escuchaba la pregunta: '*¿Cuál es el mayor tributo, el homenaje que un hombre puede ofrecer a la mujer que ama?*'[68]

> a question floated like an enigma, like those riddles that kings, in love with their daughters, set for their suitors.
>
> Princes and knights disgorged in the foolish aim of solving the complex puzzle that enabled fathers to keep their daughters for themselves. In the dream, Equis heard the question: 'What is the greatest tribute that a man can make to the woman he loves?'

As Equis's search for the answer to the enigma progresses, it becomes clear that the couching of the question within recognition of male desire for control of the female, encapsulated in the father-daughter relationship, also points to the solution of the riddle to which Equis will come through a number of encounters with disempowered women. In connection to this, and presenting an interesting connection back to my thematic concern with myth and fairy tale in Chapters One and Two, Lucia Guerra-Cunningham emphasizes the expression of the enigma through the traditional foundational moment of the fairy tale genre, whose 'phallocentric paradigms' usually revere male sagacity, but argues that Equis's approach to answering the question encountered in the dream contradicts such paradigms by being driven by 'feminine motivating forces'.[69]

Ultimately, it is due to his own experience of oppression, subsequent expulsion, and the reasons for it, that Equis is a character so sensitive to the disempowerment of women. His impotence enables him to interact with women differently than might be expected of a more normative male protagonist. The intimate encounters he shares with the Beautiful Passenger, sixty-eight-year-old woman, and Graciela are never recounted in their entirety, and the reader is left with the sensation that this incompletion of parts of his narrative is directly related to an incompletion of the sexual act during those encounters. These scenes are also, of course, examples of the avoidance of closure that is an ideological strategy at work throughout the text. This is compounded through his interactions with the prostitute he meets in a restaurant towards the end of the novel, for the sight of her beaten, swollen face is influential in his realization of the answer to his riddle.[70] The remainder of this episode is interspersed by Equis's references back to the dream and with his internalized repetitions of its central question, so that a gradual move towards the answer is insinuated throughout. Also important is the fact that it is in the room of the abused prostitute that Equis overtly acknowledges his sexual problem for the first time, telling her that he would not get undressed as she has done because '[i]t has been a long time since I've had an erection [...] And it doesn't bother me. I'm not going to talk about it now or at any other time'.[71]

The woman's response encapsulates an ideological position that, in turn, summarizes the novel's critique of gendered oppositions, the power imbalance that they inform, and exile as the ultimate result of that imbalance: she says, '[i]n case it means something to you, I find in impotence a form of harmony',[72] recalling with these words the earlier portrayal of the fragmented tapestry, where Equis saw a conceptualization of harmony as only ever possible through the destruction of anything opposing it. Now, through the eyes of the prostitute, another key female character on his journey of formation, Equis's admission of impotence is understood as a form of harmony that counters, without violence, the bias of binary thought. Thus, as he stands naked in the room with her, 'with his flaccid sex, which merited no observation on anyone's part, between his thighs',[73] this unorthodox couple come together to embody the deconstruction of the phallocentric order towards which Equis has been working, however unknowingly, throughout his global wanderings. The prostitute, now able to avoid another beating because she can convince her pimp that she has turned a trick, is at least temporarily safe in the company of Equis, who feels no need to enter into the sexualized power dynamic that would otherwise govern his interaction with her. The culmination of Equis's realization is compellingly expressed as he leaves the brothel only to find himself watching a transvestite porn show where the all-male spectators are

> [a]rrellanados en sus asientos, con esa falsa seguridad que les daba el ser mucho y anónimos, haber pagado la entrada, estar abajo y no arriba, tener el abdomen con grasa, el aliento pesado, el chiste fácil y un músculo reflejo entre las piernas [...] [P]arecían haber retrocedido a algún estado de impunidad infantil, en el cual se sentían dominadores, irresponsables.[74]

> sprawled in their seats with the false security afforded by being numerous and anonymous, by the fact of having paid to get in, being in front of the stage not on it, having a fat belly, heavy breath, jokes to hand and a muscular reflex between the legs [...] They seemed to have regressed to some state of childish impunity, in which they felt in control, without responsibility.

The depiction of the crowd here contrasts greatly with Equis's immediately preceding acknowledgement of his own non-hegemonic version of a masculine identity, and compels the reader to remember his ponderings, a few pages previously:

> ¿Qué haría una mujer con su tristeza? [...] un hombre triste entra a un bar, pide una cerveza [...] es posible que termine la noche con cualquier mujer de la vida, eyaculando tristezas en otro culo, porque para eso tiene falo y paga, ¿dónde eyaculan las mujeres, en qué culo se descargan?[75]
>
> What would a woman do with her sadness? [...] a sad man goes into a bar, asks for a beer [...] perhaps ends the night with some woman of the world, ejaculating his sadness into another's arse, because that's what he has a phallus and money for. But where do women ejaculate? Into whose arse do they empty their worries?

It is thus that Equis comes to acknowledge he has had the answer to his question for a long time, but has never dared to pronounce it. In the last pages of the novel he tells the story to the character Lucía, (whom he has previously met at the abortion clinic in London and who is now performing in the porn show), and exorcises himself of the oppression that the question carries with it while it remains unanswered: 'The answer is his virility'.[76]

What the solving of the riddle constitutes, therefore, is the suggestion that phallocentrism must be brought to an end for the exiling processes of oppositional thinking also to cease. Equis becomes, through his story, an everyman who represents the possibility of ambiguity as a way forward, and who, further still, embodies the possibility of equality through the recognition and acceptance of difference. It is ultimately the ambiguous space of dreams that carries this important message in Peri Rossi's work. In this way, the role of dreams in the structure and story of *La nave de los locos* calls to mind some of the characteristics of French feminist theories of women's writing and its engagement with psychoanalytic theory, in which, Sally Kitch summarizes, male writing has been declared to be 'linear, directed, logical', whereas the '[f]emale form, according to such an approach, is more open, fluid and simultaneous, less "terminating" and linear'.[77] These characterizations, whereas problematic in their essentialism given that *La nave de los locos* is a text with deconstructive intentions, are nonetheless applicable, and particularly to the dreams in the narrative. Crucially, this occurs in the same way that the essentialist female paradigms that have been discussed above have been deployed to work towards an undermining of the gendered logic of binary thought.

Peri Rossi does not, then, take the collectively anticipated, and therefore unchallenging, male exile only to depict him in terms that are equally unchallenging. Instead, from the very beginning, this male exile's simultaneous insider/outsider status—privy to but denied access to hegemonic discourse—is used to set him up as a postmodern, exilic *Bildungsheld*. He takes the reader with him on a journey towards a successful interrogation of the facile polarizations by means of which we define selfhood and otherness, and all of their correlations. Ultimately, his ambiguous characteristics establish Equis as the vehicle for a narrative that, whereas inescapably reliant on the orthodox readings of the gendered spaces of exile, and thus on orthodox readings of the gendered identities that such metaphors help to establish and uphold, works towards a renegotiation of gendered identity by adopting exile as a location in which hegemonic beliefs and assumptions can be challenged by the revelation of the *petit récits* of the marginalized. In this sense, exile, as art, has served as a situation at the limit of experience that facilitates radical reenvisionings of received knowledge:

> Yo tengo una predilección por los finales, por esos momentos en que el tiempo y el espacio han perdido sus características físicas y todo se tambalea [...] es entonces cuando aumenta la incertidumbre acerca de nosotros mismos [...] Estos momentos me interesan (o me obsesionan) cada vez más. En los últimos libros de narrativa estoy buscando casi exclusivamente esa situación límite, reveladora.[78]

> I have a predilection for limits, for those moments in which time and space has lost their physical characteristics and everything is unstable [...] it is then that uncertainty about ourselves increases [...] Those moments interest me (or I am obsessed by them) more and more. In my recent works of prose I have been exclusively seeking out that revelatory boundary.

Therefore, whereas Peri Rossi might have explained away the fact of her protagonist being male as simply the result of a lack of choice, what she has achieved is to use the very discourses that enforced that decision against themselves, engaging a series of norms and expectations and then countering them with, to borrow Linda Hutcheon's useful term, the 'attendant irony' by which are imbued gender characterizations and gendered conceptualizations in the text.[79]

Most effectively, by saving the final revelation of Equis's impotence, weighty with symbolism and its potential to signify radical change, to the end of the novel, Peri Rossi allows her reader to discover along with Equis that he—as they themselves—had the answer all along. The overall story told to us here is one inciting self-knowledge and knowledge of the world, achieved by the willingness to adopt different perspectives by recognizing the view of the Other as meaningful. For although I have named Equis's story an 'Anti-Bildungsroman', this is not intended to imply that there is no narrative of personal growth to be encountered here. Rather, this is an expedition whose exilic setting allows for a development in understanding of the self and of selfhood that challenges rather than accepts the status quo to which the normative Bildungsroman might have its protagonist capitulate. It is an empowering story of a journey towards agency in the form of this multiple vision of self and society, and it incites change.

NOTES

1. Cristina Peri Rossi and Diana P. Decker, 'Fragments of an Interview with Cristina Peri Rossi', *Off Our Backs*, 22.4 (April 1992), 20–21, p. 21.
2. Roberto González Echevarría, *The Voice of the Masters: Writing and Authority in Modern Latin American Literature* (Austin: University of Texas Press, 1985), p. 136.
3. See Graciela Trevisan, 'Interview with Cristina Peri Rossi' (2008) for further discussion of the events surrounding this, what Peri Rossi calls her 'second exile': http://www.citylights.com/resources/download.cfm?GCOI=87286100595160&thefile=Peri_Rossi_interview.pdf.
4. See Gabriela Mora, 'Cristina Peri Rossi', in Diane E. Marting (ed.), *Spanish American Women Writers: A Bio-bibliographical Source Book* (Westport, CT: Greenwood Publishing Group, 1990), pp. 436–445 and Peri Rossi's official website, http://www.cristinaperirossi.es/bio.htm [Accessed 07/03/2015].
5. Nicola Gilmour, 'Una entrevista con Cristina Peri Rossi', *Journal of Iberian and Latin American Studies*, 6:1 (July 2000), 117–136, p. 121. 'Sí, las mujeres no escriben, y cuando escriben se suicidan'.
6. Gilmour, 'Una entrevista con Cristina Peri Rossi', p. 122.
7. For an informative overview of late-twentieth-century Latin American Feminisms see Nancy Saporta Sternbach, Marysa Navarro-Aranguren, Patricia Chuchryk, and Sonia E. Alvarez, 'Feminisms in Latin America: From Bogotá to San Bernardo', *Signs*, 17. 2 (Winter 1992), 393–434.
8. Parizad Dejbord has also made the connection, in her seminal study of the author, between Peri Rossi's personal story and her more multifaceted approach to exile, as opposed to one focused on its geographical dimensions. See *Cristina Peri Rossi: escritora de exilio* (Buenos Aires: Galerna, 1998).
9. Sophia McClennan, *The Dialectics of Exile: Nation, Time, Language and Space in Hispanic Literatures* (West Lafayette, IN: Purdue University Press, 2004), p. 2.
10. Dejbord, *Cristina Peri Rossi*, p. 240. 'No lo quise publicar porque era demasiado quejumbroso, sólo quejumbroso. Los poemas son muy buenos [...] pero es el llanto, la llantina del exilio. Sentí que no tenía que contribuir a la ceremonia del dolor, como si fuera lo único que se podía decir del exilio. Se pueden decir otras cosas también'.
11. Dejbord, *Cristina Peri Rossi*, p. 11; 'cuestionar y desmitificar la concepción misma de la identidad unitaria'.
12. Dejbord, *Cristina Peri Rossi*, p. 14; 'el fenómeno del exilio como experiencia positiva y liberadora, nutriéndose de la noción de la ambigüedad'.
13. It is worth noting that Vercingétorix's being named after the Gallic war hero executed by Julius Caesar further links him to ideas of rebellion and repression. Leah Fonder-Solano also makes the point that due to his abhorrence of violence, Vercingétorix recalls the comic figure Astérix as the modern-day counterpart of the historic figure, famed for triumph by means of his intelligence not by physical force—a fact fitting of the novel's anti-authoritarian and pacifist discourse. See Leah

Fonder-Solano, 'Intersections Between Feminism, Film and Text: *La nave de los locos* by Cristina Peri Rossi, *Letras Femeninas*, 29.2 (Invierno 2003), 33–44, p. 36.
14. Helène Cixous, 'Sorties: Out and Out: Attacks/Ways out/Forays', in Hélène Cixous and Catherine Clément (Trans. Betsy Wing), *The Newly Born Woman* (Manchester, UK: Manchester University Press, 1986), pp. 63–132, p. 63.
15. Toril Moi, *Sexual/Textual Politics* (London: Routledge, 1985, 2002), p. 103. Moi goes on to discuss Cixous's location of '*death* at work in this kind of thought'. This concept, whereas not crucial to my use of Cixous here, is interesting in its own perpetuation of the biblical notions surrounding exile, and Eve's role in the mortality of man.
16. Julia Kristeva, 'La Femme, ce n'est jamais ça', *Tel Quel*, 59 (Automne 1974), 19–24, p. 20.
17. Moi, *Sexual/Textual Politics*, p. 165.
18. Moi, *Sexual/Textual Politics*, pp. 165–166.
19. Margaret R. Higonnet, (and citing Joni Seager, 'Blueprints for Inequality' (1993)) 'New Cartographies: an Introduction', in Margaret Higonnet and Joan Templeton (eds.), Reconfigured Spheres: Feminist Explorations of Literary Space (Amherst: University of Massachusetts Press, 1994), pp. 1–19, pp. 6–7.
20. Moi, *Sexual/Textual Politics*, p. 162.
21. Gema Pérez-Sánchez and Cristina Peri Rossi, 'Cristina Peri Rossi', in *Hispamérica*, 24.72 (December 1995), 59–72, p. 68. 'Para el inconsciente colectivo el exiliado es siempre varón [...] la figura del revolucionario sigue siendo masculina'.
22. Amy Kaminsky, *Reading the Body Politic: Feminist Criticism and Latin American Women Writers* (Minneapolis; London: University of Minnesota Press, 1993), p. 17.
23. Cristina Peri Rossi, *La nave de los locos* (Barcelona: Seix Barral, 1984; 1995), p. 10. All subsequent references are taken from this edition and all translations are my own.
24. Kaminsky, *Reading the Body Politic*, p. 39.
25. Higonnet, 'New Cartographies: an Introduction', p. 14.
26. Peri Rossi, *La nave...*, p. 38.
27. Kaminsky, *Reading the Body Politic*, p. 37.
28. Amy Kaminsky, *After Exile: Writing the Latin American Diaspora* (Minneapolis: University of Minnesota Press, 1999), p. 53.
29. Peri Rossi, *La nave...*, p. 37.
30. Raúl Rodríguez-Hernández, 'Posmodernismo de resistencia y alteridad en *La nave de los locos* de Cristina Peri Rossi, *Revista Canadiense de Estudios Hispánicos*, 19.1 (Otoño 1994), 121–135, p. 129.
31. Peri Rossi and Decker, 'Fragments of an Interview', p. 21.
32. Leah Fonder Solano, 'Intersections Between Feminism, Film and Text': *La nave de los locos* by Cristina Peri Rossi', *Letras Femeninas*, 29. 2 (Invierno 2003), 33–44, p. 38.
33. Peri Rossi, *La nave...*, p. 23.
34. Ana Basualdo and Cristina Peri Rossi, 'Fragmentos de una entrevista', *Quervo Poesía*, Monografía no.7 (Diciembre 1984), 8–12, p. 9.
35. Peri Rossi, *La nave...*, p. 3; 'La Bella Pasajera'; 'ojos verdes y ancho mar. Caderas semovientes', 'amplios costillares', p. 11.
36. Peri Rossi, *La nave...*, p. 80.
37. Peri Rossi, *La nave...*, p. 83.
38. Peri Rossi, *La nave...*, p. 85.

39. Peri Rossi, *La nave...*, p. 16.
40. Peri Rossi, *La nave...*, p. 16.
41. Peri Rossi, *La nave...*, p. 16.
42. Peri Rossi, *La nave...*, p. 85. 'en el esplendor de la edad; en el momento de radiante hermosura en que la belleza, más que una cualidad de los rasgos o de la figura, es el resultado de un pasaje a la madurez'.
43. Peri Rossi, *La nave...*, p. 89.
44. Peri Rossi, *La nave...*, p. 91. '¿Lo harías también conmigo?'.
45. Anca Vlasopolos, 'Staking Claims for No Territory: The Sea as Woman's Space' in Higonnet, *Reconfigured Spheres*, pp. 72–88, p. 75.
46. Marisa Peyreyra, 'La peregrinación hacia el paraíso: El modo utópico como viaje de retorno al origen en la narrativa de Alina Diaconú y Cristina Peri Rossi', *Confluencia*, 21.1 (Fall 2005), 168–181, p. 170. 'El hombre sale para ganar, para conquistar y dominar [...] Nadie, o pocos, esperan que la mujer descubra, conquiste o explore nuevos terrenos'.
47. Peri Rossi, *La nave...*, p. 95.
48. Raúl Rodríguez-Hernández, 'Posmodernismo de resistencia y alteridad en *La nave de los locos*, de Cristina Peri Rossi', *Revista Canadiense de Estudios Hispánicos*, 19. 1 (Otoño 1994), 121–135, p. 124.
49. Peri Rossi, *La nave...*, p. 97. 'parecen brotar de algún lejano confín, o haber nacido de sí mismos'.
50. Peri Rossi, *La nave...*, p. 97.
51. Peri Rossi, *La nave...*, p. 157.
52. Julia Kristeva, 'About Chinese Women', cited in Toril Moi, *The Kristeva Reader* (New York: Columbia University Press, 1986), pp. 148–159, p. 141.
53. Basualdo and Peri Rossi, 'Fragmentos de una entrevista', p. 11.
54. Peri Rossi, *La nave...*, p. 20.
55. Mary Beth Tierney-Tello, *Allegories of Transgression and Transformation: Experimental Fiction by Women Writing Under Dictatorship* (Albany: State University of New York Press, 1996), p. 175.
56. Tierney-Tello, *Allegories of Transgression and Transformation*, p. 175.
57. Timothy Foster, 'Transgressions in Literature, Politics and Gender: Peri Rossi's *La nave de los locos*', *Confluencia*, 13.1 (Fall 1997), 73–86, p. 78.
58. Peri Rossi, *La nave...*, p. 46.
59. Peri Rossi, *La nave...*, p. 47.
60. Jorgelina Corbatta, 'Metáforas del exilio e intertextualidad en *La nave de los locos* de Cristina Peri Rossi y *Novela negra con argentinos* de Luisa Valenzuela, *Revista Hispánica Moderna*, 47.1 (June 1994), 167–183, p. 172.
61. Peri Rossi, *La nave...*, p. 47.
62. Peri Rossi, *La nave...*, p. 9; 'La cuidad a la que llegues, descríbela'.
63. Peri Rossi, *La nave...*, p. 9. 'Obediente, pregunté: ¿Cómo debo distinguir lo significante de lo insignificante?'.
64. Peri Rossi, *La nave...*, p. 9.
65. Tierney-Tello, *Allegories of Transgression*, p. 178.
66. Tierney-Tello, *Allegories of Transgression*, p. 178.
67. Tierney-Tello, *Allegories of Transgression*, p. 178.
68. Peri Rossi, *La nave...*, p. 163.
69. Lucía Guerra-Cunningham, 'La referencialidad como negación del paraíso: Exilio y excentrismo en *La nave de los locos* de Cristina Peri Rossi', *Revista*

de estudios hispánicos 23 (1989), 63–74, p. 69; 'paradigmas falologocéntricos'; 'fuerzas motivadoras femeninas'.
70. Peri Rossi, *La nave...*, p. 184.
71. Peri Rossi, *La nave...*, p. 188; 'Hace mucho tiempo que no tengo una erección [...] Y no me importa. No voy a hablar de eso ahora ni en ningún otro momento'.
72. Peri Rossi, *La nave...*, p. 188; 'Por si te importa, encuentro en la impotencia una clase de armonía'.
73. Peri Rossi, *La nave...*, p. 188; 'con el sexo fláccido entre las piernas, que no merecía ninguna observación de parte de nadie'.
74. Peri Rossi, *La nave...*, p. 190.
75. Peri Rossi, *La nave...*, p. 178.
76. Peri Rossi, *La nave...*, p. 196; 'La respuesta es: su virilidad'.
77. Sally Kitch, 'French Feminist Theories and the Gender of the Text', in Eunice Myers and Gynette Adamson (eds.), *Continental, Latin-American and Francophone Writers: Selected Papers from the Wichita State University Conference on Foreign Literature, 1984–1985*, 1 (Lanham, MD: University of America Press, 1987), p. 3.
78. Basualdo and Peri Rossi, 'Fragmentos de una entrevista', p. 10.
79. Linda Hutcheon, *A Poetics of Postmodernism* (London & New York: Routledge, 1988), p. x.

BIBLIOGRAPHY

Basualdo, Ana, and Peri Rossi, Cristina, 'Fragmentos de una entrevista', *Quervo Poesía*, Monografía no. 7 (Diciembre W1984) 8–12.

Cixous, Hélène, 'Sorties: Out and Out: Attacks/Ways out/Forays', in Hélène Cixous and Catherine Clément (Betsy Wing, Trans.), *The Newly Born Woman* (Manchester, UK: Manchester University Press, 1986), pp. 63–132.

Corbatta, Jorgelina, 'Metáforas del exilio e intertextualidad en *La nave de los locos* de Cristina Peri Rossi y *Novela negra con argentinos* de Luisa Valenzuela, *Revista Hispánica Moderna*, 47.1 (June 1994), 167–183.

Dejbord, Parizad, *Cristina Peri Rossi: escritora de exilio* (Buenos Aires: Galerna, 1998).

Fonder Solano, Leah, 'Intersections Between Feminism, Film and Text: *La nave de los locos* by Cristina Peri Rossi', *Letras Femeninas*, 29. 2 (Invierno 2003), 33–44.

Foster, Timothy, 'Transgressions in Literature, Politics and Gender: Peri Rossi's *La nave de los locos*', *Confluencia*, 13.1 (Fall 1997), 73–86.

Foucault, Michel, *Madness and Civilization: A History of Insanity in the Age of Reason* (1961; 1964), Richard Howard (trans.) (London: Routledge, 2006).

Gilmour, Nicola, 'Una entrevista con Cristina Peri Rossi', *Journal of Iberian and Latin American Studies*, 6:1 (July 2000), 117–136.

González Echevarría, Roberto, *The Voice of the Masters: Writing and Authority in Modern Latin American Literature* (Austin: University of Texas Press, 1985).

Guerra-Cunningham, Lucía, 'La referencialidad como negación del paraíso: Exilio y excentrismo en *La nave de los locos* de Cristina Peri Rossi', *Revista de estudios hispánicos* 23 (1989), 63–74.

Higonnet, Margaret R., 'New Cartographies: an Introduction', in Margaret Higonnet and Joan Templeton (eds.), *Reconfigured Spheres: Feminist Explorations of Literary Space* (Amherst: University of Massachusetts Press, 1994), pp. 1–19.

Hutcheon, Linda, *A Poetics of Postmodernism* (London & New York: Routledge, 1988).

Kaminsky, Amy, *After Exile: Writing the Latin American Diaspora* (Minneapolis: University of Minnesota Press, 1999).

Kaminsky, Amy, *Reading the Body Politic: Feminist Criticism and Latin American Women Writers* (Minneapolis; London: University of Minnesota Press, 1993).

Kitch, Sally, 'French Feminist Theories and the Gender of the Text', in Eunice Myers and Gynette Adamson (eds.), *Continental, Latin-American and Francophone Writers: Selected Papers from the Wichita State University Conference on Foreign Literature, 1984–1985*, Vol. 1 (Lanham, MD: University of America Press, 1987).

Kristeva, Julia, 'La Femme, ce n'est jamais ça', *Tel Quel*, 59 (Automne 1974), 19–24.

McClennan, Sophia, *The Dialectics of Exile: Nation, Time, Language and Space in Hispanic Literatures* (West Lafayette, IN: Purdue University Press, 2004).

Moi, Toril, *Sexual/Textual Politics* (London: Routledge, 1985, 2002).

Moi, Toril, *The Kristeva Reader* (New York: Columbia University Press, 1986).

Mora, Gabriela, 'Cristina Peri Rossi', in Diane E. Marting (ed.), *Spanish American Women Writers: A Bio-bibliographical Source Book* (Westport, CT: Greenwood Publishing Group, 1990), pp. 436–445.

Pérez-Sánchez, Gema, and Peri Rossi, Cristina, 'Cristina Peri Rossi', *Hispamérica*, 24.72 (December 1995), 59–72.

Peri Rossi, Cristina, and Decker, Diana P. , 'Fragments of an Interview with Cristina Peri Rossi', *Off Our Backs*, 22.4 (April 1992), 20–21.

Peri Rossi, Cristina, *La nave de los locos* (Barcelona: Seix Barral, 1984; 1995).

Peyreyra, Marisa, 'La peregrinación hacia el paraíso: El modo utópico como viaje de retorno al origen en la narrativa de Alina Diaconú y Cristina Peri Rossi', *Confluencia*, 21.1 (Fall 2005), 168–181.

Rodríguez-Hernández, Raúl, 'Posmodernismo de resistencia y alteridad en *La nave de los locos* de Cristina Peri Rossi, *Revista Canadiense de Estudios Hispánicos*, 19.1 (Otoño 1994), 121–135.

Saporta Sternbach, Nancy, Navarro-Aranguren, Marysa Chuchryk, Patricia, and Alvarez, Sonia E., 'Feminisms in Latin America: From Bogotá to San Bernardo', *Signs*, 17.2 (Winter 1992), 393–434.

Tierney-Tello, Mary Beth, *Allegories of Transgression and Transformation: Experimental Fiction by Women Writing Under Dictatorship* (Albany: State University of New York Press, 1996).

Trevisan, Graciela, 'Interview with Cristina Peri Rossi' (2008) http://www.citylights.com/resources/download.cfm?GCOI=87286100595160&thefile=Peri_Rossi_interview.pdf [Accessed 07/03/2015].

Vlasopolos, Anca, 'Staking Claims for No Territory: The Sea as Woman's Space', in Margaret Higonnet and Joan Templeton (eds.), *Reconfigured Spheres: Feminist Explorations of Literary Space* (Amherst: University of Massachusetts Press, 1994), pp. 72–88.

4 En breve cárcel/Certificate of Absence *by Sylvia Molloy* (1981)

The approach I will take to Sylvia Molloy's novel in this chapter is the same as that taken in my study of Cristina Peri Rossi's *La nave de los locos* in the previous chapter, so that I read this work too as an 'anti-Bildungsroman' with deconstructive tendencies; one that seeks out new forms of self-definition by actively undermining the processes and ideologies that have dominated conceptualizations and legitimizations of selfhood. Molloy's is a very different story from Peri Rossi's, however, for as we shall see, her account of a lesbian protagonist's own personal and, in the immediate sense at least, self-imposed exile into one room takes place in a textual world that is the antithesis of that traveled by Equis and the other characters of *La nave de los locos*. Silent and primarily static, physical movement in Molloy's narrative is minimal, always short distance, and depicted only through the figure of the writer-protagonist. Arguably the most intimate of all of the novels examined in *Gender and the Self in Latin American Literature*, the reader experiences in this work a stripping bare of the self at the center of the narrative; a gradual self-exposure that accounts for the vulnerability and fragility of an individual who has suffered hurt and disappointment in personal relationships. The psychological shifts that reside at the heart of the narrative and that tap into the matter of the discursive formation of gendered selfhood, though, are just as pertinent to my interests here. The narrative is created by and through a movement *inwards* that reverses the enforced movement *outwards* of political exile, but which nonetheless exposes the mechanisms by which the very fact of 'true'—physical, ideologically—informed, geographical—exile is made possible.

In this way, the text reaches beyond its initial micro-focus in order to contribute to a macro-level social critique. In terms of my interests in genre here, Molloy's work invokes the narrative trajectory of the Bildungsroman by exposing a journey of self-development, but through a narrative arc that writes a present moment in order to be able to better read the past, and thereby exposes the ways in which the patriarchal discourses proscribing normative selfhood are enacted upon the individual. So, as opposed to narrating from the time of childhood forwards to a moment of socially acceptable maturity, Molloy presents a writer-protagonist who works backwards, excavating the foundations of selfhood in a similar way to that of Equis in *La nave de los locos* as he sought answers to his dream conundrums—but here, the conundrum is the lesbian female self that authors the text. In what follows I begin with a consideration of some of the theoretical considerations that challenge and/or enable discussion of this work as an exile text, setting up the parameters within which I read it as such, and examining how the writer-protagonist of Molloy's novel functions as a vehicle for this exilic anti-Bildungsroman. I then explore a series of the micro-spaces that are key to the text, and their role in her retrospective, self-analytical journey: the room in which she writes, its place within the social order and as a personal space; the narrative's recurrent mirror motif; and two spaces that were also given significance in Peri Rossi's exile novel in the previous chapter: the sea as a feminized space for self-exploration, and dreams as an arena apt for the deconstruction of the existing order of things.

THE PLACES AND SPACES OF EXILE: THE MATERIAL AND THE METAPHORIC

In extratextual terms there is certainly a political dimension to Molloy's text, which the author herself has said 'became a political gesture' through the context of its publication: originally published by the Barcelona-based Seix Barral in 1981, the novel was not printed and distributed in her native Argentina until 1998. In the years following its initial release it circulated instead in the form of illicit photocopies among a sympathetic lesbian readership because, she has explained, the Argentine 'Process of National Reconstruction' (*Proceso Nacional de Reconstrucción* 1976–1983) left even publishers with whom she had worked before unable to be involved in the public dissemination of a work whose focus on lesbian love affairs and implicit social critique would be perceived as subversive.[1] Further to this, the fact that *En breve cárcel* needs to be considered not just as straightforward fiction but also for its autobiographical foundations (to be discussed further below) also means that when, elsewhere, Molloy has talked of the destabilizing experience of her work being unknown in Argentina, we understand that this surely equated to a sense of being unknown herself—to being figuratively if not physically disappeared.[2]

Nonetheless, in contrast to the ease with which it was possible to discuss Peri Rossi's novel within the frame of 'exile writing' in the previous chapter, given its widely accepted identity as an ur-text in exile studies, when it comes to Molloy's work my application of a similar analytical vocabulary confronts one of the central debates in the study of exile literature. This concerns the definition of the term 'exile' itself and, in particular, the way in which it has been deployed connotatively in theoretical and critical debates. Sophia McClennan, for example, has referred to an 'increased scholarly interest in the exile as a metaphor for a new phase of social alienation', in which we encounter notions of 'inner exile, cultural migrancy, nomadism, dislocation', and she laments the fact that 'the exile was, and often still is, described as being free of the repressive state of national identity'.[3] In her own work, as a result, she aims to ensure that the material realities of empirical exile are acknowledged by 'reconciling the exile of theoretical discourse with concrete cases of exile from repressive authoritarian regimes'.[4] In a similar vein, Amy Kaminsky has challenged the metaphorization of exile in the specific context of North American feminism in which, she explains, the term was taken on to refer to the 'cultural disenfranchisement [of] even privileged women', leading to an 'evacuation of meaning of the term "exile"' and to the 'colors, shape and weight of the word [...] being eroded by the carelessness of those who picked it up and made use of it in their desire to name something else'.[5]

McClennan and Kaminsky thus seem primarily concerned about the fact that the political and physical dimensions of experiences of exile are lost through the term's theoretical and/or metaphorical application. However, both also recognize the difficulties inherent to any attempt to clearly delimit its meaning. For example, McClennan discusses the hierarchies of authenticity that have been applied to different exilic experiences, noting that 'it is clear that certain exiles are considered to be more authentic than others and that each dictatorship or repressive regime produces "representative" exiles'.[6] Writing against this kind of hierarchizing, and despite her concerns about the loose application of the term in critical works, she pertinently asks: 'If the state of exile is a result of the individual's perceived threat to the status quo, why should we expect the condition of exile to carry its own status quo?'[7] There is also a significant gendered dimension to take into account here, of course, for the 'real' exile that Kaminisky and McClennan might wish to hold on to is a *political* exile that remains symbolically tied to a male-dominated realm, as Peri Rossi has also commented.[8] In fact, setting aside Equis's gradually revealed unorthodoxy and standing him alongside Molloy's woman writer-protagonist, the two actually embody the notion of political exile as 'male', and metaphorical exile as 'female'—so that to fail to enquire after the distinct natures of the isolation depicted in these novels surely entails a failure to enquire after the formulation of gender itself.

I defend the treatment of Molloy's work as an exile text because the 'inner exile' depicted by her evinces and magnifies the insularity of woman's position within patriarchal culture. It may well, therefore, be a metaphorical exile, but, as Kaminsky is also careful to recognize, 'in language there is no "beyond metaphor," [...] metaphor not only is the inevitable condition of language but is, at times, a gift of beauty and wisdom'.[9] What she acknowledges here is something of which Cixous, too, has made us aware through the list of dualistic oppositions presented in *La jeune née* and discussed in the introduction to the previous chapter. Later on in this piece Cixous returns to metaphor to further emphasize for us the connections between it and gender in the formation of the symbolic order that Molloy targets in her writing:

> The (political) economy of the masculine and the feminine is organized by different demands and constraints, which, as they become socialized

> and metaphorized, produce signs, relations of power, relationships of production and reproduction, a whole huge system of cultural inscription that is legible as masculine and feminine.[10]

And her co-author Catherine Clément further points to the necessity of enacting symbolic shifts as a way of achieving tangible changes in the social order, underlining that to '[assume] the *real* subjective position that corresponds to [a woman's] discourse',

> [o]ne would [have to] cut through all the heavy layers of ideology that have borne down since the beginning of the family and private property: that can only be done in the imagination. And that is precisely what feminist action is all about: to change the imaginary order to be able to act on the real, to change the very forms of language which by its structure and history has been subject to a law that is patrilinear, therefore masculine.[11]

The 'feminized' exile depicted by Molloy is both a space of marginalization and an opportunity to contest those 'heavy layers of ideology'.

MARGINAL PERSPECTIVES: EXILE IN *EN BREVE CÁRCEL*

It is upon these terms, then, that I treat Molloy's work as a 'novel of exile'—keeping in mind the importance of the points made by McClennan and Kaminsky regarding our ethical responsibility not to diminish the dangerous and painful experiences of political exiles, whereas also engaging the parallels between the various forms of Othering whose recognition takes us to the roots of authoritarian discourses. I adopt the term 'exile' and its connoted vocabulary here as a frame of reference for the marginalized but not necessarily physically ousted individual: if a person is perceived as a threat, the fact of their ideological 'otherness' does locate them 'outside'; it ostracizes them. Avoiding the prioritization of certain types of exilic experiences therefore facilitates the use of exile as metaphor in the description and portrayal of experiences of marginalization, and so also its insertion into the theoretical vocabulary that is necessary to the full reading of *En breve cárcel*. In particular, this enables me to account for the way in which the writer-protagonist's lesbian sexuality informs the text and what we as readers can take from it. For as Elena M. Martínez reminds us in her study *Lesbian Voices from Latin America: Breaking Ground* (1996), 'in Latin America, like everywhere else' there has been 'a denial of lesbian existence and thus, of the possibilities of lesbian literature'.[12] To query the use of exile as 'a [literary] metaphor for the exclusion that lesbians experience in their lives [...], for the disenfranchisement of lesbians, for the experiences of outsiders in a society that is hostile to non-conventional forms of love and desire',[13] would surely be to contribute yet further to that experience of isolation. And so I align myself with this critic's approach to exile 'not just as a geographical separation from one's land' but also as a frame of reference for the 'emotional and psychological attitudes of those who live at the margins of society'.[14]

Exile as it is discussed here, then, is a matter of social alienation and the negative effects of the discourses that establish the margins in which non-normative individuals will eventually always be located—either physically or metaphorically. (Although I would maintain that those two different conceptualizations are utterly intertwined—a place is just a place until labeled as centric or non-centric, and such labeling is never empty of discourse.) This means that there is a deeply spatial aspect to Molloy's work; one which she has herself delineated as a recurrent quality in Latin American women's narratives:

> a *dislocation in order to be*—that could well be the main impulse behind their writing. One is (and one writes) elsewhere, in a *different* place. A place where the female subject chooses to relocate in order to represent itself anew.[15]

And I have found a particularly helpful way of articulating how this more connotative exile is deployed in her novel in black feminist bell hooks's notion of, in the words of Edward Soja, 'choosing marginality'.[16] For hooks, marginality signifies not something

> one wishes to lose, to give up, but rather [...] a site one stays in, clings to even, because it nourishes one's capacity to resist. It offers the possibility of radical perspectives from which to see and create, to imagine alternatives, new worlds.[17]

Importantly, in terms of addressing the concerns of exile literature theory discussed above, her approach here is grounded in the statement that '[t]his is not a mythic notion of marginality. It comes from *lived experience*' [my emphases].[18] And following from Soja's description of it, the relevance of her approach to my interest in the Bildungsroman is heightened by 'hooks's consciousness [being] rooted in the everyday life experiences of youth, home and family'.[19] I feel that this notion of a 'chosen marginality' is extremely useful to a reading of Molloy's story as it helps to negotiate the ethical quandaries discussed above via Kaminsky and McClennan without obfuscating the role of the voices of others, of social discourses, in placing the text's writer-protagonist where she is found.

ANON.: MOLLOY'S WRITER-PROTAGONIST

En breve cárcel is absolutely a response to the experience of marginalization by others, then, but initially not of social marginalization enacted by institutional forces. It begins with much more intimate experiences: the failure of romantic relationships. It quickly becomes clear to the reader that the retreat into the room that is the only setting of the first half of the novel (it is only in Part Two that the writer-protagonist begins to make forays outside of these four walls), and the scene of the story's actual creation (the present tense narrative means that we read seemingly as she is writing), has been catalyzed by the need to work through the traumas of a relationship and its eventual breakdown. We encounter a feeling of her own personhood having been diminished and pushed aside by the dominant personalities of two ex-lovers, leaving her 'outside' in terms of a lack of self-recognition, as well as in terms of a lack of agency in those relationships. The narrative begins, in a sense, then, as a story about love, first and foremost, but my interest is in the wider discursive context that is revealed via the ensuing self-analysis of the writer-protagonist, for the deeply personal tale penned here gradually leads a close reader to a narrative of broader social relevance; in particular to an exploration of the discourses by which female sexuality and selfhood are constituted and defined right from childhood.

This is enabled by Molloy's writer-protagonist being attributed a number of what I would term 'by-extension qualities'—characteristics that enable her reading as an individual (thanks to the intimate details provided of her family, lovers and emotions) at the same time as representative and revelatory of common experiences of female self-development and selfhood. At this point it is useful to bring into play the novel's aforementioned autobiographical dimensions, for whereas critics such as Virginia Muzquiz have rightly pointed out that the novel cannot be classified as a straightforwardly autobiographical text, 'we can interpret [it] as a sort of fictional autobiography in that it takes as its subject the autobiographical process'.[20] Marcia Stephenson has added to the consideration of this aspect of *En breve cárcel* that it, in fact, problematizes the autobiographical genre through its non-linear presentation of the ontology of an individual life, and reminds us of the moment in which the writer-protagonist explicitly defies classification of her text along such lines—a moment that also heightens the representative nature of the story and hints at the aims of Molloy as author:

> Autobiografías: qué placer seguir a un yo, atender a sus mínimos meandros, detenerse en el pequeño detalle que, una y otra vez, lo constituye [...] Estas líneas no componen, y nunca quisieron componer, una autobiografía: componen—querrían componer—*una serie de violencias salteadas, que le tocaron a ella, que también han tocado a otros.* [Emphases mine.]

> Autobiographies: what pleasure she feels in following a self, paying attention to its little meanderings, pausing over the tiny detail that, time and time again, gives it shape [...] What she writes does not constitute, and will never constitute, an autobiography: *rather, it tries to reproduce a disjointed series of acts of violence that befell her, that also befell others.*[21]

The novel is clearly not intended solely as an exploration of one selfhood, but of the formulation of selfhood through a discursive matrix that establishes the shared context for self-development, and whose violences shade and shape the lives of others also.

In terms of the broader frame of my interest in the Bildungsroman, one of the major challenges presented to discursive identity formation by Molloy is her implicit retention of a self-knowing, self-articulating subject at the heart of the narrative, in place of the passive written-into-history protagonist growing towards a prescribed form of social acceptance. This narrative strategy is one of the key reasons why her work is of interest to the present study, for it represents an important example of the role of literature in claiming a space for female agency, and is as such an illustration of what Molloy, who is a well-established critic of the autobiographical mode in Latin American literature, has described as 'the imagination of self' (a turn of phrase that also recalls hooks's evaluation of the space of the margins as a place of new perspectives).[22] Her own evaluations of the role of autobiography as used by regional authors provide a number of interesting insights into what her protagonist might be intended to achieve, even in light of the intratextual refutation of the genre, and also point to further ways in which the realm of the imagination is embraced here as a space from which to challenge the gendered metaphorics of the patriarchal symbolic order. To begin with, reflecting on examples of Spanish American autobiography, Molloy notes a 'clear need [therein] to be representative (of a country, of a social group, of a sex) in ways more extreme than one might expect', and that the 'Spanish American "I" [...] seems to rely more than other "Is" [...] on a sort of national recognition'.[23] In other words, as we would expect, the self of the autobiographical text is grounded in localities, but Molloy is keen to underline that the Spanish American autobiographer needs also to feel, to justify, a connection with other selves at various levels of identity. It is curious therefore that in her novel she takes the opposite approach but with, I would argue, the same aim: the writer-protagonist of *En breve cárcel* is purposefully removed of markers of identity, but it is exactly this that enables her to function allegorically. Firstly, she never names herself nor is she ever named by any other character because, aside from two instances of direct speech, (one brief statement at the start of the text and the second a slightly more extended one very near to the end), the only narrative voice is her own.[24] She remains anonymous throughout the book and bears similarities to Peri Rossi's Equis by thereby remaining unfixed by the patrilineal language of names and surnames and their traceable roots.

Next, the absence of geography in the narrative further contributes to the symbolic nature of the protagonist. There is an avoidance of place names that persists right until the end, so that Molloy evades pinning her story to any specific, mappable location or connecting her writer-protagonist to a specific point of origin. Both the number of spaces depicted and their descriptions are constrained: most are domestic and private in nature, aside from a couple of references to meetings in the more social spaces of bars or cafés in the second half of the story, and there is certainly no mention of clearly public, political arenas. Yet, where in Peri Rossi's *La nave de los locos* it was important to consider this vague depiction of place as a sign of the characters' imposed nomadism, because the writer-protagonist of *En breve cárcel* is in control of her own story, and because the story is one very much centered on the self, we are able to read this choice as an active attempt to sever ties, so that the spaces configured within the novel and deployed as loci for her intense self-exploration are purposefully unloosened from specific national, and therefore historical, cultural and sociopolitical ties. Molloy has commented on the role of geography in Spanish American autobiography in terms that are of interest here, writing that:

> The reworking of the birthplace autobiographeme—home, city or country—doubtlessly blends individual and collective memory the most successfully [...] Thus in remembering a city, the autobiographer will necessarily count on a collective memory of that city against which he will play his or her individual recollections, giving a particular, personalized reading of a common experience.[25]

Yet here, there seems to be no such sense of a common experience. Established in its place is a more open space from which to begin the journey of self-negotiation, and this is surely usefully related to the matter of the writer-protagonist's lesbian sexuality; to her disconnect from collective memories at the level of gender because of her 'otherness' in those terms. (We will see this come into play in particular in relation to the archaic figures who appear in the dreamscapes discussed at the end of this chapter.) Very simply, if we imagine this story of selfhood differently, as one invoking and then embracing the national map (geographical, sociopolitical, cultural, historical), the subsequent alignment of self and nation would establish very different literary parameters and fundamentally change the story of selfhood that can be narrated. For as Molloy and Robert McKee Irwin remind us in their introduction to *Hispanisms and Homosexualities* (1998), 'relations between nationalities and sexualities are uneasy at best', but those 'between nationalities and homosexualities [...] are downright problematic, even personally dangerous'.[26] The factor of national identity that McClennan was keen to underline above is a presence in absence here, whose recognized power is precisely what makes valuable a clearing of the map and the relocation of selfhood in a space as unmarked as possible by those discourses that predefine the individual. In its place is established a site from where lesbian identity can be included in, and accounted for as a part of, the redefinitions of selfhood that will be enacted.[27] A space that will allow for the reversal of the denial of lesbianism remarked upon by Martínez, above, and the creation of a form of relative autonomy.

'A PAUSE IN THE FLOW OF HISTORY': CHOOSING MARGINALITY AND THE ROOM OF ONE'S OWN

I say 'relative' because it is important to recognize that it does not make sense to assume it is possible to establish a which that is truly outside of discourse—and this is another reason why I find hooks's 'chosen marginality' an apt descriptor for what is depicted in/enacted by Molloy's novel: the empowering space of chosen marginalization in which the autonomous writer-protagonist creates her story is a small rented apartment, grasped as an opportunity to privilege individual experience and to thereby begin to reveal and unpick the threads by which her selfhood is constituted. It is embraced as a sanctuary, therefore, rather than experienced as a prison, but its portrayal nonetheless evinces the impossibility of simply stepping outside of the hegemonic matrix: the room is a liminal space; a threshold encapsulating that to 'be on the margin is to be a part of the whole but outside the main body'; a location permitting the development of 'a particular way of seeing reality'—a way of looking 'both from the outside in and from the inside out'.[28] A curious detail in the descriptions of this nodal space is especially interesting in these terms, for the way it quietly encourages the reader to keep in mind the space's duality, and its relationship with the culturally and politically specific backdrop of this Argentine woman's narrative: at the start of her story the writer-protagonist explains how '[w]hen she looks at the walls covered with a greenish-brown fabric (a martial color that she would never have chosen), she remembers her childhood'.[29] There are two important aspects of this easily missed detail. The first is the way in which the décor of the room evokes a military context and, by extension, a patriarchal one, and the second is that staring at those walls causes her to recall early memories. Given the significant role that a revision of childhood comes to play in the self-analysis on which the writer-protagonist embarks, it is intriguing that these two foundational elements are intertwined, and I would argue that it incites the reader to make the connections between the individual and the public realms between which the room stands. This description, given some thought, contributes meaningfully to a setting of the scene and to a revelation of intentions on the part of Molloy as author, allowing a view beyond the four walls into which she has her protagonist retreat, towards the exterior forces whose influence needs to be better understood by the end of her period of voluntary isolation.

In effect, the power of the room as a space of renegotiation rests upon its provision of an interstice in which the effect of dominant forces can at least be diluted. Those forces cannot be given privilege in this personal realm, but rather must be kept at an objective distance in order to be seen clearly for their influence upon the world and the self. My reading here is evinced by the nature of the single reference to what we can assume (although only in hindsight, at the end of the narrative when the writer-protagonist's childhood home is finally named as Buenos Aires), to be the Dirty War:

> En esa casa oyó un día, mientras la mujer seleccionaba los huevos y su hija Elise le mostraba con orgullo una cicatriz de apendicitis, un discurso que inauguraba una larga dictadura.
>
> It was in that house, while the woman was picking out the eggs and her daughter Elise was proudly showing off her appendectomy scar, that she heard a speech that marked the beginning of a long dictatorship. [30]

Here, the writer-protagonist is describing a childhood summer holiday with her family and remembering a small farm where she was sent to buy eggs. But the dictatorship that would give very particular shape to her 'dissidence'—as a lesbian and as a writer—is sidelined by a focus instead on the domestic setting, the routine task of choosing eggs, and a female body bearing a scar. Immediately the narrative moves on, and the more micro, but no less significant focus exemplified in this passage is sustained throughout the novel—a discursive move and mood that makes of both the room and the textual realm to which it, in turn, provides access, spaces in which to disrupt hegemonic power structures. Effectively banished are the proscriptive voices that enact control over selfhood, pushed back into realms of memory (and as shall be discussed later) dreams, from whence they can be addressed and reconfigured.

It is in instances like this that Molloy's work entails what Francine Masiello has called a turning to 'privatized experience to claim a pause in the flow of history';[31] making of that experience an opportunity through which to see more clearly, and begin renegotiating, the impact of social discourse, reading it through the lens of the personal and delineating its impact on the shaping of the individual. Here we see yet again the value of hooks's spatial vocabulary to reading Molloy's aims and achievements: her depicted space permitting new perspectives and the opportunity to explore the implications and revelations of such fresh ways of seeing is thoroughly grounded in lived experience. Upon this background, the exilic, the socially marginal, is embraced as a 'space of opportunity and action' to be occupied by the female writer-protagonist, and as one in which she is enabled to examine the formulation of her female selfhood by 'reconceptuali[zing] the problematic of subjection by deconstructing and disordering both margin and center'.[32]

Also relevant to my interests here, of course, is the fact that the gendered connotations of the space within which she chooses to go into exile are brought clearly into view. On the very first page of the novel, the writer-protagonist describes the room in which she sits down to write as one where the

> exagerado cuidado de algunos detalles, la falta de otros, señala que ha sido previsto para otro uso del que pensaba darle; de hecho para el que

> ocasionalmente le da. Cuarto y amores de paso. No hay bibliotecas [...] no hay mesa para escribir y la luz es mala. Suplió esas deficiencias y ahora libros y lámparas la rodean, apenas eficaces. Sabe con todo que la protegen, como defensas privadas, marcando un espacio que siempre llamó suyo sin hacerse plenamente cargo de él. Como máscaras la ayudan: adentro, para salirse de ella misma: afuera, para protegerse de los demás.
>
> exaggerated attention to certain details, the lack of others, are signs that it was intended for a purpose other than the one she planned for it: indeed, for the very purpose she occasionally makes of it. A place of transit for transitory loves. There are no bookshelves [...] no desk, and the light is bad. She made up for these defects and now books and lamps surround her, without much change. She knows, however, that they protect her, like defensive weapons, marking off a space that she has always called her own without fully taking possession of it. They help her like masks: from within, to free her from herself; from without to free her from others.[33]

Because the narrative is situated in this very clearly domestic space, the labeling of domesticity as woman's realm is called into play in this novel right from the start, engaging traditional gendered, spatial associations. However, normative gender/place relations are not simply deployed here and then left uninterrogated. This room is a space of autonomy in which the protagonist purposefully creates an environment for herself that is founded upon her own needs at the present time—not those of others.

The primary consequence of this is that even while remaining geographically located within the sociopolitical patriarchal sphere, and inescapably characterized by that phallocentric order (remembering the implications of the green walls), the interior spaces of both the room and the text created within it enable the creation of a gynocentric world. Most significant in these terms is the matter of the woman's sexuality. In the above citation, she refers to the fact that this is occasionally the site of the fleeting romantic encounters, which the reader is soon given to understand are part of lesbian rather than heterosexual affairs that we cannot fail to recognize as transgressive within the vocabulary of the patriarchal economy. This female-centered universe is sustained throughout the novel by various means, including the elimination of all male characters save as portrayed through the recollections of her father and very fleeting memories of an uncle who, it is hinted, was also homosexual and labeled as mad by the family.[34] (So that his disappearance is not actually carried out by her in writing, but was effected by the family unit's adherence to the rule of patriarchy.) And even when her father is recalled there is no use of direct speech to recount his words, he is allowed into her text only passively, never attributed the agency of speech/voice. As part of an interesting commentary on the novel's qualities as an example of women's writing that must both stand alongside and challenge the male tradition, Michael Hardin astutely highlights that one of the dreams in which her father is portrayed he is missing a hand, and interprets this as the writer-protagonist having denied him the parallel position of writer.[35] Yet more intriguingly, such purposeful removal of male influences is also depicted via references to childhood games in which that same refutation of the father figure is enacted by her and her younger sister, Clara, in their play-time imaginings of scenarios where 'there were never fathers or husbands', because they had all died in the masculinized pursuit of war 'or had simply never existed'.[36]

> Sólo estaban ellas dos—madres viudas, tías solteras o hermanas huérfanas—para organizar y llevar adelante al mezclado grupo de muñecas y animales de trapo que componían la familia.
>
> Only Clara and herself—widowed mothers, maiden aunts, or orphaned sisters—were left to organize and support the motley group of dolls and stuffed animals that made up their family.[37]

This tracing back of such a desire to her formative years contributes to a normalization of a world in which gender roles remained untethered to sex; where the absence of male counterparts means that little girls take on the roles of both men and women in caring for a disparate group of creatures whose description further hints at a desire to preserve the childhood innocence that facilitates acceptance of difference.

This normalization is then driven home and expanded beyond the realm of childhood memories by the fact that the word 'lesbian' never actually appears in the story. The refuge represented by the room and set up from the start of the narrative is crucial to this because in a story where the woman herself were not in charge of the words that produced the text, such an omission would surely be oppressive—a silencing of that which is considered subversive and unspeakable, as represented by her uncle Arthur. Instead, this discursive choice is both purposeful and fascinating. It achieves a freeing-from-discourse that we as readers and critics then find ourselves forced to undo as soon as we wish to speak of the text: it is we who bring the term 'lesbian' to bear on the story, along with its connotations of otherness. Molloy's text places us in a position whereby it is *we* who demonstrate the inescapability of the heterosexual linguistic and symbolic matrix by requiring the term in order to speak of her work. This is just one thread in the text's inherent metatextuality, a quality by which Molloy incites an active reader through leaving gaps we must fill ourselves; and it is important to make our own 'pause in the flow of history', to borrow Masiello's words once more, and think about the ways in which we respond to that task; to consider what informs our responses.

THE TEXTUAL SPACE: THIRD PERSON NARRATIVE AND DIALOGUE WITH SELF

To return to the key space of the room as the center of this gynocentric universe, its identity and purpose is furthered precisely via recourse to a tradition of women's writing from the margins because it is surely intended to evoke a Woolfian 'Room of One's Own'; a space that facilitates the writer-protagonist's contact with the herself, inspiring writing for herself, about herself, in order to understand herself. This self-situating within a female literary canon is furthered also by one of Molloy's choices of epigraph: a citation from Virginia Woolf's *An Unwritten Novel* (1921), in which the British author refers to 'the eyes of others' as 'our prisons' and 'their thoughts, our cages'.[38] Here, her writer-protagonist will be able to respond to her need

> de empujar, de irritar, para poder ver. Escribe hoy lo que hizo, lo que no hizo, para verificar fragmentos de un todo que se le escapa. [...] Encerrada en este cuarto, todo parece más fácil porque recompone. Querría escribir para saber qué hay más allá de estas cuatro paredes; o para saber qué hay dentro de estas cuatro paredes que elige, como recinto, para escribir.
>
> to probe, to provoke, the better to see. Today she is writing down what she has done, what she has not done, trying to grasp the fragments of a whole that escapes her. [...] Shut up in this room everything seems easier because she can piece things together. By writing, she would like to find out what lies beyond these four walls; or perhaps she would like to find out what lies within them, in this closed space where she has chosen to write.[39]

Challenging the traditional configuration of the domestic realm of which it is undeniably a part, in this room, despite its inadequacies, there exists a sense of agency not implicit in understandings of the domestic/private as counterpart to the public/political. When the writer-protagonist referred to the space as one 'that she always called her own without fully taking possession of it', she began embracing her present state of exile (however voluntary it might be judged to be), as an opportunity to claim back something that is always connected with and to her through her gendered identity, but that, because 'the home which is usually thought to be gendered feminine has also traditionally been subject to patriarchal authority of the husband and father',[40] has never truly been hers. Here, then, it is useful to compare Molloy's character with Tita in *Como agua para chocolate*, discussed in Part One, who is portrayed by Laura Esquivel as reclaiming the hub of the domestic space, the kitchen, as a means to empowerment because therein she could exploit her magical cooking skills, but who nonetheless remains defined by the gender roles imposed upon her through the patriarchal symbolic association of femininity and that space. In light of this, Esquivel's story might well be said to share with Molloy's the notion of 'choosing marginality' that I have discussed here, but it is also clear that their approach differs in its radicalness. In *Como agua para chocolate* we witness a retreat into a positivized gendered space in order to establish ground for the visibility of women and to gain purchase on a space that can then serve as a creative outlet for self-expression. In contrast, what is achieved in *En breve cárcel* is a much more direct self-exploration that entails the purposeful problematization of imposed identity categories and their far-reaching implications both symbolic and real, because to simply 'reclaim' such a feminized space is not an obvious strategy for the lesbian subject whose points of reference and identification do not necessarily align with those embodied by heterosexual characters like Tita. Molloy's character needed to be placed in a position of autonomy within the homespace that is described here, but without the aid of magic, and without its characterization via feminine tropes of hearth and home; cooking and nourishment of others; fertility and motherhood, and so on. This space had to be imbued with greater signs of the independence that would facilitate a more deeply critical, more drastic rethinking of gender identifications and identities; to be representative of a space outside of the family hierarchy that, 'as understood within the context of authoritarian [/patriarchal] rule, is not to be perceived as a haven in a heartless world, but as a managerial system that upholds repressive ideology'.[41]

It is also for these reasons that, as I have suggested, the room is best seen as sitting at the threshold of the opposing forces of the individual, interior world, and the exterior, social world; a kind of liminal, third space that embraces both sides of the dualism central to the narrative trajectory of the Bildungsroman. In terms of traditional generic conventions that might be usefully applied as categories of analysis, therefore, the process of *Bildung* that takes place in this novel is one that reflects a retreat inwards shown to be typical of female characters in novels that have been read as female Bildungsromane. For example, Abel et al. have observed that European nineteenth- and twentieth-century novels of female development show how '[c]onfinement to inner life, no matter how enriching, threatens a loss of public activity; it enforces an isolation that may culminate in death'.[42] Yet there is an important difference in this Spanish American text, in that here what is portrayed is a necessary but *chosen* and *temporary* social death aimed at generating a self-knowledge that enables the woman to then contend with hegemonic ideologies by being fully cognizant of her positioning by them:

> Comienza a escribir una historia que no la deja: querría olvidarla, querría fijarla. Quiere fijar la historia para vengarse, quiere vengar la historia para conjurarla tal como fue, para evocarla tal como la añora.
>
> She begins to write a story that will not leave her alone. She would like to forget it; she would also like to give it shape, and, in shaping it, find

> revenge: for herself, for her story. She wants to exorcise that story as it was, in order to recover it as she would like to remember it.[43]

For Molloy's anonymous protagonist, cathartic recipes are replaced with cathartic, stream-of-consciousness bouts of writing that work towards undoing the 'crisis in self-knowledge' that Masiello has rightly signaled to be a central thematic concern of the novel.[44] Thus, both room and text are spaces in the sanctity of which she can learn about what exists beyond them, enabling contact with the sociopolitical arena through the facilitating mechanism of narrative distance. In both the original text and in the translation of the above citation, a lexis is adopted that evokes notions of spatiality and tangibility: the story that she desires to 'fix' (fijar) in place, rendered in English as 'to give shape to', gradually comes into view as that of a failed romantic relationship and of the emotional traumas caused by its problems and eventual collapse. (The choice of words here is compelling given it seems to directly contradict the process of deconstruction that is enacted in the novel, and seems to me to hint at the appeal (and subsequent strength) of the static nature of binary oppositions as an organizational framework—we are aware of their danger and yet their clear delineation of black and white offers a source of comfort in a world of complexity and contradiction.)

Necessarily, the revision of failed relationships entails a revision of selfhood in broader terms and so the narrative develops along the lines of a dialogue with the self in which the writer-protagonist is, as Cristina Ferreira-Pinto has observed, at once patient and analyst.[45] In light of this and the room's characterization as a kind of third space, it is wholly appropriate that a third person narrative perspective is adopted throughout the novel, imbuing the text with precisely the kind of objective distance necessary to the completion of the aims of this 'contestatory monologue'.[46] This is also the traditional narrative voice of the Bildungsroman, and it should be recalled that in the novels discussed in this study, that voice is adapted and manipulated in a variety of ways: exchanged for an empowered first person in Allende's *Eva Luna*, Mastretta's *Arráncame la vida*, and Valdés's *La nada cotidiana*; given over to a female inheritor of the oral tradition in *Como agua para chocolate*; fractured by the inclusion of a multiplicity of *petits récits* in Peri Rossi's *La nave de los locos*. Here, as Ana Figueroa describes it, the third person is taken on by Molloy as a means by which her writer-protagonist can play with the conventions of canonical writing by 'parodying the logic of the omniscient narrator that proposes its own vision of the world as a truth'.[47] Mielly adds to this that, when read in the context of exilic experiences, this use of a third person perspective and the elision it creates between the 'She' and the 'I' of the narrative is a strategy allowing for an account of selfhood to take place that is protected from the gaze of others;[48] it means that no other presence is needed and the writer-protagonist thereby functions self-sufficiently. However, even if claiming this narrative authority and disguising with it the implicit 'I' provides a protected and protective standpoint from which to speak, I would argue that the speaking self here never falls into the trap of assuming that position unquestioningly; she remains, thanks to the multiple perspectives provided by her chosen marginality and the self-awareness it procures, cognizant of the state of constant motion that is the self's only certainty. Lastly, Roberto Echevarren concurs with this reading by conjecturing that the third person voice disguises but does not dissolve the autobiographical aspect of the text.[49] Not just an author, the writer-protagonist is the author of her 'self'—the 'act of writing relates therefore to the composition of a story and simultaneously to the process of constituting the subject that writes'.[50]

ON REFLECTION

With regard to the simultaneously writing and written self, Michael Hardin highlights the significance of the trope of the writer-protagonist as a metafictional technique that enables authors like Molloy to 'write against a male tradition that is validated by its insistence on distinctions between self and other, subject and object, reader and author'.[51] This prioritization of similarity over otherness is figuratively and metaphorically reflected in the text through a number of meaningful episodes in which mirrors feature strongly. These begin early on in the novel, when the woman writer recalls the penchant her ex-lover Renata had for looking in the mirror—an act that she sees as connected to an equal proclivity for 'the vague, the lack of limits' and to a 'zeal for ambiguity', that the narrator-protagonist (in whom such things instill fear at the start of her text) finds exasperating.[52] While away together on a holiday by the sea (one of the first appearances of this other important motif), they had stayed in a first floor room whose landing area was decorated with two interfacing mirrors, in which 'Renata, when going up just as when going down, looked at herself [...] in one, in the other, in both at the same time'.[53] Renata thus seems to possess a proliferation of selves, and in her love for ambiguity is happy for the image of that self to appear in the empty spaces of the mirrors whose location opposite one another, moreover, enables the repetition of that image to become infinite. In contrast, the writer looks for herself in the mirrors

> de manera distinta, fingiendo desgano y como para corregir, para imponer un orden, no sabe cuál. En todo caso el orden que pretendía y aún pretende justificar a Renata [...] el orden que quiere imponer al sentir la amenaza de una vaguedad compartida, de un vacío que invada el suyo.

> in a different way, feigning reluctance, as if to correct the image, or perhaps to restore some kind of order. In any case it was order she aimed for, even trying [...] to persuade Renata of the need for it. Order is what she wants to impose whenever she feels the threat of a shared vagueness, of an emptiness invading her emptiness.[54]

That the mirror is a site of a self-confrontation which the narrator-protagonist finds difficult to encounter in her current state of insecurity vis-à-vis her selfhood is made clear by the fact that this first memory leads her to think of another lover, Vera, and the 'pleasure that Vera used to feel talking about herself, in front of her, in front of others: the security with which she offered herself as a fiction'.[55] In the Spanish original the choice of the verb 'contarse' is nuanced, and might also be translated as 'recounting herself', evoking thereby a clear alignment between selfhood and narration, and drawing together the matter of narrative perspective discussed above and the repeated motif of the mirrors. In the face of the self-assuredness of these two women the writer-protagonist appears as someone who is self-effacing—inert and cautious, rather than active and vocal, for she describes herself as remaining 'passive in the face of this storytelling' and

> a menudo irritada buscando la pausa que le permitiría entrar, introducir su propio relato, componer su cara, detener las palabras ajenas de Vera, obligarla a mirar: quería defenderse de la agresión que veía en esas anécdotas que se le brindaban, donde hasta la indecisión era compacta, impenetrable.

> often annoyed, searching for the pause that would allow her a way in: she needed to introduce her own story, compose her own face, halt Vera's alien words and force Vera to look at her. There was aggression in the anecdotes proffered her—even their indecisiveness was solid, impenetrable—and she felt the need to defend herself.[56]

These emotional responses evoke a desire to protect herself from the barrage of 'alien words' and to remind Vera of her own presence by forcing her to look, just as Renata looked at herself in the mirror, rendering clear that it is her desire to feel the same ability to 'contarse' that drives the production of the text we are now reading.

In terms of the matter of the protagonist's sexuality, which in spite of the gynocentric universe created in the text clearly remains an aspect of the gradual acceptance of self towards which the writer-protagonist is working—evinced by the need for acceptance by her lovers and by the presence of the ideologies whose influence is, as has been argued, still palpable even with the haven of the writing space—the particular qualities of the reflections offered by the mirror trope have an added dimension of interest: Hardin conjectures that Molloy can use the mirror to 'question the integrity of the categories of self and other' because

> [u]nlike conventional opposites, male/female, black/white, on/off, mirror opposites are 'opposite' only in handedness—when one looks in a mirror and raises one's right hand, the mirror-self raises its left hand. As such, phallic binaries do not enter into the equation: there is no

> female/male function. A woman can see herself in the mirror and her other in the mirror at the same time; it is her and not her.[57]

As regards the lesbian identity depicted here, Hardin's point compels a reading of sexuality in these terms of sameness and difference. If in the mirror the woman can see herself and her non-self at once, so that sameness and difference become conflated, it becomes possible to understand the otherness around which interpersonal relationships are constructed in equivalent terms. Simply put, her reflection in the mirror encapsulates *homo*sexuality and because it becomes a trope that exemplifies the possibility of sameness and difference existing in tandem, it effectively delegitimizes the organizational terms of the hegemonic, heterosexual order, predicated on the coupling of *differences*, as the only possible ones. Foucault's conceptualization of 'heterotopias' as spaces that enact a refusal of the norms surrounding them is useful in further exploring this idea, because he specifically uses the object of the mirror to exemplify his neologism. Foucault defines heterotopias as

> real places—places that do exist and that are formed in the very founding of society—which are something like counter-sites, a kind of effectively enacted utopia in which the real sites, all the other real sites that can be found within the culture, are simultaneously represented, contested and inverted.[58]

His definition of heterotopic spaces chimes well with the needs of exile theory, discussed at the start of this chapter, to elucidate an account of exile as both tangible and metaphorical—as place and non-place. The pertinence of his term to the consideration of exile and exilic spaces is then furthered by the fact that his definition is predicated on the counterpointing of 'utopia', which in theorizations of exile always figures as the desired point of return that remains forever out of reach, and heterotopia. Yet more usefully, Foucault goes on to connect these two initially oppositional places through the space of the mirror that 'is, after all, a utopia, since it is a placeless place':

> In the mirror I see myself there where I am not, in an unreal virtual space that opens up behind the surface; I am over there, there where I am not, a sort of shadow that gives my own visibility to myself, that enables me to see myself there where I am absent: such is the utopia of the mirror. But it is also a heterotopia in so far as the mirror does exist in reality, where it exerts a sort of counteraction on the position that I occupy. From the standpoint of the mirror I discover my absence from the place where I am since I see myself over there. Starting from this gaze that is, as it were, directed toward me, from the ground of this virtual space that is on the other side of the glass, I come back toward myself; I begin again to direct my eyes toward myself and to reconstitute myself there where I am.[59]

His description of the mirror portrays a site of encounter with the self that encourages the recognition of sameness and difference and of presence and absence all at once, and his presentation of it as being able to give visibility back to the subject is also very meaningful to the reading of Molloy's story, in which the writer-protagonist clearly wishes to recover her own by delineating herself through her writing. In more straightforward terms, the confrontation of the self within the mirror is a highly legible metaphor for the process of self-recognition with which this text engages in a more nuanced manner. Its added depth comes through the fact that the mirror trope is expanded and deployed to articulate the possibility of same-sex relationships, ones simultaneously constituted by sameness and difference, at the same time as standing as a sign for recovery and recognition of the self. Such successful questioning of the categories of self and other ultimately affords a critique of subject positions more broadly so that whilst focusing on gender and sexuality, this novel utilizes the free space of self-imposed exile to underline the limitations of all identity categories. Thus, exile, both spatially and symbolically, here is made a space and place of contestation of hegemonic norms—a heterotopia.

THE TROPE OF LIQUIDITY: FLUIDITY AND EXCESS AS WAYS FORWARD

The mirror trope and the elision of self and other that it entails is also significant in respect of the frameworks of meaning produced within the novel through the woman's preoccupation with the imposition of order on a self that is frequently described in terms of boundlessness and superfluousness (as we saw above, 'Order is what she wants to impose whenever she feels the threat of a shared vagueness...'). The reflective surface of the mirror allows for useful boundaries to be established without constraining selfhood. It implies and incites a sense of self that is ordered, because it is known and self-knowing—the clear delineation of self provided by the vision of its own reflection comes into view not because of a mandate on identity imposed from without, but as the result of a dialogue carried out at the boundary of inside/outside.

The mirror is, then, a place of self-encounter whose inherent fluidity is a quality that we learn has always been appealing to the woman protagonist, but which as she grew up she felt compelled to control. She writes very early on in the novel that:

> Aprendió de chica a controlar la zozobra, a negar cuanto pudiera llevarla del lado del desorden, del desmán, de la locura: se defendía con sus fantaseos, con su aislamiento, sobre todo con una conducta ejemplar. No sabe si soñaba; sí sabe que su necesidad para las reglas era tal que alguna vez preguntó si para rezar había que pensar en Dios—en la cara de Dios—o pensar en las palabras que decía.

> She learned as a girl to control the foundering feeling, to deny anything that could carry her over into disorder, excess, madness: she defended herself with her daydreaming, with her aloofness, above all with her perfect behavior. She does not know if she dreamed; she does know, however, that the need she felt for rules was so strong that once she asked whether, when praying, it was necessary to think of God—of God's face—or of the words that one was saying.[60]

She perceived a division in her childhood that taught her that the choice to be made, when presented with the opposing options of control, regulation and regularity, and disorder, excess, or madness, was clear, and she had to work hard in order to steer herself away from the appeal of anything that might lure her into making the wrong choice.

The sea, when it appears in her writing, is presented as the antithesis to this rigidity; a fluid space akin to the mirror for its enabling of a contact with herself freed from the demands made on her identity. We are told that 'as a child she wished for it fervently ten months of the year' and that whenever 'she went in for a swim, the water made her forget her head (so full, so insecure in its thinking), her clumsy left-handedness, her straight hair (very different from her sister Clara's blond curls), her spying eyes, her questions'.[61] The ocean provided a protective distance in much the same way that the room in which she writes now does; distance between herself and others that is precisely what is required for her to be able to locate her self on her own terms:

> Juega a atacar el mar (lo sigue haciendo), atraviesa la rompiente, necesita encontrar ese lugar preciso donde surgen las olas y se mantienen suspendidas, tan lejos del fondo, antes de desmoronarse. Ella se busca y se encuentra allí, es parte de esa inmovilidad única, y luego se entrega al buen regreso que la lleva entre la espuma a la costa desde donde volverá a buscar ese movimiento suspendido, que la devuelve completa. Dentro del mar vivía, ignoraba con deliberación los llamados de su madre quien, desde la costa, gesticulaba impacientemente (agitando una toalla roja) para que volviera.

> She pretended to attack the sea (still does), crossed the breakers, needing to find the exact spot where the waves swell and crest, for one tenuous moment, before collapsing. She feels in touch with herself there, held in that unique stillness: yielding to the good flow that sweeps her with the foam back to the shore, she will then go out again in search of that moment of fullness that makes her whole. She felt alive in the sea, and would deliberately ignore the red towel her mother waved impatiently at her from the beach to call her.[62]

The attempts of her mother to call her back in, as Marcia Stephenson writes, see the maternal figure 'cast as the lifeguard who will cut off the daughter's exploration of self, symbolized by her solitary excursions into the sea'.[63] Stephenson also notes that, although the mother figure is sometimes infantilized in the text through her neediness, she is also 'aggressive and "castrating"', so that '[i]dentification with the mother is painful because [the daughter] locates in her at once an entrenched passivity and neediness that are unbearable to her'.[64] In light of the attributes awarded to the sea in the writer-protagonist's own personal symbolic imaginary, her mother's disassociation with it is indicative of what she represents to her daughter: the internalization of the hegemonic order; the rejection of a fluidity that, in the terms of that order, is understood as an excess, an uncontrollability, an otherness that must be constrained. Thus, her time in the sea equates to a positive loss of self, because it is the loss, as Stephenson goes on to say, of 'the self that is structured and regimented by the daily schedule, the rules and regulations of the "correct" way to live'.[65]

In the second section of the novel the reader gains insight into further childhood memories of other watery spaces that become associated with both defiance of the regulations imposed on her life, and times of self-discovery and understanding. Again during the summertime, but this time on a farm rather than at the village by the sea, she is told that there is a water tank in which she must not go swimming, and the fear instilled in her by these warnings, (however practical nonetheless representative of an order in which she has no voice), push her to stay away from the aquatic places with which she feels such an affinity. It is not long, however, before a desire to investigate that forbidden place overcomes her and one afternoon,

> se atrevió a acercarse al tanque [y] metió la mano derecha en el agua verdosa, después la zurda [...] Durante un largo momento no movió las [manos], sumergidas, hasta que se le ocurrió agitarlas, chapotear, jugar con ellas [...] Recuerda que hasta se agarró las manos, dentro del agua, como si se saludara, y se sintió muy contenta.
>
> She resolved to go to the tank [and] she stuck her right hand into the greenish water, then her left one [...] For a long time she did not move her hands in the water, until it occurred to her to stir them about, splash, play with them [...] She remembers that she even clasped her hands together, under the water, as if greeting herself, and that she felt very happy.[66]

In this second solitary excursion, the young girl symbolically confronts once more the demands that had cut her off from points of self-contact and seeks out thereby self-knowledge, here represented by the image of her joining her own hands together under the water. These forays into childhood memory entail not only a retracing of the roots of selfhood, but also a recuperation of the inquisitiveness inherent to that time in life—the audacity that is necessary to cutting our own path but which is lost through the gradual internalization of hegemonic ideologies. Neatly encapsulated by the focus on a part of the body that is so suggestive of autonomy, this scene points towards the need to at least *question* the validity of rules that seem not to make sense; to not blindly accept what we are told is appropriate.

One final point to be made in reference to the two episodes discussed here is that they also exemplify a fixation with the body and with embodiment that is a feature of Molloy's text throughout—one that I have not centered on here because it is the topoi to which I turn in the next and final section of *Gender and the Self...* via a consideration of Ángeles Mastretta's *Arráncame la vida* and Zoé Valdés's *La nada cotidiana*, but which has been discussed at length by other critics. References to the body are rife in this narrative, and the body as the site of subjectivity is at the heart of its recuperating project. For if this voluntary exile is undertaken with the aim of finding a free space in which to explore and come to an understanding of her own identity, what must first be achieved is contact with her own body—the contact that is represented by the time spent playing by herself in the water, but which has apparently been lost as the writer has become an adult. In this way her connection to water, and especially the sea, is once again emphasized, so that a yearning for the ocean and other watery spaces is tantamount to a yearning for her own body. Kaminsky, for example, points out that it is through writing as a mode of recuperation that this body is gradually brought into focus for the woman, saying that the 'pages of the text become like layers of skin or scales—text as bodily secretion that contains, protects, and gives form to the body'.[67] The desire to 'contain' and 'protect' is generated by the fear of excess that has grown in her since childhood (referred to briefly above in relation to the story of her uncle Arthur). The contradiction that is thus found at the heart of her narrative project is that whereas she wants to give form to her body through her writing, she also desires the excess that she remembers so fondly and that is associated with a true knowledge of, and relationship with, herself and her identity, outside of the boundaries imposed on that identity by her parents, her sister, her romantic relationships, or indeed the social schema of which all of those people are a part:

> Una clave, un orden para este relato. Sólo atina a ver capas, estratos [...] como las diversas capas de piel que cubren músculos y huesos, imbricadas, en desapacible contacto. Estreñimiento, erizamiento de la superficie: ¿quién no ha observado, de chico, la superficie interior de una costra arrancada y la correspondiente llaga rosada, sin temblar? En ese desgarramiento inquisidor se encuentran clave y orden de esta historia.

> A key, an ordering principle for this story. She can only see layers, strata, [...] as in the segments of the earth's crust shown in schoolbooks. No, more like the various layers of skin that cover muscles and bones, overlapping, in unpleasant contact. Quivering, bristling surfaces. Who has not observed as a child, after pulling off a scab,

> the inner surface and the pink sore that goes with it—and looked at it without trembling? In that inquisitive act of destruction she finds the key and ordering principle for this story. [68]

Kaminsky also recognizes this contradiction, writing that 'simultaneous with her desire for the order imposed by narration is the writer's urge to break out of that which confines her'.[69] Ultimately, however, given that by the end of the story her desire to create such order in her life has not been accomplished, excess remains as a trait of her identity. It cannot be said that she has come to a place of self-acceptance by internalizing the systems of control and organization that she has needed to interrogate, but rather by learning to embrace the excesses—those qualities that make her a social outsider—that are fundamental to her selfhood.

DREAMS AND THE REIMAGINATION OF SELF

This gradual journey to self-acceptance is best exemplified by a close examination of one particular example of the final space of renegotiation in Molloy's text that I wish to consider in this chapter: I find it compelling that dreams play a key role in *En breve cárcel* just as they did in Peri Rossi's *La nave de los locos*; adopted in both texts as powerful tools for the examination and deconstruction of fixed identity categories. Molloy's narrative as a whole retains a rather oneiric quality as a result of its generation through a free-flowing, Proustian process of memory connections, inflecting the highly personal nature of the writing. The inclusion of dreams within the narrative only compounds this personalization of the text, homing in on the interior spaces of the individual psyche, its memory-scapes, and thereby revealing some of the external frames of reference that it has internalized. They are a crucial element of the project of self-discovery and self-understanding that the text entails, and are a point at which the alignment of gender and sexuality is made the direct target of the work's deconstructive project.

The writer-protagonist recognizes her dreams as 'coded images in which she often reads herself',[70] and has saved accounts of dreams from her formative years.[71] Early on in the novel these serve to reveal particular areas of interest or concern for her. The sea motif discussed above, for example, is present in her dreamscapes,[72] and then there are dreams of scenarios clearly depicting the romantic triangle in which she is embroiled and her feeling of having been pushed out of that triad.[73] The most significant of the dreams described, though, functions very similarly to Equis's final conundrum in *La nave de los locos* in that it carries a message that the writer-protagonist outrightly says she will work towards answering, and provides a force of motivation to continue her exploration of self.[74] It is a thread that resurfaces at points where the narrative undergoes key shifts: first recounted at the transition point between Parts One and Two, where there begins a more active engagement with the world beyond the writing space,[75] and then again referred to at the end of the narrative where the writer-protagonist has finally decided to leave the city where she has been living in order to carry out her writing project (which we now know to be Buffalo, New York), and is setting off to a new, again undisclosed, location. Its association with such significant changes in direction clearly points towards its value within the developmental trajectory of the self-analyzing female figure at the heart of the text. In this dream, the writer-protagonist hears the voice of her dead father, who calls her on the telephone:

> la comunicación es mala, oye apenas su voz. Con dificultad empieza a distinguir palabras aisladas: primero la palabra Egeo, urgente, luego la palabra Éfeso, repetida varias veces. Es necesario dejar todo—le dice la débil voz de su padre—y viajar para ver a Artemisa.
>
> the connection is bad; she can hardly hear his voice. She slowly begins making out individual words: first the urgent word Aegues, then the word Ephesus, which is repeated several times. It is necessary to leave everything—her father's faint voice is telling her—and travel to see Artemis.[76]

Reflecting on this moment in the novel and connecting it to a scene not previously discussed here in which, as a child, the protagonist dresses up in her father's clothes and looks at herself in the mirror,[77] Stephenson contends that '[t]he father represents the law, the heterosexual norm, to whom the [writer-protagonist] continually looks for affirmation and guidance', and that in this scene

> the narrator's identification with the father, with masculinity, seemingly enables her to enact a desire for the female object as if to suggest that desire originates from a masculine, heterosexual position.[78]

Even in this first occurrence of the dream, however, we see her question the fixity of gendered identities towards which this patriarchal voice directs her, and which assume that sexual opposition must underpin sexual desire: the Ephesian Artemis towards whom her father directs her is a distinct Greek formulation of Artemis and of her Roman equivalent Diana, wherein the deity's role as goddess of fertility is emphasized above and beyond her other associations as goddess of the wild, of nature, of hunting. The figure stands, therefore, for orthodox womanhood, and inhabits the position that the writer-protagonist is here encouraged to take—a position whose logic would require her to continue to dress in her father's clothes in order to legitimately act upon her lesbian sexual desire. In other words, the Ephesian version fails to provide a meaningful point of reference for lesbian subjectivity. Disconcerted, the writer-protagonist recognizes that 'this biological monotony' (the enforced identification with orthodox femininity as subject position, not as object of desire) 'seems to lead her astray. She should travel to Ephesus by other routes, not only the ones indicated to her by memories'.[79] Because far more significant for her is the

> otra Artemisa, otra Diana, la cazadora suelta, no inmovilizada por un pectoral fecundo, pero *para esa figura no parece haber santuario estable*. Sí la deleitan los pechos de esa otra Diana, pequeños y firmes, apenas perceptibles bajo la túnica [...] Disponible, armada de arco y flecha [...] *no se detiene*; no la lastran los racimos de pechos, maternales y pétreos, de su contrafigura, la enorme figura de Éfeso, cifra de la fecunda. No, la otra Diana, la que ella prefiere—la Diana suelta –, no es fecunda.

> [other] Artemis, [other] Diana—the free huntress, not weighed down by a breastplate of fertility—although *no fixed sanctuary seems to have been built to her*. Indeed, she delights in the small, firm breasts of that other Diana, barely visible beneath the tunic [...] Poised for action, armed with bow and arrow [...] *she is on the move*: not burdened by the clustering stone breasts of her mothering counterfigure, the huge image of Ephesus, symbol of fertility. No, this other Diana, the one she prefers—the free Diana—is not fertile. [Emphases added.][80]

It is recounted that Artemis 'resented any kind of intrusion into her domain', and that she changed male mortal Actaeon into a stag for stumbling upon the place in which she was bathing.[81] It is not difficult, therefore, for the reader to understand the implied alignment between the writer-protagonist and this mythical figure, whose retreat into a private room actively claimed as her own has been the scene of production of the narrative, for whom we understand the loss of virginity to be irrelevant, and its correlative assumption of fertility/motherhood not a given at all.

I also have emphasized in the above citations key references to matters of fixity versus movement or nomadism, in part due to the matter of exile both real and metaphoric as the point of departure for my own discussion here, but also because of their meaningfulness in terms of the deconstruction of fixed identity categories and the supposition of clear alignments of sexuality and gender that they entail. It seems to me very telling that Molloy has her writer-protagonist immediately identify with the version of the goddess that is not held in place by the existence of a permanent shrine to her, preferring instead the freedom of movement inherent to Diana the huntress and seemingly making of her an emblem of self-determination on all levels. Moreover, it is significant that in referring to these different descriptions of the deity, she reminds us precisely of the possibility of *versions*—there is not one Artemis/Diana, just as there is not one female gendered identity, and the possibility of female identification is maintained.[82] Thus, Molloy underscores plurality of identity and defies rigid heterosexual and patriarchal norms not only by taking on narratives about gender, but by engaging some of the foundational myths of patriarchy and reminding us that even in those early narratives gendered identifications were not so fixed as they have been made to seem in more modern contexts—they maintained an easy relationship with ambiguity; with the 'multiplicity and contradiction' that the writer-protagonist herself desires and towards which she works throughout her narrative.[83] And so it is that in the dream's recurrence:

> Diana, de nuevo inasible. Percibida en escorzo entre dos árboles, fugaz y rodeada de penumbra, al acecho; o la otra Diana, de nuevo estática y abrumadora, la que lastrada por sus pechos de piedra se impone, culmina bajo un cielo azul mediterráneo. No puede orientarse ya hacia una o hacia otra, combinando restos o recuerdos que la ayuden en su camino, como lo hubiera hecho antes, porque el pasado ya empieza a dejarla. O más bien: porque *ha elegido desasirse de cierta composición de su pasado*. Despojada, tantea itinerarios diversos hacia Diana, con el fin de descubrir el suyo.

> Diana appears, once again untouchable. She sees her fleetingly between two trees, elusive, wrapped in shadow, on the lookout. Or she sees the other Diana, massive and overwhelming, imposingly weighed down by her stone breasts, against a blue Mediterranean sky. She can no longer direct her steps towards one or the other, combining fragments or memories that would help her on her way. The past is beginning to leave her, or rather *she has chosen to free herself from a certain version of her past*. Dispossessed, she considers different routes towards Diana, trying to discover which one she should take, which one to make her own. [Emphases added.][84]

There is a real sense of greater agency in this account; an emphasis on choice and of being comfortable with the ambiguity that is ultimately necessary to opening up new possibilities of being.

And so although, as other critics have commented, the end of the novel is not one of outright positivity, it is undeniably the case that the writer-protagonist's project, initially rooted in the examination of personal, romantic relationships but ultimately a revelation of the far more wide-reaching problematic of fixed identity categories, has been begun in earnest. The spaces that have been encountered have been both real and imagined spaces of exile—cities and rooms, memories, mirrors, the sea, and dreamscapes—and the self-exploration that they have permitted is by no means over. It would make no sense for a text that does so much to fracture such notions of fixity to then end with a completely stable female self, buoyed by total clarity regarding who she is and where she fits within the complex social and symbolic matrix. This would be an unsafe stance to take in a world whose tangible reality has yet to catch up with the kind of imaginative recreations of it depicted in the novels considered in this study. Far more fitting is the writer-protagonist's self-recognizing description as alone and afraid, waiting in an airport—a transitory space that further infuses the scene and the woman herself with a sense of continued movement and momentum—to begin the next phase of her journey towards self-knowledge.

NOTES

1. Patricia Kolesnicov and Sylvia Molloy, *Sylvia Molloy: 'Me sentiría defraudada si mi novela fuera reconocida sólo por las lesbianas'* (11/18/2012), http://www.revistaenie.clarin.com/literatura/sentiria-defraudada-novela-reconocida-lesbianas-sylvia-molloy_0_812918995.html [Accessed 06/30/2014] 'Sí, se volvió un gesto político. En primer lugar, tuvo un rechazo muy fuerte dadas las circunstancias: era plena dictadura. Ninguna editorial quería publicarla, ni siquiera Sudamericana, donde yo ya había publicado, donde tenía amigos, pero eran épocas difíciles para sacar un libro que, se sentía, iba a ser percibido como subversivo'.
2. Sylvia Molloy, '*En breve cárcel*: pensar en otra novela', *Punto de vista: Revista de cultura* 21 (December 1998), 29–32, p. 29.
3. Sophia McClennan, *The Dialectics of Exile* (West Lafayette, IN: Purdue State University, 2004), p. 1.
4. McClennan, *The Dialectics of Exile*, p. 1.
5. Amy K. Kaminsky, *After Exile: Writing the Latin American Diaspora* (Minneapolis; London: University of Minnesota Press, 1999), p. xi.
6. McClennan, *The Dialectics of Exile*, p. 21. She gives the example of Juan Goytisolo, 'often considered to be a self-exile, since he was not forcefully thrown out of Spain', in order to show how this kind of standardization marginalizes other exilic experiences, and also mentions Cabrera Infante's coining of the term 'invisible exile', used in reference to the status of Cuban exile in studies of the Latin American Diaspora.
7. McClennan, *The Dialectics of Exile*, p. 21.
8. Gema Pérez-Sánchez and Cristina Peri Rossi, 'Cristina Peri Rossi', *Hispamérica*, 24.72 (December 1995), 59–72, p. 68. 'Para el inconsciente colectivo el exiliado es siempre varón [...] la figura del revolucionario sigue siendo masculina'.
9. Kaminsky, *After Exile*, p. xi.
10. Helène Cixous, 'Sorties: Out and Out: Attacks/Ways out/Forays', in Hélène Cixous and Catherine Clément (Trans. Betsy Wing), *The Newly Born Woman* (Manchester, UK: Manchester University Press, 1986), pp. 63–132, p. 81.
11. Catherine Clément, cited in Gayatri Chakravorty Spivak, 'French Feminism in an International Frame', *Yale French Studies*, 62, Feminist Readings: French Texts/American Contexts (1981), 154–184, pp. 171–2.
12. Elena M. Martínez, *Lesbian Voices from Latin America: Breaking Ground* (New York; London: Garland Publishing, Inc., 1996), p. 3.
13. Martínez, *Lesbian Voices*, p. 36.
14. Martínez, *Lesbian Voices*, p. 38.
15. Sylvia Molloy, 'Part 2: Introduction', in Sara Castro-Klarén, Sylvia Molloy, and Beatriz Sarlo (eds.), *Women's Writing in Latin America: An Anthology* (Boulder, CO; San Francisco; Oxford: Westview Press, 1992), pp. 107–124, p. 107.

16. Edward Soja, *Thirdspace: Journeys to Los Angeles and Other Real- and-Imagined Places* (Cambridge, UK: Blackwell, 1998), p. 96.
17. bell hooks, *Yearning: Race, Gender and Cultural Politics* (Boston, MA: South End Press, 1990), pp. 149–150.
18. hooks, *Yearning*, p. 150.
19. Soja, *Thirdspace*, p. 99.
20. Virginia Muzquiz, 'Boundaries Around Identity: Sylvia Molloy's *Certificate of Absence* and the Autobiographical Process', *Monographic Review* 9 (1993), 176–188, pp. 176–177.
21. Sylvia Molloy, *En breve cárcel* (Barcelona: Seix Barral, 1981), p. 68; *Certificate of Absence*, Trans. Daniel Balderston (Austin: University of Texas Press, 1989), p. 49. All subsequent references are taken from these editions, with the Spanish version page number first, the English edition page numbers second. (Where I have, for other texts, preferred to use my own translations, given Molloy's personal involvement in the English language version of her novel I have made use of that, accounting for any impact this might have on the clarity of my analyses where necessary).
22. Sylvia Molloy, 'At Face Value: Autobiographical Writing in Spanish America', *Dispositio*, 9.24/26 (1984), 1–18, p. 3.
23. Molloy, 'At Face Value', p. 3.
24. Molloy, *En breve cárcel,* p. 131; p. 102. In Chapter One of Part One and Chapter Five of Part Two her ex-lover Vera's comments on the writer-protagonist's personality are directly cited, and the comments are related. This is an interesting feature of the text for the fact that the more extended citation appears after the halfway stage of the story, at which point the writer-protagonist has begun to occasionally leave the sanctity of her apartment and to socialize once more. It suggests that it is only at this stage, having had the time to galvanize her sense of selfhood through the revisions of childhood and of failed romantic relationships carried out in Part One, that she feels able to begin allowing the voices of others back into her text in a meaningful way. Secondly, it is curious that the words allowed into spoken assessments of the writer-protagonist are not positive (she is described as uncomfortable in her own skin, and then called insular and narcissistic), but do provide clarification on clashes in approaches to communication between her and Vera. She therefore now seems comfortable in facing criticism without losing herself to the opinion of others because of a greater self-knowledge and the greater objective distance facilitated by her retreat into writing.
25. Molloy, 'At Face Value', p. 15.
26. Robert McKee Irwin and Sylvia Molloy, 'Introduction', *Hispanisms and Homosexualities* (Durham, NC, & London: Duke University Press, 1998), pp. ix–xvi, p. xii.
27. Elena Castro, 'Identidad lésbica y sujeto femenino: El papel de la escritura en *En breve cárcel* de Sylvia Molloy', *Letras Femeninas,* 26.1/2 (Primavera-Otoño 2000), 11–26, p. 24.
28. bell hooks, *Feminist Theory: From Margin to Center* (Boston, MA: South End Press, 1984), p. ix.
29. Molloy, *En breve cárcel*, p. 18; p. 7. 'Al mirar las paredes de marrón verdoso, un color marcial que jamás hubiera elegido, recuerda fantasías de infancia'.
30. Molloy, *En breve cárcel*, p. 66; p. 47.
31. Francine Masiello, 'Subversions of Authority: Feminist Literary Culture in the River Plate Region' in *Chasqui* XXI.1, pp. 39–48, p. 40. Here, Masiello is

describing the approaches of best seller works from the River Plate region to the question of feminist resistance to authoritarian discourses, not avant-garde works like *En breve cárcel*. It is therefore interesting that a similarity in approach can be seen between disparate kinds of women's writing, in terms of reference to the private, domestic space and its potential role in facilitating social critique.

32. Soja, *Thirdspace*, p. 98.
33. Molloy, *En breve cárcel*, p. 13; p. 3.
34. Molloy, *En breve cárcel*, pp. 27–28; p. 15. She recalls this uncle being referred to as 'A bit of a dandy', and herself thinks of him as 'mad Arthur' ('Arturo loco'). He was rendered unmentionable by the family, and she is told by her mother not to ask her father the 'forbidden question' of how his eldest brother died. Her desire to control her own 'madness'—read potential for transgression—as a child is overtly connected to the fear instilled by knowledge of this uncle's ostracization.
35. Michael Hardin, 'Dissolving the Reader/Author Binary: Sylvia Molloy's *Certificate of Absence*, Helena Parente Cunha's *Woman Between Mirrors*, and Jeannette Winterson's *Written on the Body*', *The International Fiction Review*, 29 (2002), 84–96, p. 85.
36. Molloy, *En breve cárcel*, p. 77; p. 56; 'nunca habían padres ni maridos: se habían muerto en alguna guerra o simplemente nunca habían existido'.
37. Molloy, *En breve cárcel*, p. 77; p. 56.
38. It is worth noting that for the English translation Molloy not only replaced the citation from Quevado that served as her first epigraph in the original Spanish text with the Emily Dickenson poem *We'll pass without the passing* (1863), but also took from it the title *Certificate of Absence*. Michelle Mielly has noted, in line with my own arguments about the room's dualistic qualities and roles, that 'common to all three [...] epigraphs is an appeal to the sense of enclosure and captivity as well as a desire to recreate or recover the presence of what is intrinsically absent'. Michelle Mielly, 'Filling the Continental Split: Subjective Emergence in Ken Bugul's *La baobab fou* and Sylvia Molloy's *En breve cárcel*, *Comparative Literature*, 54.1 (Winter 2002), 42–57, p. 45.
39. Molloy, *En breve cárcel*, p. 13; p. 3.
40. Nancy Duncan, 'Renegotiating Gender and Sexuality in Public and Private Spaces', in Nancy Duncan (ed.), *BodySpace: Destabilizing Geographics of Gender and Sexuality* (London & New York: Routledge, 1996), pp. 127–144, p. 131.
41. Masiello, 'Subversions', p. 45.
42. Elizabeth Abel, Marianne Hirsch, and Elizabeth Langland, *The Voyage In: Fictions of Female Development* (Lebanon, NH: Dartmouth College Press, 1983), p. 9.
43. Molloy, *En breve cárcel*, p. 13; p. 3.
44. Francine Masiello, '*En breve cárcel*: La producción del sujeto', in *Hispamérica* Año 14, No. 41 (Aug., 1985), pp. 103–112, p.107.
45. Cristina Ferreira-Pinto, '*En breve cárcel*: escribiendo el camino del sujeto', *Letras Femeninas*, 15.1/2 (Primavera-Otoño, 1989), 75–82, p. 77.
46. Martínez, *Lesbian Voices*, p. 527.
47. Ana Figueroa, *Escritoras hispanoamericanas: Espejos, desplazamientos, fisuras, dobles discursos* (Madrid: Editorial Cuarto Propio, 2001), p. 75.
48. Mielly, 'Subjective emergence', p. 4.
49. Roberto Echevarren, 'La literariedad: *En breve cárcel* de Sylvia Molloy', in Rose S. Minc (ed.), *El cono sur: Dinámica y dimensiones de su literatura. A symposium* (Upper Montclair: Montclair State College, 1985), pp. 205–212, p. 205.

50. Cristina Ferreira-Pinto, 'El rescate de la figura materna en *En breve cárcel*' in *Romance Notes*, XXXVI.2 (Winter 1996), 155–162, p. 156. '[E]l acto de escribir representa por tanto la composición de un relato y simultáneamente el proceso mismo de constitución del sujeto que escribe'.
51. Hardin, 'Dissolving the Reader/Author Binary', p. 84.
52. Molloy, *En breve cárcel*, p. 21; p. 10. 'lo vago, la falta de límites'; 'fervor por la ambigüedad'.
53. Molloy, *En breve cárcel*, pp. 21–22; p. 10. 'Renata tanto al subir como al bajar, se miraba [...] en uno, en otro, en los dos juntos'.
54. Molloy, *En breve cárcel*, p. 22; p. 10.
55. Molloy, *En breve cárcel*, p. 22; p. 10. 'El placer que sentía Vera al *contarse*, ante ella, ante los otros: la seguridad con que se ofrecía como ficción' (my emphases).
56. Molloy, *En breve cárcel*, p. 22; p. 10. 'pasiva ante ese relato'.
57. Hardin, 'Dissolving the Reader', p. 92.
58. Michel Foucault, '*Of Other Spaces*, Heterotopias' (1967), http://foucault.info/documents/heteroTopia/foucault.heteroTopia.en.html [Accessed 07/16/2014].
59. Foucault, '*Of Other Spaces*, Heterotopias'.
60. Molloy, *En breve cárcel*, pp. 28–29; p. 16.
61. Molloy, *En breve cárcel*; p. 63; p. 45. 'De chica lo deseaba con fervor diez meses del año [...] En el agua desaparecían, en cuanto se sumergía, la gran cabeza de la que no sabe si piensa, la torpeza de su mano zurda, el pelo lacio tan lejano de los rulos rubios de su hermana Clara, los ojos que espían, sus preguntas'.
62. Molloy, *En breve cárcel*, pp. 63–4; p. 45.
63. Marcia Stephenson, 'Lesbian Trajectories in Sylvia Molloy's "En breve cárcel"' in *MLN*, 112.2, Hispanic Issue (March 1997), 253–268, p. 265.
64. Stephenson, 'Lesbian Trajectories', p. 264.
65. Stephenson, 'Lesbian Trajectories', p. 265.
66. Molloy, *En breve cárcel*, p. 109; p. 83.
67. Amy Kaminsky, *Reading the Body Politic: Feminist Criticism and Latin American Women Writers*, (Minneapolis; London: University of Minnesota Press, 1993), p.103.
68. Molloy, *En breve cárcel*, p. 23; pp. 11–12.
69. Kaminsky , *Reading the Body Politic*, p. 103.
70. Molloy, *En breve cárcel*, p. 102; p. 78. 'las imágenes cifradas en las que con frecuencia se lee'.
71. Molloy, *En breve cárcel*, p. 20; p. 9.
72. Molloy, *En breve cárcel*, p. 20; p. 9.
73. Molloy, *En breve cárcel*, p. 63; p. 45. She dreams of being in a three carriage train able to fly through the sky, but becomes decoupled from the other two carriages in which two separate figures sit. They fall to the ground and she though knows they will be safe, she remains floating in the air.
74. Molloy, *En breve cárcel*, pp. 79–80; p. 58.
75. Molloy, *En breve cárcel*, p. 82; p. 61. At the beginning of Chapter One of Part Two the writer-protagonist accepts an invitation from a friend for a weekend away at his country house. Prior to this locations beyond the rented apartment have appeared only through memory. She writes of the invitation: 'She barely hesitated [...] an outing, to be sure, but a safe one. It was one way, she told herself, of breaking out of her seclusion, of putting herself in motion'. (Dudó apenas [...] se trataba de una salida, sí, pero una salida protegida. Una manera, se dijo, de empezar a romper el encierro, de ponerse en movimiento'.) There are two

interesting aspects of this citation: firstly, given the way in which the fact of going out is described (the English translation is perhaps especially helpful in making this point), the reader is drawn to think of the question of being 'out' in relation to sexuality, and the need for this first foray beyond the homespace to be a protected one is thereby connected to the matter of lesbian identity and its social acceptance. (The expression 'to be out of the closet' is used in both Spanish and English.) Secondly, her desire to be 'in motion' speaks of a desire to shift towards a greater level of activity that, as we shall see, is then echoed by the portrayal of the mythical figures of Artemis and Diana in the dream discussed here.

76. Molloy, *En breve cárcel*, p. 77; p. 56.
77. Molloy, *En breve cárcel*, p. 14; p. 4.
78. Stephenson, 'Lesbian Trajectories', pp. 258–259.
79. Molloy, *En breve cárcel*, p. 79; p. 58. 'Siente que al caer en estas monotonías biológicas inicia un camino en falso. Tendrá que cumplir el viaje a Efeso según otros rumbos, no sólo los que le indican estos recuerdos'.
80. Molloy, *En breve cárcel*, p. 78; p. 57.
81. Arthur Cotterell, *The Encyclopaedia of Mythology* (London: Hermes House, 1996; 2003), p. 23.
82. Ferreira-Pinto notes that the multiple versions of Diana can be drawn parallel with the other women figures in the novel—the writer-protagonist's mother, sister, Aunt Sara and lovers. Cristina Ferreira-Pinto, 'El rescate de la figura maternal en *En breve cárcel* de Sylvia Molloy', *Romance Notes*, XXXVI.2, 155–162, p. 161.
83. Molloy, *En breve cárcel*, p. 150; p. 118.
84. Molloy, *En breve cárcel*, pp. 149–150; p. 118.

BIBLIOGRAPHY

Abel, Elizabeth, Hirsch, Marianne, and Langland, Elizabeth, *The Voyage In: Fictions of Female Development* (Lebanon, NH: Dartmouth College Press, 1983).

Castro, Elena, 'Identidad lésbica y sujeto femenino: El papel de la escritura en *En breve cárcel* de Sylvia Molloy', *Letras Femeninas,* 26.1/2 (Primavera-Otoño 2000), 11–26.

Castro-Klarén, Sara, Molloy, Sylvia, and Sarlo, Beatriz (eds.), *Women's Writing in Latin America: An Anthology* (Boulder, CO; San Francisco; Oxford: Westview Press, 1992).

Cixous, Hélène, 'Sorties: Out and Out: Attacks/Ways out/Forays', in Hélène Cixous and Catherine Clément (Betsy Wing, Trans.), *The Newly Born Woman* (Manchester, UK: Manchester University Press, 1986), pp. 63–132.

Cixous, Hélène, and Clément, Catherine, (Betsy Wing, Trans.), *The Newly Born Woman* (Manchester, UK: Manchester University Press, 1986).

Cotterell, Arthur, *The Encyclopaedia of Mythology* (London: Hermes House, 1996; 2003).

Duncan, Nancy, 'Renegotiating Gender and Sexuality in Public and Private Spaces', in Nancy Duncan (ed.), *BodySpace: Destabilizing Geographics of Gender and Sexuality* (London & New York: Routledge, 1996), pp. 127–144.

Duncan, Nancy (ed.), *BodySpace: Destabilizing Geographics of Gender and Sexuality* (London & New York: Routledge, 1996).

Echevarren, Roberto, 'La literariedad: *En breve cárcel* de Sylvia Molloy', in Rose S. Minc (ed.), *El cono sur: Dinámica y dimensiones de su literatura. A symposium* (Upper Montclair, NJ: Montclair State College, 1985), pp. 205–212.

Ferreira-Pinto, Cristina, 'El rescate de la figura materna en *En breve cárcel*', *Romance Notes*, XXXVI.2 (Winter 1996), 155–162.

Ferreira-Pinto, Cristina, '*En breve cárcel*: escribiendo el camino del sujeto', *Letras Femeninas*, 15.1/2 (Primavera-Otoño, 1989), 75–82.

Figueroa, Ana, *Escritoras hispanoamericanas: Espejos, desplazamientos, fisuras, dobles discursos* (Madrid: Editorial Cuarto Propio, 2001).

Foucault, Michel, '*Of Other Spaces*, Heterotopias' (1967), http://foucault.info/documents/heteroTopia/foucault.heteroTopia.en.html [Accessed 07/16/2014].

Hardin, Michael, 'Dissolving the Reader/Author Binary: Sylvia Molloy's *Certificate of Absence*, Helena Parente Cunha's *Woman Between Mirrors*, and Jeannette Winterson's *Written on the Body*', *The International Fiction Review*, 29 (2002), 84–96.

hooks, bell, *Feminist Theory: From Margin to Center* (Boston, MA: South End Press, 1984).

hooks, bell, *Yearning: Race, Gender and Cultural Politics* (Boston, MA: South End Press, 1990).

Kaminsky, Amy K., *After Exile: Writing the Latin American Diaspora* (Minneapolis; London: University of Minnesota Press, 1999).

Kaminsky, Amy, *Reading the Body Politic: Feminist Criticism and Latin American Women Writers*, (Minneapolis; London: University of Minnesota Press, 1993).

Kolesnicov, Patricia, and Molloy, Sylvia, *Sylvia Molloy: "Me sentiría defraudada si mi novela fuera reconocida sólo por las lesbianas"* (11/18/2012), http://www.revistaenie.clarin.com/literatura/sentiria-defraudada-novela-reconocida-lesbianas-sylvia-molloy_0_812918995.html [Accessed 06/30/2014].

Martínez, Elena M., *Lesbian Voices from Latin America: Breaking Ground* (New York; London: Garland Publishing, Inc., 1996).

Masiello, Francine, 'Subversions of Authority: Feminist Literary Culture in the River Plate Region', *Chasqui* XXI.1, 39–48.

McClennan, Sophia, *The Dialectics of Exile* (West Lafayette, IN: Purdue State University, 2004).

McKee Irwin, Robert, and Molloy, Sylvia, *Hispanisms and Homosexualities* (Durham, NC, & London: Duke University Press, 1998).

Mielly, Michelle, 'Filling the Continental Split: Subjective Emergence in Ken Bugul's *La baobab fou* and Sylvia Molloy's *En breve cárcel*, *Comparative Literature*, 54.1 (Winter 2002), pp. 42–57.

Molloy, Sylvia, 'At Face Value: Autobiographical Writing in Spanish America', *Dispositio*, 9.24/26 (1984), 1–18.

Molloy, Sylvia, '*En breve cárcel*: pensar en otra novela', *Punto de vista: Revista de cultura* 21 (December 1998), 29–32.

Molloy, Sylvia, 'Introduction', in Robert McKee Irwin and Sylvia Molloy, *Hispanisms and Homosexualities* (Durham, NC, & London: Duke University Press, 1998).

Molloy, Sylvia, 'Part 2: Introduction', in Sara Castro-Klarén, Sylvia Molloy, and Beatriz Sarlo (eds.), *Women's Writing in Latin America: An Anthology* (Boulder, CO; San Francisco; Oxford: Westview Press, 1992), pp. 107–124.

Molloy, Sylvia, *Certificate of Absence*, Trans. Daniel Balderston (Austin: University of Texas Press, 1989).

Molloy, Sylvia, *En breve cárcel* (Barcelona: Seix Barral, 1981).

Muzquiz, Virginia, 'Boundaries Around Identity: Sylvia Molloy's *Certificate of Absence* and the Autobiographical Process', *Monographic Review* 9 (1993), 176–188.

Pérez-Sánchez, Gema, and Peri Rossi, Cristina, 'Cristina Peri Rossi', in *Hispamérica*, 24.72 (December 1995), 59–72.

Soja, Edward, *Thirdspace: Journeys to Los Angeles and Other Real- and-Imagined Places* (Cambridge, UK: Blackwell, 1998).

Spivak, Gayatri Chakravorty, 'French Feminism in an International Frame', *Yale French Studies*, 62, Feminist Readings: French Texts/American Contexts (1981), 154–184.

Stephenson, Marcia, 'Lesbian Trajectories in Sylvia Molloy's *En breve cárcel*' *MLN*, 112.2, Hispanic Issue (March 1997), 253–268.

Part III

Reconstruction

The Female Body and Agency

5 Arráncame la vida/ Tear This Heart Out *by Ángeles Mastretta* (1985)

This final section is dedicated to the exploration of the last stage of *Bildung* as it has been articulated through the structure of *Gender and the Self in Latin American Literature*—that of 'reconstruction', which will be explored using the topos of the body as the primary point of reference. In many ways this part of the threefold process of the dialectic is the most complex and difficult to define, for it is a point of culmination, yet not an ending per se. Rachel Blau DuPlessis has succinctly evaluated the importance of endings in *Writing Beyond the Ending: Narrative Strategies of Twentieth-Century Women Writers*, remarking that 'one of the great moments of ideological negotiation in any work occurs in the choice of a resolution for the various services it provides'.[1] And whereas this moment of reconstruction is the end point of this study, it is also a site of potentiality that needs to be left in a state of openness through its literary representation, so it is apt that both of the works examined here in Part Three end at a point of nonclosure.

The main prism through which I wish to search out this point of simultaneous conclusion and continuation is the female body (although reference will also be made to depictions of the male body as a counterpoint), incorporated here as the 'locus for feminist identities and concerns' that it represents for authors and literary critics alike.[2] The body is understood in my readings of the novels as the site upon which gender is brought to bear and inscribed *as* identity; located at 'the boundaries of the physical and psychoanalytic, the linguistic and the material' and read for both its materiality—physical sensations, capabilities, limitations—and attributed symbolisms;[3] outlined as the physical form that has been deployed in the foundation of dominant gender ideals within patriarchal symbolic orders, and as the tangible mechanism via which those ideals are expressed, acted out, and made part of everyday life in Western cultures.

Judith Butler's contribution to the theorization of the body is one of particular value here as a result of its focus on the role of repetition in the formulation of gendered identity—a formative pattern that, I argue, can be positively interrupted by the triadic formulation of the Hegelian dialectic. In *Gender Trouble* (1990) Butler defines gender as an identity category that is brought to bear through the repetition of acts and ideas that legitimate some identities and exclude others:

> Gender is the repeated stylization of the body, a set of repeated acts within a highly rigid regulatory frame that congeal over time to produce the appearance of substance, of a natural sort of being. A political genealogy of gender ontologies, if it is successful, will deconstruct the substantive appearance of gender into its constitutive acts and locate and account for those acts within the compulsory frames set by the various forces that police the social appearance of gender.[4]

The formulation of an identity through repetitive acts that are legitimized by, and which effectively reinforce, the social order, is a process paralleled by the generic regulation of the Bildungsroman as discussed in the Introduction, and in the resultant models for identity development produced by its (now contested) normative versions. As I have discussed, the recognition of other kinds of Bildungsromane and so Other kinds of identities to which this project seeks to contribute can therefore also be interpreted as a desire to underline the meaningful relationship between genre and gender, where both are understood as regulatory practices governed by the repetition of certain traits. In this way, the relationship between gender and genre brought about through the notion of the 'Other' Bildungsroman furthers an understanding of Butler's idea that it is possible for identities to be 'done' differently—for *Bildung* to take place differently.

Returning to the role of the dialectic in drawing forth these realizations, the stage of 'synthesis' to which this study now turns can be conceived of as a space in which repetition without difference itself is brought to an end. Instead, the antagonism inherent to the opposition thesis/antithesis is negated by a push forward towards an accepted element of difference, even while retaining repetition through the inclusion of old elements in the creation of something new. In many ways, this recalls the dream that began *La nave de los locos*, in which the confusion of a mixed, non-binary organizational system is portrayed to have been brought about by the insertion of an active, female element. In the critical study of Mastretta's novel presented in this chapter (and Zoé Valdés's *La nada cotidiana* in the next, and final, chapter), that active female element is the body and, expressed and explored via the body of the text, it serves as the space in and through which synthesis occurs. Moreover, it is through the rendering visible of this synthesis that agency is gained, as the ever-more (self-)knowing female protagonist is able to recognize her identity as discursively constructed, and to retain the agency afforded by that knowledge by adapting and reengaging those very same discourses. The body here then, is not simply the material form upon which gendered identities are inscribed. Rather, it is the nodal point at which identity comes to be; to be done, to be undone, and to be redone.

The story told in *Arráncame la vida* is set against the backdrop of the politically turbulent post-revolutionary Mexico of the 1930s and 1940s. It recounts from her early years the life of Catalina Guzmán, a young girl from Puebla coerced into marrying, at the age of fifteen, a formidable and ambitious politician more than twice her age named Andrés Ascensio. A traditional Bildungsroman in terms of its trajectory, because of the span of its plot and for its depiction of the protagonist's entrance into the Bourgeois social class that is returning to dominate at this time in the country's history, the twist in this story of *Bildung* is found in Catalina's ambiguity. In no way a straightforward character, Mastretta's leading lady has been recognized time and again for her inconsistent relationship with the power structures by which her life is governed—themselves embodied by her husband, as we shall see. Like her contemporary and fellow Mexican Laura Esquivel, Mastretta has been accused of producing *literatura lite*; her use of melodrama and popular cultural texts, such as the *Bolero* from which the novel's title is taken, residing at the heart of such critique. Nonetheless, just as I argued was the case for *Como agua para chocolate*, the lack of radical stylistic experimentalism in this work does not equate to ideological laziness, and the recourse to modes such as the melodrama that characterizes this novel does not necessarily incur the formulation of a Manichean fictional world. Rather, the ambivalence adopted as a narrative strategy in the characterization of the protagonist in this novel draws on that term's inherent potency, as so saliently pointed out by Nuala Finnegan in her own critical application of it:

> Ambivalence is popularly defined as the simultaneous coexistence of contradictions (often emotional). In many cases this leads to a state of uncertainty or fluctuation between two opposites. I use the term here, conscious of its etymology from the Latin *ambi* ('both') and *Valentia* ('strength'). Used in this context, it evokes notions of strength and vigour as well as connoting fluctuation and contradiction. Over the course of my research into the writing by Mexican women, it seemed to capture effectively the impossible situation of many of the fictional characters explored in these writers' texts. Furthermore, by linking it in a more general way to the writers' own position vis-à-vis traditional structures of cultural power, it seemed extraordinarily apt.[5]

In terms of the thematic and theoretical interests of this last section of the present study, the dualistic qualities with which Catalina is made into a vehicle for social critique echo, therefore, the qualities of the body as an interface for the discursive and the tangible—because, in Butler's words, 'language and materiality are not opposed, for language both is and refers to that which is material, and what is material never fully escapes from the processes by which it is signified'.[6] In fact, as will be explored in this chapter, it is the push and pull generated by the contradictory, double location of the body, that stimulates growth and change in this novel; the kind of progress towards self-consciousness and social agency that is the common feature of all of the works explored in *Gender and the Self*. Catalina's development into a female figure of greater autonomy, rather than remaining defined solely by the parameters of her social context, is depicted in parallel with the experiences lived through her gendered body, many of which function as key rites of passage in female *Bildung*.

EMBODYING THE NATION

I begin this discussion of the female body as deployed in Mastretta's work at its broadest dimensions as a socially codified symbolic entity, before gradually drilling down to examine the depiction of Catalina's own more intimately lived embodiment and the portrayal of the sexed and gendered body as a locus for change. At the macro level, one of the key ways in which the notion of *Bildung* finds its place in this narrative is via the alignment of Catalina's person with the Mexican nation at the time of the novel's setting, itself in a stage of what might be described as a kind of adolescence following the tumult of the Revolution. This thematic intertwining is stylistically engaged via the first person narrative point of view through which the story is told. Recounting the life of its protagonist in hindsight, therefore, the mature analytical perspectives of the now grown narrator-protagonist seep through into the story, and this

> foregrounding of the woman's voice personalizes history to reveal both Catalina and Mexico as the result of change and experience; they are neither eternally docile social, political, and economic subjects nor stagnant identities. Rather, they embody the dynamic forces between the control and expression of one's own 'desires' (either national or individual), and the imposition of limits or restrictions from 'outside' (dictated norms that exclude, repress or forbid by public proscription or private internalized self-censorship).[7]

Claudia Schaefer's observations here recall those of Bakhtin, discussed in the Introduction, who describes the Bildungsroman as a novel in which 'time is introduced into man',[8] so that the coming-to-be of the genre's protagonist parallels the coming-to-be of the world more broadly. Yet the male-focused genre which Bakhtin studied has been greatly changed here, and the creation of a narrative that elucidates a relationship between the female gender, the female body, and the sphere of politics, puts in evidence a valuable shift in representational possibilities. More precisely, as Schaefer puts it, this narrative structure enables the incorporation of 'Mastretta's contemporary questioning voice' into that of Catalina, resulting in a 'retrospective portrait of a string of epiphanies', through which

> discoveries of the foci of power are combined in a process of demystifying traditional cultural values which if adopted would, in theory, make the adult Catalina merely repeat the role of previous generations of women.[9]

Powerfully, what Mastretta succeeds in doing is to connect social change at a national level to the necessity of change at the level of gendered identities, and to place women at the center of that initiative: 'That year, many things happened in this country. For one, Andrés and I were married'.[10] From its very first sentences Mastretta's text foregrounds *Bildung* national and personal, that change immediately encapsulated in the pairing of Catalina with her male counterpart. Thus, when the reader is shortly afterwards told by Catalina that 'I was fifteen, and really wanted things to happen to me',[11] we are led to understand that her and Andrés's marriage is the principal arena in which the battle for change will be enacted: that social institution serving as a neat metonym for the sex/gender system, as Blau Duplessis has highlighted,[12] which is also deeply informative of national identities (to be explored further in Chapter Six).

The marriage is also Catalina's initiation into the deeply conservative values of the social class to which Andrés has been able to rise from his initially poor roots. (In fact, it is curious how much Andrés's own back story might be read as a traditional male Bildungsroman narrative in line with the critiques aimed at the genre by feminist literary theory, for he utterly embodies the white male bourgeois narrative, successfully seeking social mobility and embracing dominant power structures.) The detail with which Mastretta depicts the physical appearance of the people with whom Catalina and Andrés socialize is a meaningful instance not only of the Post-Boom 'return to realism' that characterizes her work, but also of the foregrounding of the body as a social entity that is ideologically codified. Before delving down into the story's depiction of the sexualized body, therefore, it is worthwhile considering occasions when the narrative demonstrates just how, to cite Sidonie Smith, 'bodies locate us topographically, temporally, socioculturally as well as linguistically in a series of transcodings along multiple axes of meanings'.[13]

One salient example of this is when, five years into their marriage and during Andrés's campaign for the Governorship of Puebla, Catalina accompanies him on his rallies throughout the state but remains, at this time, happily disengaged from the politics that are the motivation for the trip. She nonetheless plays her role perfectly, however unintentionally, by choosing to dress herself and their children up in the traditional Indian clothing of Andrés's hometown:

> se me ocurrió que Marcela se vería linda con un traje como el de las inditas. Organicé que todas nos vistiéramos como ellas [...] Volvimos a la plaza en la que Andrés iba a empezar un discurso para los pocos mirones que había. Caminábamos con trabajo, nos costaba mantener firme la cabeza llena de estambres, nos veíamos extrañas, pero a la gente le gustamos. Empezaron a seguirnos al cruzar el mercado. Cuando llegamos a la plaza le llevábamos al general Ascencio tres veces más público del que habían logrado conseguir sus acarreadores.[14]

> it occurred to me that Marcela would look pretty dressed like the Indian women. I organized for us all to dress up like them [...] We

> started back to the square where Andrés was going to address the few onlookers there were. We found it difficult to walk and hold our heads up straight with the headdresses on and we looked strange to each other, but people liked us. They began to follow us through the market. When we arrived at the square we were bringing to General Ascencio three times more people than his assistants had gathered.

This episode is intriguing because of the cultural particularities it depicts, but also because of the very obvious 'dressing up' as the Other that it portrays. Catalina's accidental facilitation of her husband's acceptance by the townspeople distills a more general manipulation of women within the political class to which the couple now belongs; something to which Catalina becomes increasingly sensitized:

> Para mucha gente yo era parte de la decoración, alguien a quien se le corren las atenciones que habría que tener con un mueble si de repente se sentara en la mesa y sonriera. Por eso me deprimían las cenas. Diez minutos antes de que llegaran las visitas quería ponerme a llorar, pero me aguantaba para no correrme el rimel y de remate parecer bruja. Porque así no era la cosa diría Andrés. La cosa es ser bonita, dulce, impecable. [...]
>
> De todos modos me costaba disimular el cansancio frente a aquellos señores que tomaban a sus mujeres del codo como si sus brazos fueran el asa de una tacita de café.[15]

> For many I was part of the décor, someone to whom as much attention was owed as to a piece of furniture that suddenly sat at the table and smiled. That's why the dinners [hosted by Andrés] depressed me. Ten minutes before the arrival of the guests I felt like crying, but I held back so as not to make my eye makeup run and end up looking like a witch on top of everything else. Because that was not the way to be, Andrés would say. The thing is to be pretty, sweet, impeccable. [...]
>
> Nonetheless, it was hard for me to disguise my weariness when faced with those men who led their wives by the elbow as if their arms were the handle of a teacup.

Both this and the above scene are worth citing at length, then, for the way in which they so clearly highlight the performative nature of identity at a number of its constituent levels, and precisely because of their insistence on dressing- and making-up the surface of the body in order to then be seen to *em*body a recognizable, socially appropriate kind of femalehood, in the very theatrical sense by which Butler's theory was first inspired: In a 2006 documentary about her work, Butler discusses the concept of 'Gender Trouble' as influenced by her own upbringing and gradually developing perceptions of gender and gendered identities during that time. She comments that her parents and grandparents were from generations of 'American Jews who understood that assimilation meant conforming to certain gender norms that were presented in Hollywood movies'. As a result, she says,

> looking around me, trying to make sense of gender, I saw these extremely exaggerated notions of what gender was. But I think these were notions of Hollywood gender that came through Jewish assimilation and maybe 'Gender Trouble' is actually a theory that emerges from my effort to make sense of how my family embodied those Hollywood norms [...] and how they also didn't. You know, they tried to embody them, and then there was some way in which they couldn't possibly. And my conclusion was that anyone who strives to embody them also perhaps fails in ways that are more interesting than their successes.[16]

The gendered identities Butler witnessed her relatives adopting came about through persistent reference back to preexistent models just like that which Cati, as she is affectionately known, and her fellow wives are guided to carry out by their patriarchal counterparts. And of course Catalina herself has, on some levels, also bought into this discursive arrangement, as is seen in her obedience to the standards of femininity set by Andrés, and evinced throughout the work by her cutting judgments of other women's shapes, sizes, features and clothes—woman-on-woman judgements that are a key mechanism in the upholding of patriarchal beauty ideals, as Naomi Wolf has so compellingly argued in *The Beauty Myth* (1990).[17] Both negative and positive, her critiques voice, as Salvador A. Oropesa has observed, Catalina's command over 'the cultural codes of her gender and the genres associated with femininity'.[18]

Crucially, though, command is an active, not a passive act. Rather, the fact is that Catalina 'knows how to textualize her behavior and how to map her body in order to get the effects she pursues'.[19] In other words, her behaviors give evidence to her simultaneous awareness of, and entrapment by, those discourses, so that she is at once a mouthpiece for hegemonic ideals and for the possibility of their revelation as artifice by means of their not being 'done' properly. This is neatly hinted at the in the last citation from the novel by the 'Nonetheless' with which the second paragraph begins: despite her well-informed intention to play the part, Catalina is a character imbued with a glint of rebellion from the very beginning of her story. Thus, just as Butler's parents and grandparents were not completely disempowered by what she noted as their meaningful *failures* to completely embody the models they looked to as vehicles for social integration, Mastretta's protagonist is enabled to discover some element of agency through her dualistic location at once inside and outside, central and marginalized, active and passive, material and symbolic. In short, Catalina is written as a space of synthesis that shows doubleness, not fixity or certainty, to be the essence of a transformative agency, expressed in Butler's philosophical mode as follows:

> The abiding gendered self will then be shown to be structured by repeated acts that seek to approximate the ideal of substantial ground of identity, but which, in their occasional *dis*continuity, reveal the temporal and contingent groundlessness of this "ground." The possibilities of gender transformation are to be found precisely in the arbitrary relation between such acts, in the possibility of a failure to repeat, a de-formity, or a parodic repetition that exposes the phantasmatic effect of abiding identity as a politically tenuous construction.[20]

POSSESSING THE BODY: MARRIAGE AND MOTHERHOOD

The foregrounding in the above scenes of the physical body as a portmanteau for a range of appropriately formulated identities—national, classed, gendered—also reveals that body's central role in the objectification of women; as an indispensable building block for the foundational binary oppositions of the patriarchal symbolic order that are challenged by Mastretta's protagonist: male/female, subject/object, mind/body, active/passive. As the tangible locus of identity, the body is the locus of objectification also. In line with Blau DuPlessis's above-cited comments on marriage as metonym for the sex-gender system at large and as a traditional rite of passage to orthodox womanhood, Catalina's retrospective account of her wedding ceremony emphasizes its legitimization of Andrés's already presumed ownership of her: she tells how he appears at the family home unannounced, goes inside, says 'three words' to her father and reappears with her family in tow ready to accompany them to the service.[21] Catalina explains how her parents' unpredictable financial future meant they were, above all, grateful that at least one of their children had a future secured for her, and we understand by now that in any case her milk farmer father had no way of challenging the power of a figure like General Ascencio. The language deployed in hindsight to recount Andrés's actions at the ceremony further underscores her presence there purely as 'thing': he 'yanks' her away from her mother and brusquely vows to the judge, 'I accept her, I promise the protection that the strong owes to the weak and all that, so you can save yourself the trouble of the speech. Where do we sign?'[22] The signature serving to finalize the ceremony then quite literally inscribes Catalina's new identity, echoing Foucault's description of the body as 'the inscribed surface of events'.[23] Her transformation into another of her husband's possessions is thus made official; as she signs her name Andrés leans over her shoulder and tells her to add the patronymic 'de Ascencio' to her own names. 'Did you write *de Guzmán*?' she questions,[24] only to receive an unequivocal reply: 'No my dear, because that isn't how it goes. I protect you, not you me. You become a part of my family; you become mine'.[25]

Narratively, this initial owner-possession dynamic is encoded in the fact that the first three chapters of the novel read somehow as more about Andrés than about Catalina—the narrative seems filtered through her attempts to bring into view for her implied reader and, cathartically, I would argue, for herself, the man she married. Because to understand him is to understand her better, such is the nature of the life she lives with him and the influence on her development that he has. This is not to say that his influence disappears after that point in the story, for such is certainly not the case. But it is very meaningful that the story begins with his appearance in her life and that the narrative ends when *his* life does. He is the first character we are given any sense of—despite the novel being a self-narrated story of self-development it does not begin with 'I'. And it ends with a more fully formulated and textually present 'I' that exists at that point precisely because of Andrés's death. Read symbolically, the overall trajectory of the novel thus implies that selfhood for women begins only with the death of patriarchy. Catalina comes into full ownership of herself only when her possessor is no longer around to continue possessing.

Thus, as evidence of her increased consciousness regarding her discursive context, Catalina's mature reflections on her official coupling to him, written after Andrés has died, are telling:

> Siempre me río en las bodas. Sé que tanta faramalla acabará en el cansancio de todos los días durmiendo y amaneciendo con la misma barriga junto. Pero la música y el desfile señoreados por la novia todavía me dan más envidia que risa. [Una boda así] no me hubiera cambiado la vida pero podría haber jugado con el recuerdo como juegan otras. Podría evocarme caminando el pasillo de regreso, apoyada en Andrés y saludando desde la altura de mi nobleza recién adquirida, desde la alcurnia que todos otorgan a una novia cuando vuelve del altar.[26]

> I always laugh at weddings. I know that all that fanfare will end in the boredom of going to bed and waking up every day with the same person. But the music and the procession dominated by the bride still make me more envious than they make me laugh. [A wedding like that] would not have changed my life but I could at least have held onto the memory as other women do. I could picture myself walking back down the aisle leaning on Andrés and greeting the guests from the lofty heights of my newfound nobility, basking in the reverence that everyone awards to a bride leaving the altar.

As well as inflecting Nuala Finnegan's observations regarding the aptness of ambivalence as a lens through which to examine the challenge presented by

Mexican women writers (she includes Mastretta in her study), this passage also furthers *Arráncame la vida*'s exemplification of Butler's performativity; especially the formulation of agency within it. The critical portrayal of the marriage ceremony as a rite of passage through which gendered identities are legitimized is interesting as an exemplification of Butler's theory because its demarcation as a 'ceremony' is acquired precisely through the *repetition* of its constituent rituals and words. Catalina's recognition that it was not the fairytale episode she alludes to above—i.e., that her wedding was a *failed* reproduction of the standard—and that as a result she cannot simply, nostalgically, enjoy the memory, is a liberating factor. For instead of obfuscating the power dynamic instigated with the marriage ceremony, memories of her wedding actually align with the realities of a marriage whose metonymic role in the novel makes its critique fundamental to a more general deconstruction of the symbolic order.

Evocative as they are of Catalina's powerful ambivalence, these reflections communicate both refusal and recognition of the various kinds of social legitimization provided by the marriage ceremony. That she, to a degree, laments not having been able to enjoy this orthodox rite of passage reminds the reader that Mastretta has not created in Catalina a protagonist who personifies a radical rejection of the hegemonic order—as the author has commented herself, 'Catalina is not consciously feminist. She enjoys relative freedom because she is wealthy'.[27] To serve as a tool for feminist critique, however, a character does not always need to be able to articulate their ideas by labeling them as of a particular ideological standpoint. And within the frame of the female Bildungsroman this is even more so the case, because the story itself is most useful when articulating the gradual development of a particular mindset in response to a specific sociopolitical context. As Carol Pearson succinctly puts it, 'there are multiple avenues to resistance',[28] and this protagonist most certainly serves to incite reflection on those institutions that continue to serve as the building blocks of patriarchy. In the words of Aída Apter-Cragnolino:

> Como personaje Catalina adhiere al comportamiento que le asigna la cultura, aunque como narradora encuentra la capacidad de criticar ese papel y denunciar el modelo. La narración no se limita entonces a denunciar los moldes a los que la sociedad ha sometido a la mujer, sino que indaga en los roles femeninos y sus relaciones con las maquinaciones del poder y los valores de la clase social en que se desarrolla el relato. Expresa de esta manera toda la ambigüedad con que las mujeres se han solidarizado y han apoyado y ayudado a consolidar las mismas estructuras que les han sometido.[29]

> As a character Catalina adheres to the behavior that is culturally assigned to her, although as narrator she finds the capacity to criticize that role and denounce the established model. The narration

is not, therefore, limited to criticizing the molds by which society has subjugated women, but rather examines those female roles and their relationships to the power structures and the values of the social class depicted in the story. She thus expresses all of the ambiguity with which women have aligned themselves with, supported, and helped to consolidate the same structures that have oppressed them.

Her objectification ostensibly completed by her now being 'de Ascencio', Andrés's possession of Catalina is linguistically inflected on a number of occasions where Catalina specifically deploys inanimate objects as similes and metaphors for describing her husband's attitude towards her, as in the dinner party scene discussed above. She becomes to her husband 'a burden', 'a thing you buy and put away in a drawer'; 'like a toy he talked nonsense with'.[30] Andrés mocks her naivety and, at the start of their life together at least—this changes as the novel progresses, as shall be seen—appears to see her only for her material being. As all body, no mind:

> Andrés se levantaba con la luz [...] Yo me quedaba quieta tapándome los ojos y pensando en el mar o en bocas riéndose. A veces me quedaba tanto tiempo que Andrés volvía del baño en el que se encerraba con el periódico, y gritoneaba
>
> —Orale güevoncita. ¿Qué haces ahí pensando como si pensaras? Te espero abajo, cuento a 300 y me voy.[31]

> Andrés got up at the crack of dawn [...] I used to stay in bed, still, covering my eyes and thinking about the sea and laughing mouths. Sometimes I stayed there so long that Andrés would come back from the bathroom where he shut himself away with the newspaper and shout
>
> —Oy lazybones. What are you doing lying there pretending you can think? I'll wait for you downstairs. I'm counting to 300 and then I'm leaving.

But of course Catalina can think—the whole narrative is construed precisely as the result of her dominion over her own mind.

And so it is especially interesting that the profoundly bodily experience of pregnancy is deployed by Mastretta as one of the major catalysts for Catalina's critical thinking vis-à-vis her situation. This female rite of passage, important to all feminist formulations of gendered identity regardless of their perspective because of its complete specificity to women's lives, is experienced and depicted by the narrator-protagonist as a further 'possession' of her being:

> Tenía yo diecisiete años cuando nació Verania. La había cargado nueve meses como una pesadilla. Le había visto crecer a mi cuerpo una

> joroba por delante y no lograba ser una madre enternecida. La primera desgracia fue dejar los caballos y los vestidos entallados, la segunda soportar unas agruras que me llegaban hasta la nariz. Odiaba quejarme, pero odiaba la sensación de estar continuamente poseída por algo extraño. Cuando empezó a moverse como un pescado nadando en el fondo de mi vientre creí que se saldría de repente y tras ella toda la sangre hasta matarme.[32]

> I was seventeen when Verania was born. I had carried her for nine nightmarish months. I had watched a hump form on the front of my body and just couldn't be the archetypal tender mother. The first hardship was having to give up horse riding and fitted dresses, the second was putting up with a heartburn that seemed to reach my nose. I hated to complain, but I hated the sensation of being continually possessed by something foreign. When she started moving around inside me like a fish swimming at the bottom of my stomach I felt as if she would suddenly burst out and all my blood would follow her, leaving me for dead.

In an article about the representation of this theme in fiction by three Mexican women writers (including Mastretta), Finnegan examines pregnancy as an enforced element of the female complicity with the patriarchal system summarized by Apter-Cragnolino above. Because of their biological role as reproducers, she writes, women 'are the [...] vehicles through which the existing tyrannical power structures are perpetuated and upheld'; a fact that 'raises the crucial question of the complicity of women in the maintenance of the systems of power that oppress them'.[33] The descriptions of Catalina's experiences of pregnancy align with this reading because they are made to function in the narrative as one of the impetuses for her recognition of the subjugation she suffers at Andrés's hands. Up until the point in her marriage where she falls pregnant for the first time she demonstrates extreme dependence on her husband in even the most banal details of her daily life. At that stage she still relates to him in part as a kind of benevolent father figure—understandably so, given the combination of her young age, his comparative seniority, and their sociocultural positioning via normalized gender and power relations. So when, for example, very early in their marriage Andrés is arrested as a suspect in a murder case, rather than focusing on the possibilities of his involvement and the meaning of that, as she later learns to do, one of Catalina's first concerns is: 'Who will I go to bed with? Who will wake me up in the morning?'[34]

It is significant, therefore, that when reflecting on her pregnancy Catalina reveals the start of a somewhat more confident separation of herself and her husband: 'Andrés was the reason all this was happening to me, and he wouldn't even put up with hearing me talk about it'.[35] In effect, in the aftermath of pregnancy and birth, her sense of selfhood, still very much in the process of formation, is required to take on the new gender and social roles she realizes she must now adopt if she is to conform to the Mexican social norms aligning womanhood with motherhood. But recalling the birth of her second child she persists with the same attitude as the first time around: 'When [Sergio] began to cry and I felt that I was finally rid of the stone that I had been carrying in my belly, I swore that that would be the last time'.[36]

As part of the novel's challenge to the assumptions made in orthodox understandings of identity formation, these portrayals of pregnancy as a series of uncomfortable physical sensations recall Butler's summary of the role of boundaries in any notion of fixed selfhood:

> 'Inner' and 'outer' make sense only with reference to a mediating boundary that strives for stability [...] Hence 'inner' and 'outer' constitute a binary that stabilizes and consolidates a coherent subject. When that subject is challenged, the meaning and necessity of the terms are subject to displacement. If the 'inner' world no longer designates a topos, then the internal fixity of the self and, indeed, the internal locale of gender identity becomes similarly suspect.[37]

The depiction of the pregnant female body in *Arráncame la vida* focuses our attention on that body's fluid boundaries; one of the features of it that more radical feminist critiques have seen to inspire patriarchal fear, and subsequent desire for control of, that powerful entity. Cixous, for example, has described the possibility of female identities' defiance of patriarchally imposed limits as 'bisexual', and writes that 'for men this permeability, this non-exclusion is a threat, something intolerable'.[38] Parallels can be found between this conceptualization of 'bisexuality', and the concepts of 'inner' and 'outer' that Butler also assesses in terms relating to danger, saying that '[r]egardless of the compelling metaphors of the spatial distinctions between inner and outer, they remain linguistic terms that facilitate and articulate a set of fantasies, feared and desired'.[39] Pregnancy and its related processes—the sexual act, conception, the growth of a child inside its mother, and birth—are dependent on the permeability of the female body; on its existence as a boundary that can be crossed and its ability to draw masculine elements into its own confines. Thus, pregnancy is understood to call into question the 'coherent subject' that binary divisions work to establish.[40] Consequently, women are seen to challenge their own existence as subjects by performing a creative process that is reliant upon and yet destabilizes that very subject status. In line with Finnegan and Apter-Cragnolino's earlier assertions regarding the complicity of women in the order that subjugates and marginalizes them, this might be perceived as the consummate irony of woman's place in the hegemonic symbolic order: through these symbolic associations she comes to be feared and controlled, so that the bodily abilities that permit her to reproduce the subjects necessary to the perpetuation of the system that oppresses her, also reassert her own subjugation.

Cixous, however, develops her notion of 'bisexuality' as a positive force that works against the patriarchal indictment of 'unboundedness'; as an ability to traverse the artificially imposed divisions of male/female, active/passive, subject/object, inner/outer both performed and metaphorized by the female physical form:

> But there is a nonclosure that is not submission but confidence and comprehension; that is not an opportunity for destruction, but for wonderful expansion. Through the same opening that is her danger, she comes out of herself to go to the other, a traveller in unexplored places; she does not refuse, she approaches, not to do away with space between, but to see it, to experience what she is not, what she is, what she can be.[41]

NONCLOSURE AND EXPANSION: RIGHT TO PASSAGE AND THE RECLAIMING OF THE SELF

And of course it is the question of what Catalina *can* be, and by extension of what women *can* be, that is the driving force of *Arráncame la vida*. That the narrative itself is left open-ended, leaving the matter of her future entirely open to the 'almost happy' Catalina's own definition, means that the question remains unanswered, and implies that *an* answer is not desirable. More important is the process that leads both her and her reader to that point. Continuing on from the above discussion of pregnancy and its role in the development of Catalina's self-awareness and self-contextualization, her refusal to adopt the role of perfect mother as corollary to perfect wife takes some time to come into full force. Her statement about never getting pregnant again after her second child is a promise to herself the she keeps. Read in context of the ideas discussed above, this is an important step in terms of taking control of her body and therefore her identity. But her refusal to go through pregnancy again does not equate to a refusal of motherhood altogether, and for a long time after her children's birth, and after she is also forced to adopt the role of mother for Andrés's children from previous relationships (relationships and children she knew nothing of until the day he appears at their home with his offspring), Catalina enjoys the role of parenting, spending 'years closely intertwined with them [...] my passion [...] my diversion'.[42]

Her eventual, more forceful rejection of motherhood itself comes instead through a desire to protect her children. When her five-year-old son Sergio nonchalantly mentions that Andrés had told him 'killing is hard work', Catalina's body registers more quickly the horror that her mind will eventually come to process and she vomits up her evening meal. 'After that' she says, 'I decided to close the chapter on motherly love'.[43] She leaves their care to the servants from then on, and the next chapter begins with the phrase 'In exchange, I set myself the task of finding out about Andrés's dealings'.[44] The role of mother is left aside in order to facilitate an increased understanding of the corrupt world in which she is embroiled as 'the official accomplice'.[45] And in terms of the strategy implied in the novel of a reclaiming of her body as the reclaiming of her selfhood, Catalina's next moves are key. Early on in their relationship Andrés had enjoyed talking to Catalina about his political ambitions, as she recalls when describing a trip they take to the coast not long after she has earned his attentions; a trip (to be discussed further below) on which she loses her virginity to him and on which he talked at her 'as if to a wall, without waiting for a response, without asking my opinion, motivated purely by having an audience'.[46] Recounted early on in the narrative this scene portrays clearly both Andrés's stereotyped hypermasculinity and then Catalina's concurrent ignorance and capacity for rebellion. Despite his lack of interest in her opinions, she dares to share one with him after listening to his monologues on a particular political opponent. Again, his response clearly reaffirms his view of their respective roles:

> —[...] 'Y tú qué te metes, ¿quién te pidió tu opinión?
> —Hace cuatro días que hablas de lo mismo, ya me dio tiempo de tener una opinión.
> —Vaya con la señorita. No sabe ni cómo se hacen los niños y ya quiere dirigir generales. Me está gustando.[47]

> —[...] 'And what do you have to say about this? Who asked your opinion?
> —You've been talking about the same thing for four days now; I've had time to form an opinion.
> —Well look at the little señorita. She doesn't even know how babies are made and yet she already wants to give orders to Generals. I'm liking this.

Seeming to enjoy the challenge presented by Catalina's 'insolence', at this time Andrés remains unthreatened by her self-expression because he can still see her as he expects her to be; an ignorant woman whose lack of sexual knowledge and experience equate to a general and unchangeable ignorance towards life. And Mastretta, too, seems to make the same equivalence throughout the story, because of the clear parallel between Catalina's coming to know her physical self and her coming to know the realities of her sociopolitical surroundings. The underlying message, therefore, is that knowledge of the world begins with self-knowledge, which in turn begins with knowledge of the body that is the locus of selfhood. And as an outcome of this textual strategy, as Catalina's knowledge of sociopolitical realities increases, so does her awareness of the fact that she can use her body as a site of political resistance, precisely because it is one of the main things that her manipulative and dominant husband wants from her.

Chapter Seven and the events following her decision to find out more about her husband's activities see Catalina come to terms for the first time with the evidence of Andrés's cruelty and corruption; evidence of which, by her own admission, she has preferred to ignore:

> Yo preferí no saber qué hacía Andrés. Era la mamá de sus hijos, la dueña de su casa, su señora, su criada, su costumbre, su burla. Quién sabe quién era yo, pero lo que fuera lo tenía que seguir siendo por más que a veces me quisiera ir a un país donde él no existiera, donde mi nombre no se pegara al suyo.[48]

> I preferred not to know what Andrés was up to. I was the mother of his children, the mistress of his household, his wife, his servant, his wont, his joke. Who knows what I was to him, but I had to keep being it however much I wanted to take myself off to a country where he didn't exist, where my name was not connected to his.

In the space of this one chapter, however, she recounts becoming witness to the murder of an Indian man in which she is convinced her husband has had a role, and also learns of the death of a man whom she had seen in discussion with Andrés and whose daughter had asked for her help in solving the mystery of his disappearance. Through these events, she is confronted with and finally confronts the truth about Andrés's character, and her own role as passive bystander and potential enabler. Catalina interrogates Andrés about his involvement in the murder and, as a result of his denial and her disbelief, refuses him access to her body for the first time:

> —Quítate este vestido que pareces cuervo, déjame que te vea las chichis, odio que te abroches como monja. Ándale, no estés de púdica que no te queda.
>
> Me trepó el vestido y yo apreté las piernas. Su cuerpo encima me enterraba los broches del liguero.
>
> —¿Quién lo mató? —pregunté.
>
> —No sé. Las almas puras tienen muchos enemigos –dijo mientras sobaba su cuerpo contra mi vestido. Pero yo seguí con las piernas cerradas, bien cerradas por primera vez.[49]

> —Take that dress off, you look like a crow [priest]. Let me see your tits; I hate it when you button yourself up like a nun. Hurry up and don't be coy, it doesn't suit you.
>
> He grabbed at my dress and I squeezed my legs together. The weight of his body on top of me pressed the fastener of my suspender belt into my flesh.
>
> —Who killed him?—I asked.
>
> —I don't know. Pure souls have many enemies—he said as he squeezed his body up against my dress. But I kept my legs tightly together, really tightly together for the first time.

Andrés's first choice of metaphor for describing Catalina in this dress, a slang term for a priest, is interesting because of the negative symbolism attached to these birds, and because it recalls the Spanish idiom 'Cría cuervos y te sacarán los ojos'—'If you raise crows expect them to peck out your eyes'. It inflects his impending realization that he might not be able to control the rebellious qualities that only made her amusing to him before, and is starting to fear her ability to challenge his authority.

This is the potential for resistance that was in evidence in the scene, referred to above, from the trip to the coastal town of Tecolutla that depicts the first of the novel's moments of foci on the body as a nodal point for identity formation and for the establishment of the thematic thread that aligns knowledge of and dominion over one's body with more worldly knowledge and power. During the trip, Catalina is indeed a 'traveller in unexplored places', both geographically and more intimately:

> Yo no conocía al mar, él me contó que se ponía negro en las noches y transparente al mediodía. Quise ir a verlo. Nada más dejé un recado [para mis padres] diciendo: 'Queridos papás, no se preocupen, fui a conocer al mar'.
>
> En realidad, fui a pegarme la espantada de mi vida. Yo había visto caballos y toros irse sobre yeguas y vacas, pero el pito parado de un señor era otra cosa. Me dejé tocar sin meter las manos, sin abrir la boca, tiesa como muñeca de cartón, hasta que Andrés me preguntó de qué tenía miedo.[50]

> I didn't know the ocean. He told me that it turned black at night and became transparent at midday. I wanted to go and see it. I just left a note for my parents saying: 'Dear mum and dad, don't worry, I went to meet the ocean.'
>
> In reality, I went off to get the fright of my life. I'd seen stallions and bulls mount mares and cows, but a man's erect prick was a different matter altogether. I allowed myself to be touched without touching back, without opening my mouth, stiff as a cardboard cutout, until Andrés asked me what I was afraid of.

Catalina's narrative reflections on this moment in her life reveal her lack of comprehension of what was expected of her—to begin with she tells Andrés that she isn't sure his penis will fit inside her.[51] In response to her obvious dumbfoundedness at his sexual performance, Andrés asks Catalina 'Don't you feel anything? Why don't you feel anything?', to which she responds: 'I feel something, but I didn't understand the end'.[52] 'The end is what matters', Mastretta has Andrés insist, serving to intertwine yet further Cati's sexual self-knowledge with her *Bildung*, because, as has already been noted, his notion is countered entirely by the narrative structure of the story and its open-ended account of Catalina's life.

In her interpretation of these scenes, Jane Lavery reads 'the virgin's reliance on the male's sexual expertise as a reflection of traditional gender and hierarchical power roles based on binary divisions', and proposes that Catalina's failure to reach orgasm functions as a form of resistance to Andrés's attempted sexual appropriation.[53] In line with this, Catalina's first sexual experience serves to initiate a discovery of the possibilities for female sexual autonomy that are openly explored in the novel. For although she did not then know to articulate it as such, Catalina's failure to reach orgasm inspires in the protagonist a desire to know more. She admits to Andrés that she does not know what it is that she is supposed to have 'felt', and asks him to 'teach her'. His reply is paradoxical: that is not something that can be taught, it is something that is learnt.[54] Andrés's reaction to her request—a quick shutting down of a topic of conversation that he is not interested in pursuing—suggests that, despite being much older and very much more sexually experienced, he is as oblivious as the fifteen-year-old Catalina to the female body's capacity for sexual enjoyment—or at least much more uninterested in finding out about it. That both sexes are ignorant to the possibility of female sexual pleasure also, therefore, comes to implicate within the fictional world a broader, socially interred disregard for the female body as anything more than a vessel for reproduction. Andrés's final comment in particular compounds this ignorance, reading as an evasion tactic through which he is able to disregard the fact that he knows nothing about Catalina's sexuality, body, likes or dislikes. In this way the episode takes on a more subversive meaning, for rather than simply reflecting orthodox power imbalances between male and female gendered identities, it serves to turn the female body into a space within which such hierarchical oppositions can be refuted. Most precisely, Andrés unwittingly admits here that there exists a part of Catalina that he is unable to know or control. Alicia Llarena refers to this notion of the unreachable in Catalina as essential to the feminist merits of Mastretta's novel, remarking that it is not Catalina's progressive aversion to social norms, nor her demands for equality that matter most, but rather 'her acceptance of those intimate regions, different and authentic, that the General saw—feared, perhaps—as the only unreachable, uncontrollable, unknown element of the multiple women that there are in his wife'.[55] It is the self-acceptance of those parts of herself that are denigrated by the patriarchal social code as 'feminine' and therefore emotional before rational, passive before active, weak before strong, superfluous before necessary, etc., etc., that transforms Catalina's story into a valuable narrative of *Bildung*—a point that we shall return to later on.

The key role of the Tecolutla episode in the movement towards such self-knowledge and self-acceptance is compounded by what it inspires Cati to do next. Upon her return home, in an episode whose significance has been frequently noted in studies of Mastraetta's work, Catalina turns to another female in her desire for knowledge: a gypsy woman whose multifaceted marginality injects into the middle-class-, white- and male-dominated fictional world a correlative counter-discourse that provides much impetus for the overall challenge to the hegemony (and which will recur again in the final stages of the story and be implicated in Andrés's death). Catalina seeks out this woman, famed for being an expert in matters of the heart, in order to learn precisely what it was that Andrés was referring to when he asked her if she could 'feel'. The frank response she receives lifts the veil of secrecy placed over the female body even for women themselves:

> —Aquí tenemos una cosita—dijo [la gitana] metiéndose las manos entre las piernas.—Con ésa se siente. Se llama el timbre y ha de tener otros nombres. Cuando estés con alguien piensa que en ese lugar queda el centro de tu cuerpo, que de ahí vienen todas las cosas buenas, piensa que con eso piensas, oyes y miras; olvídate de que tienes cabeza y brazos, ponte toda ahí.[56]

> —We have a thing here—[the gypsy] said, putting her hands between her legs.—With this we feel everything. It's known as 'the bell' but must have other names too. When you are with someone think of this place as the center of your body, that from there come all good things, think as if you think, hear and see from there; forget that you have a head and arms, put all of yourself there.

Lavery rightly affirms the importance of this scene as one that 'anticipates the autonomy and self-control which Catalina will later exert over her own body'.[57] And crucial to this is the fact that Catalina does not reserve this information for her next encounter with Andrés (or anyone else), as the gypsy woman suggests, but deploys her newly gained knowledge in solitary sexual experimentation. In doing so, she further derides traditional male/female logos/pathos binaries by using her newly gained knowledge of her own physicality in order to *learn* how to *feel* pleasure—despite Andrés's insistence that this was not possible. Lavery's subsequent assertion that 'the focus on the 'physical' derives from [Mastretta's] determination to challenge the concept of woman as a site of lack, and to examine the 'dark continent' of female sexuality from a feminist perspective, is put in evidence by this moment of the narrative, which comes to represent a significant moment in the *Bildung* of this female protagonist.[58] Catalina's lack of a phallus is not simply remedied, but rendered irrelevant by the fact that she (woman) does not need to be penetrated by the male sex in order to reach orgasm—the moment of the sexual act that, according to paradigmatic macho male Andrés, was what mattered.[59] As opposed to a site from which something is missing, the uniqueness of the female body is portrayed here in such a way that that this 'lack'—an abnormality only when placed in comparison with a masculinized norm—is turned into a positivized difference, and Catalina's sexual liberation is yet again connected to her desire to be autonomous and through that autonomy construct her own identity.[60]

That all of the above is instigated, and therefore underpinned by, a trip to the sea, is an aspect of Mastretta's novel that I find intriguing not least because it brings into play once a feminized trope that is a thematic recurrence in a number of the novels studied in this project. Through her desire for that voyage of discovery and the obviously important impact upon her of what happens there, the reader is encouraged to start associating Catalina with the qualities of 'nonclosure' and 'expansion', to borrow Cixous's terminology once more, so well embodied by the ocean itself. This established link is perpetuated throughout *Arráncame la vida* from this point on, as the sea is eventually deployed as a simile for her beloved Carlos, the man with whom she has an affair (to be discussed below) and falls in love, it is evoked in songs they sing together, and kept present through her appropriation of a house by the sea at Acapulco that Andrés buys but to which she is more often than not able to escape alone (and where she spends time with another lover after Carlos's death), given Andrés's dislike of the water.

As an approach to the analysis of this connection, I turn to Elizabeth Grosz's interrogation of the female body's association with liquidity as one of the symbolic modes through which not female subordination per se, but the *need* for female subordination within the patriarchal symbolic order, is expressed. Her pithy summary of this idea is worth citing in full:

> Can it be that in the West, in our time, the female body has been constructed not only as a lack or absence but with more complexity, as a leaking, uncontrollable, seeping liquid; as a formless flow; as a viscosity entrapping; secreting; as lacking not so much or simply the phallus, but self-containment—not a cracked or porous vessel, like a leaking ship, but a formlessness that engulfs all form, a disorder that threatens all order? I am not suggesting that this is how women are, that this is their ontological status. Instead, my hypothesis is that women's corporeality is inscribed as a mode of seepage. My claim is not that women have been somehow desolidified but the more limited one which sees that women, in so far as they are human, have the same degree of solidity, occupy the same genus, as men, yet insofar as they are women, they live themselves as seepage, liquidity. The metaphorics of uncontrollability, the ambivalence between desperate, fatal attraction and strong revulsion, the deep-seated fear of absorption, the association of femininity with contagion and disorder, the undecidability of the limits of the female body (particularly but not only with the onset of puberty and in the case of pregnancy), its powers of cynical seduction and allure are all common themes in literary and cultural representations of women. But these may well be a function of the projection outwards of their corporealities, the liquidities that men seem to want to cast out of their own self-representations.[61]

The metaphors and tropes that Grosz points out are interlinked with the female body in *Arráncame la vida* at a number of different points in the work, and not least by Andrés. As if in recognition of the potential for autonomy that Catalina's sexual self-explorations and consequent gain in self-knowledge afford her, Andrés overtly connects the female gender with the sea. As Schaefer has also noted, he remarks that 'The sea irritates me, it never shuts up. It's like a woman';[62] a negative comparison that indicates fear of an incessancy he cannot control.

THE FEMALE GAZE: SEEKING AUTONOMY

For Catalina, the associations are directly the opposite. The sea is connected to 'fleeting instants of liberation' and associated with a 'constant murmur' that 'seem[s] to remind her continually of her inner desires, in spite of and in contrast to the surrounding society'.[63] And in this way, it is aligned with the depiction of the female gaze in the novel, equally connected to the powerful sexuality that is coming clearly into view here as a foundation of female identity in this narrative, and equally responsible for the challenge to hegemonic structures that Cati comes to enact. Arguably her greatest act of rebellion against both her husband and the social structures he personifies are the three extramarital affairs that she embarks upon, engaging in a stereotypically male behavior that is depicted with frankness, and which keeps her sexuality and sexual appetites in the foreground of her characterization as much as it does her nonconformist attitudes. Underlining in particular the role of these affairs as a means of enjoying her body purely as a source of physical pleasure and rejecting its abuse as a means of reproduction of the hegemonic order, is the fact that the first of them happens when she is *already* expecting her first child. Andrés has become uninterested in her pregnant body but an old school friend, Pablo, was, she tells us, willing to 'soothe my anxieties'.[64] Moreover, it is she who takes *his* virginity, and the whole time Catalina is protected from some of the worst likely consequences by the fact that she is already pregnant. In other words, the capacity for reproduction explored by Mastretta as a mode of subjugation of women is inversely made use of by Catalina here as a means to heighten her freedom and autonomous pleasure-seeking. Such highly unorthodox behavior flies in the face of a number of social mores and overturns various elements of the assumed male/female dynamic.

Her second affair continues these challenges to the hegemonic order but plays a far greater role in Catalina's life, becoming a turning point and serving as a forceful eye-opener to a character who, although increasingly willing to see, is never truly committed to any cause more than to her own search for freedom and self-definition. Catalina falls in love with Carlos, the son of an old revolutionary mentor of Andrés's, but whose own political sympathies oppose the General's. What is most meaningful about this relationship in terms of the corporeal thematic that I am focused on here, is that the affair furthers the positioning of Cati in the traditionally male role of onlooker and seeker of sexual pleasure, and using the safe textual space of the female Bildungsroman to undermine the reductiveness of the virgin/whore dichotomy. The challenge to the characterization of female sexuality as passive has obviously been present throughout the novel, even depicted as part of her relationship with Andrés, as in the important scene where she refuses to sleep with him.[65] However with Carlos, she is the initiator, not just a willing participant. After her chance encounter with him at work conducting the newly established National Orchestra, the second time Cati and Carlos cross paths it is entirely down to her decision to go back and seek him out at the Opera House. She describes how

> Me gustaba cómo movía las manos, cómo otros lo obedecían sin detenerse a reflexionar si sus instrucciones eran correctas o no. Daba lo mismo. Él tenía el poder y uno sentía claramente hasta dónde llegaba su dominio. Iba por la sala, se metía en los demás, en mi cuerpo recargado sobre el barandal del palco, en mi cabeza apoyado sobre los brazos, en mis ojos siguiéndole las manos.[66]

> I liked how he moved his hands, how others obeyed without hesitating to ask whether or not his instructions were right. It didn't matter. He was in control and one could feel precisely to what extent. He moved around the room, he entered other people, entered my charged body as I leaned on the balcony rail, entered my head as I rested it on my folded arms, entered my eyes as they followed his hands.

Her focus on Carlos's hands here is very interesting in its repetition of her early observances of Andrés, whose large hands she tells us she liked from the outset, and about which she later says: 'He had large hands. I liked them as much as others feared them. Or perhaps that's why I liked them. I don't know'.[67] Then, all of these depictions call to mind the episode in Esquivel's *Como agua para chocolate*, discussed in Chapter One, in which we saw that body part clearly outlined as a sign of autonomy within the symbolic vocabulary of that Bildungsroman. Given the primary driving force of Mastretta's narrative is Catalina's search for autonomy, the fact of Catalina being particularly drawn to that body part is legible also as a desire to possess the independence, power and privilege of her male counterparts. Her adultery, initially at least, is a strategy for achieving that aim.

Although her sexual attraction to Carlos is described in terms that reinvoke a familiar heterosexual power dynamic, it is nonetheless difficult not to notice a sense of fluidity in her depictions of him and how he makes her feel that invokes the discourse of liquidity discussed above. Thus, he comes to embody the possibility of a positive union of opposites rather than the problematic antagonism of the power play between her and Andrés. Mapped onto the novel's political plane, this sees Carlos as representing a left-wing liberalism that directly contradicts the despotism of Andrés and his cronies, and the power with which his masculinity endows him does not force Catalina into a passive position. Quite the opposite is true, as she remains the onlooker, gaining visual and physical pleasure from the sight of the object of her desires. The traditional divisions of male/female and passive/active are thus broken down in her pairing with Carlos, which engenders a form of synthesis not usually legible, as noted by Blau DuPlessis at the start of this chapter, in portrayal of heterosexual romantic scenarios. What is more, and vitally in terms of the story's development, the entrance of Carlos into the Andrés-Catalina pairing creates a triangle that echoes the structure and dynamic of the triadic structure deployed in this study, and which opens up new possibilities by presenting Catalina with a fork in the road. Danny J. Anderson concurs with this reading of Carlos's role in Catalina's *Bildung*. He suggests that Mastretta's novel can be divided into two blocks of thirteen chapters, the first of which he argues are dedicated to Catalina's 'sentimental and political education',[68] the second showing how she 'has to depend on her ever evolving political and sentimental savvy in order to negotiate the triangle among herself, Andrés and [Carlos]' (whom she meets in chapter thirteen).[69] In the same way that the witness and discovery of acts of murder, discussed above, served to initiate her distrust of Andrés and her physical and ideological distancing from him, Andrés's eventual murder of Carlos, and the subsequent removal of all he has come to mean to Catalina, Anderson observes, 'is the catalyst that motivates her to take action'.[70]

BODY OF PROOF

At this point, for the first time, she denounces Andrés to the authorities, deploying the political knowledge she has gained thus far to take a stand against the tyrannical figure upon whom she was once completely reliant. Just prior to this key event taking place, however, the empowered female gaze attributed by the author to her protagonist is already revealing a shift in worldview. Where her critique of his *behavior* is a feature of the text from the very beginning, this change in his portrayal is noteworthy for its appearance now, at a time where Catalina can no longer pretend not to see what she sees. And so her physical descriptions of Andrés stop portraying the strong pseudo-paternal figure that she talks about in the earlier chapters, painting instead a portrait of a ridiculous figure who seems incapable of inspiring still the fear upon which he has founded his empire of power: 'he fell asleep with his hands on his belly and his mouth half open, one shoe on and one shoe off, trouserless and with his shirt undone'.[71] Andrés's reign is not quite over yet—at the very moment she describes him in this way his henchmen are murdering the love of her life, so that by the end of that chapter Carlos is dead and Catalina heartbroken and embittered. But the state of disarray in which we see him above does foreshadow the beginning of his end, for the central role of the body in the story, its delineation as the locus of selfhood, means that bodily portrayals must also be read as indicative of less tangible, more profound shifts. For example, even before Carlos's murder, Catalina's body physically communicates before she is able to in words an increasing awareness of the realities of her existence and of Andrés's power:

> A veces en las noches despertaba temblando, suda y suda [...] miraba a Andrés con la boca media abierta, roncando, seguro de que junto a él dormía la misma boba con la que se casó [...] un poco más vieja y un poco menos dócil, pero la misma. Su misma Catalina para reírse de ella y hacerle la cómplice, la misma que le adivinaba el pensamiento y no quería saber nada de sus negocios. Esos días, todas las cosas que había ido viendo desde que nos casamos se me amontaron en el cuerpo de tal modo que una tarde me encontré con un nudo debajo de la nuca. Desde el cuello y hasta el principio de la espalda se me hizo una bola, una cosa tiesa como un solo nervio enorme que me dolía.[72]

> Sometimes at night I would wake up trembling and sweating [...] I used to look at Andrés with his mouth half open, snoring, sure that the same idiot he had married lay sleeping next to him [...] a little older and a bit less docile, but the same. His same Catalina, who he could laugh with and make into his accomplice; the same one that read his mind and never wanted to know about his business. During those days, all of the things that I had seen since we got married accumulated in my body until one afternoon I had a knot at the nape of my neck. A painful, solid ball, like a single mass of nerves.

In a narrative that resounds with references to the physical body and that presents it as an active force for change, the translation of Catalina's nervousness into physical tension is more than a realist description of the potential effects of stress on an individual. Instead, the metaphorical value of that is exploited as a narrative strategy; as a means of underlining the importance of her physical form as a motivational source of power. Reinforcing such an interpretation is the fact that this scene becomes a narrative link that again connects Catalina's body and her increasingly informed outlook: encouraged by her friend Bibi to go for massages to assuage her muscular pain, Catalina befriends a woman named Andrea at the spa she attends. One day the two women have an argument about the possible consequences of an adulterous affair on Catalina's part, into which interjects the masseuse, Raquel, naming a woman that Andrés had murdered because she tried to end her affair with him.[73] Again, traditional discourses and organizational structures relating to gender and power are undermined by Mastretta, as the wholly feminized world of the beauty parlor is transformed into a site of revelation and resistance—a space informed by and created by hegemonic notions of masculinity and femininity, and the rituals that define and maintain bodies in an appropriately heterosexual series of oppositions, but which subverts from within by creating a safe space for the crossing of boundaries; for the synthesis of masculinized knowledge with feminized feeling. Thus, the physical effects of Catalina's growing realization about the kind of man she has married and the entrapment of the marriage itself lead her to discover yet more worrying evidence about Andrés's violent capabilities, and continues her growth towards the knowledge that will give her the agency and autonomy she seeks.

In light of the novel's focus on corporeality as the locus of identity formation and vehicle for lived existence, it is not at all surprising that the downfall of the main villain of the piece comes about not through means such as his revelation as corrupt and subsequent removal from power by his peers, or through a life lesson that allows him to see the error of his ways, repent and change for the better, but through the gradual disintegration of his body. Neatly tying together the thematic threads of an active female body and sexuality, the feminized trope of liquidity as a means of pushing beyond the delimitations of dominant power structures, and the physical body as the site of gendered identity formulation and the embodiment of power, the despot's eventual demise is instigated by his addiction to nothing more than an herbal tea given to Catalina by one of the women whose lives Andrés has ruined, and whom she had helped in the aftermath. Cati regulates her own intake of the tea, given to her to help with 'headaches *and other ills*',[74] and which is said to have beneficial effects on the health when taken in moderation, but also known to prove addictive and fatal if overconsumed. Andrés, on the other hand, refuses to invest in such folkloric beliefs, or in the idea that a simple tea could cause him any harm, and drinks it in large amounts in the period leading up to his death. The reader knows from earlier appearances in the plot of such marginalized discourses—as represented by the gypsy woman who helps initiate Catalina's sexual autonomy, and also by the instinctual, feminized 'feelings' or presentiments with which her mother rightly foretells events—that they require heeding,[75] and thus we are encouraged not to be surprised that Andrés pays a heavy price for his refusal of the knowledge gleaned from Other perspectives.

One thing that he is able to recognize in the view from his deathbed, however, is the powerful multiplicity of his wife:

> Nunca he podido saber lo que quieres tú. Tampoco dediqué mucho tiempo a pensar en eso, pero no me crees tan pendejo, sé que te caben muchas mujeres en el cuerpo y que sólo conocí unas cuantas.[76]

> I have never been able to know what you want. Not that I've dedicated much time to thinking about it, but don't assume I'm an idiot. I know that you are made up of many women and that I only knew a few of them.

In this way, even while serving as an extreme example of patriarchal thought and its social power, the character of Andrés is used by Mastretta here to voice a belief in female capacities beyond those to which their traditional gender roles limit them; to acknowledge the existence of multiple versions of womanhood, of female selfhood, and to remind the reader of Catalina's role as an embodiment of multiplicity, ambivalence and ambiguity; as a body of proof that the oversimplifications of a Manichean worldview fail greatly to account for the contingencies of identity formation. Far from idealized, Catalina is a potent literary creation much more for her ability to bring into play the reader's own prejudices than because of any role she might have as representative of a new model for womanhood. If we judge her behavior, we must ask ourselves why, for we are not led to easy conclusions that fit carefully within the confines of any particular ideological stance on the matters she engages. She enjoys being beautiful and happily judges other women's physical appearance by marking them against the yardstick of patriarchal assumptions about what beauty is; she loves her children but she refuses to venerate pregnancy and motherhood; she hates Andrés for his unfaithfulness and lack of honesty but she is unfaithful and dishonest in her own ways. However we respond to, judge or excuse those actions, we do so via the terms imposed by our own socialization and we are required by this novel to be aware of that important fact.

The story finally ends with the funeral of Andrés, whose textual demise cannot easily be disconnected from the narrative's obvious sociopolitical motivations, thus pointing hopefully towards a future without the form of patriarchal control embodied by him throughout the novel but questioned right at the end of his life, in the words cited above. Compounding this demise, and directly suggesting its necessity, a friend at the funeral tells Catalina that 'Widowhood is the ideal state for a woman [...] She places the deceased at the altar, honors his memory each time it's deemed necessary and dedicates herself to doing all the things she couldn't do with him around'.[77] In line with this forward-looking statement, Catalina's open-ended narrative finishes with her appearing almost childlike, 'sitting on the ground and playing with the wet earth around the edge of Andrés's grave. Enjoying my future. Almost happy'.[78] Borrowing from the key Bildungsroman motifs of youth and the promise it holds for the future, this final description of Catalina strongly implies a new beginning; that she has reached the end of one cycle, synthesized both the positive and the negative of the lessons taught to her about who she should and who she could be, and is about to embark on a whole new journey of self-discovery.

NOTES

1. Rachel Blau DuPlessis, *Writing Beyond the Ending: Narrative Strategies of Twentieth-Century Women Writers* (Bloomington: Indiana University Press, 1985), p. 5.

2. Avril Horner and Angela Keane (eds.), 'Introduction', in *Body Matters: Feminism, Textuality, Corporeality* (Manchester, UK; New York: Manchester University Press, 2000), pp. 1–14, p. 4.
3. Horner and Keane, 'Introduction', p. 4.
4. Judith Butler, *Gender Trouble: Feminism and the Subversion of Identity* (1990) (London; New York: Routledge, 1999), p. 44.
5. Nuala Finnegan, *Ambivalence, Modernity, Power: Women and Writing in Mexico Since 1980* (Bern: Peter Lang, 2007), p. 22.
6. Judith Butler, *Bodies That Matter: On the Discursive Limits of Sex* (London; New York, 1993), p. 68.
7. Claudia Schaefer, *Textured Lives: Women, Art and Representation in Modern Mexico* (Tucson; London: University of Arizona Press, 1992), pp. 91–2.
8. Mikhail Bakhtin, 'The Bildungsroman and Its Significance in the History of Realism (Toward a Historical Typology of the Novel)', in Vern W. McGee (trans.), Carol Emerson and Michael Holquist (eds.), *Mikhail Bakhtin: Speech Genres and Other Late Essays* (Austin: University of Texas Press, 1986), pp. 10–59, p. 21.
9. Schaefer, *Textured Lives*, p. 91.
10. Ángeles Mastretta, *Arráncame la vida* (1985) (New York: Random House, 1997), p. 1. 'Ese año pasaron muchas cosas en este país. Entre otras, Andrés y yo nos casamos'. All subsequent references are from this edition and all translations are my own.
11. Mastretta, *Arráncame...*, p. 11. 'Tenía quince años y muchas ganas de que me pasaran cosas'.
12. Rachel Blau DuPlessis, *Writing Beyond the Ending*, p. 3.
13. Sidonie Smith, 'Identity's Body', in Kathleen M. Ashley, Leigh Gilmore, Gerald Peters (eds.), *Autobiography & Postmodernism* (Boston: University of Massachusetts Press, 1994), pp. 266–292, p. 267.
14. Mastretta, *Arráncame...*, pp. 59–60.
15. Mastretta, *Arráncame...*, p. 74.
16. Paule Zajdermann, Dir., *Judith Butler: Philosophe en tout genre*, Documentaire Arte France & Associés, 2006.
17. Naomi Wolf, *The Beauty Myth* (1990) (London: Vintage, 1991), pp. 13–14. For examples of Catalina's scathing observations of other women's appearance in *Arráncame la vida* see p. 42; pp. 130–131; p. 174. There are, equally, instances of her praising women for their conformity to orthodox notions of beauty, for example her comments on the ex-girlfriend of her daughter Lilia's fiancé, p. 242.
18. Salvador A. Oropesa, 'Popular Culture and Gender/Genre Construction in *Mexican Bolero* by Ángeles Mastretta', in David William Foster and Roberto Reis (eds.), *Bodies and Biases: Sexualities in Hispanic Cultures and Literature* (Minneapolis; London: University of Minnesota Press, 1996), pp. 137–164, p. 147.
19. Oropesa, 'Popular Culture', p. 147.
20. Butler, *Gender Trouble*, p. 179.
21. Mastretta, *Arráncame*, pp. 17–18; pp. 9–10.
22. Mastretta, *Arráncame*, p. 18 'La acepto, prometo las diferencias que el fuerte le debe al débil y todas esas cosas, así que puedes ahorrarte la lectura. ¿Dónde te firmamos?'
23. Michel Foucault, 'Nietzsche, Genealogy, History' (1977), in Paul Rabinow (ed.), *The Foucault Reader* (1984) (London: Penguin, 1991), pp. 76–100, p. 83.

24. Mastretta, *Arráncame...*, p. 19. '¿Tú pusiste *De Guzmán*?'
25. Mastretta, *Arráncame...*, p. 19. 'No m'ija, porque así no es la cosa. Yo te protejo a ti, no tú a mí. Tú pasas a ser de mi familia, pasas a ser mía'.
26. Mastretta, *Arráncame...*, p. 13.
27. Braulio Peralta and Ángeles Mastretta, 'Interview: "Mi novela es una historia, no un ensayo feminista": Ángeles Mastretta', *La jornada* (11 June 1985), p. 25. Cited in Anderson, pp. 22–23. 'Catalina, no es una mujer conscientemente feminista: es bastante libre porque es rica'.
28. Carol Pearson, 'Resistance from Within: Feminism and Politics in the Work of Angeles Mastretta', *Confluencia*, 18.2 (Spring 2003), 83–94, p. 84.
29. Aída Apter-Cragnolino, 'Jugando con el melodrama: género literario y mirada femenina en *Arráncame la vida* de Ángeles Mastretta' in *Confluencia*, 11.1 (Fall, 1995), 126–133, p. 131.
30. Mastretta, *Arráncame...*, p. 35; p. 37. 'a veces como una carga, a veces como algo que se compra y se guarda en un cajón'; 'como un juguete con el que platicaba tonterías'. It is also worth noting that Catalina seems to privately undermine the unidirectional nature of this possession by sardonically referring to Andrés throughout the novel as '*my* General', and then often reverting to the more distanced 'the General' at times when she wishes to distance herself from his activities or power—just as he does with their children, who are hers when it suits him but his when 'important' decisions need to be made (see p. 207).
31. Mastretta, *Arráncame...*, pp. 23–24.
32. Mastretta, *Arráncame...*, p. 39.
33. Nuala Finnegan, 'Reproducing the Monstrous Nation: A Note on Pregnancy and Motherhood in the Fiction of Rosario Castellanos, Brianda Domecq, and Angeles Mastretta', *The Modern Language Review* 96.4 (2001), 1006–1015, p. 1006.
34. Mastretta, *Arráncame...*, p. 29. '¿Con quién me iba a acostar? ¿Quién me iba a despertar en las mañanas?'
35. Mastretta, *Arráncame...*, p. 39. 'Andrés era el culpable de que me pasaran todas esas cosas y ni siquiera soportaba oír hablar de ellas'.
36. Mastretta, *Arráncame...*, p. 56. 'Cuando [Sergio] empezó a llorar y sentí que me deshacía de la piedra que cargaba en la barriga, juré que ésa sería la última vez'. It seems noteworthy that in the 2008 film based on Mastretta's novel, with which the author was involved, the order of birth of Catalina's children is reversed, with son Sergio coming first. This aligns with a very conservative investment in Hispanic cultures, historically relevant to the plot, in the birth of a male heir—a theme explored in depth, for example, in the novel *Balún Canán* (1957) by Mastretta's fellow Mexican writer Rosario Castellanos. But what is curious is that this change around is not made in any way relevant to the film plot, which begs the question of why it was deemed necessary.
37. Butler, *Gender Trouble*, p. 170.
38. Hélène Cixous, 'The Newly Born Woman', in Susan Sellers (ed.), *The Hélène Cixous Reader* (London: Routledge, 1994),pp. 35–46, p. 42.
39. Butler, *Gender Trouble*, p. 170.
40. Butler, *Gender Trouble*, p. 170.
41. Hélène Cixous, 'Sorties: Out and Out: Attacks/Ways Out/ Forays', in Hélène Cixous and Catherine Clément, *The Newly Born Woman* (London: Routledge, IB Tauris & Co. Ltd., 1996), p. 86.
42. Mastretta, *Arráncame...*, p. 81; p. 88.
43. Mastretta, *Arráncame...*, p. 81; p. 88.

44. Mastretta, *Arráncame...*, p. 82; p. 89.
45. Mastretta, *Arráncame...*, p. 65; p. 72.
46. Mastretta, *Arráncame...*, p. 17.
47. Mastretta, *Arráncame...*, p. 13.
48. Mastretta, *Arráncame...*, p. 72.
49. Mastretta, *Arráncame...*, pp. 98–99. Eva Nuñez-Méndez also references this connection, in 'Mastretta y sus protagonistas: Ejemplos de Emancipación Femenina', *Romance Studies*, 20.2 (December 2002), 115–128, p. 116.
50. Mastretta, *Arráncame...*, p. 13.
51. Mastretta, *Arráncame...*, p. 12.
52. Mastretta, *Arráncame...*, p. 12. '¿No sientes? ¿Por qué no sientes?—preguntó después. Sí siento, pero el final no lo entendí'.
53. Jane Lavery, 'The Physical and Textual Bodies in the Works of Ángeles Mastretta and Elena Poniatowska', *Romance Studies*, 19.2 (December 2001), 173–186, p. 174.
54. Mastretta, *Arráncame...*, p. 13. '- ¿Por qué no me enseñas?—le dije. - ¿A qué? - Pues a sentir. - Eso no se enseña, se aprende—contestó'.
55. Alicia Llarena, '*Arráncame la vida* de Ángeles Mastretta: El universo desde la intimidad', in *Revista Iberoamericana*, LVIII.159 (Abril-Junio 1992), 465–475, p. 471. 'lo esencial no es su progresivo aversión hacia las normas sociales, ni la declaración de la igualdad' sino al contrario, la aceptación de esas regiones íntimas, diferentes y auténticas, que el general veía—temía, quizás—como lo único inasible [sic], incontrolable, desconocido, en las múltiples mujeres que hay en su mujer'.
56. Mastretta, *Arráncame...*, p. 15.
57. Lavery, 'Physical and Textual Bodies', p. 175.
58. Lavery, 'Physical and Textual Bodies', p. 174.
59. Mastretta, *Arráncame...*, p. 12.
60. Lavery, 'Physical and Textual Bodies', p. 175. In this article, Lavery cites an interview that she held with Mastretta, in which the author describes female sexuality as 'rica, prolongada y distinta' ('rich, prolonged and distinct'), highlighting 'the importance of the multiplicity of female orgasm' in contrast with the singularity of male orgasm (p. 180). It seems clear that these ideas inform her portrayal of Catalina's sexuality in the episodes discussed here, in which the trope of excess is connected to female sexuality within the novel.
61. Elizabeth Grosz, *Volatile Bodies: Towards a Corporeal Feminism* (Bloomington: Indiana University Press, 1994), p. 203.
62. Mastretta, *Arráncame...*, p. 288. 'Me molesta el mar, no se calla nunca, parece mujer'.
63. Schaefer, *Textured Lives*, p. 103.
64. Mastretta, *Arráncame...*, p. 41; p. 35.
65. For example, when Carlos comes home after his brief arrest in Chapter Two, the first thing Catalina does upon seeing him is start undressing and initiate sex. See p. 33.
66. Mastretta, *Arráncame...*, p. 165.
67. Mastretta, *Arráncame...*, p. 84.
68. Danny J. Anderson, 'Displacement: Strategies of Transformation in *Arráncame la vida* by Ángeles Mastretta', in *The Journal of the Midwest Modern Language Association*, 21.1 (Spring 1988), 15–27, p. 16.
69. Anderson, 'Displacement: Strategies of Transformation', p. 17.

70. Anderson, 'Displacement: Strategies of Transformation', p. 17.
71. Mastretta, *Arráncame...*, p. 224. 'Se quedó dormido con las manos sobre la barriga y la boca media abierta, con una bota sí y otra no, sin pantalones y con la camisa desabrochada'. Although not directly implicated in the story of Catalina's self-development, there is another scene in the novel very noteworthy for its involvement of the empowered female gaze as part of a broad strategy for the deconstruction of the patriarchal order. Catalina's friend Bibi is helped by a woman brothel owner to disguise herself as a leprous prostitute wrapped in bandages, thereby being enabled to sit in as a kind of fetish figure during a bizarre bachelor party in which her husband participates. During this, Bibi's husband and the other men challenge one another to a game of measuring their erect penises to see whose is largest. The irony of the situation, that they believe themselves to have gone there to look at, and be sexually stimulated by, pleasing female figures, but in the end are subjected to both the pitying gaze of a woman they do not know is there and to their own macho evaluations of one another, makes this one of the most interesting moments in the novel's in-depth examination of the role of the physical body in identity formation. In terms of the depiction of male bodies in the narrative, the ridiculing of the erect phallus in Bibi's account of what she saw may also be read as a ridiculing of the system for which it stands as symbol/metonym. See pp. 264–266.
72. Mastretta, *Arráncame...*, p. 197.
73. Mastretta, *Arráncame...*, p. 199.
74. Mastretta, *Arráncame...*, p. 258.
75. Mastretta, *Arráncame...*, p. 17.
76. Mastretta, *Arráncame...*, p. 288.
77. Mastretta, *Arráncame...*, p. 297. 'La viudez es el estado ideal de la mujer [...] Se pone al difunto en un altar, se honra su memoria cada vez que sea necesario y se dedica una a hacer todo lo que no pudo hacer con él en la vida'.
78. Mastretta, *Arráncame...*, p. 305.

BIBLIOGRAPHY

Anderson, Danny J., 'Displacement: Strategies of Transformation in *Arráncame la vida* by Ángeles Mastretta', in *The Journal of the Midwest Modern Language Association*, 21.1 (Spring 1988), 15–27.

Apter-Cragnolino, Aída, 'Jugando con el melodrama: género literario y mirada femenina en *Arráncame la vida* de Ángeles Mastretta' in *Confluencia*, 11.1 (Fall, 1995), 126–133.

Bakhtin, Mikhail, 'The *Bildungsroman* and Its Significance in the History of Realism (Toward a Historical Typology of the Novel)', in Vern W. McGee (trans.), Carol Emerson and Michael Holquist (eds.), *Mikhail Bakhtin: Speech Genres and Other Late Essays* (Austin, TX: University of Texas Press, 1986), pp. 10–59.

Blau DuPlessis, Rachel, *Writing Beyond the Ending: Narrative Strategies of Twentieth-Century Women Writers* (Bloomington: Indiana University Press, 1985).

Butler, Judith, *Bodies That Matter: On the Discursive Limits of Sex* (London; New York: Routledge, 1993).

Butler, Judith, *Gender Trouble: Feminism and the Subversion of Identity* (1990) (London; New York: Routledge, 1999).

Cixous, Hélène, 'Sorties: Out and Out: Attacks/Ways Out/ Forays', in Hélène Cixous and Catherine Clément, *The Newly Born Woman* (1975) (London: Routledge, IB Tauris & Co. Ltd., 1996).

Cixous, Hélène, 'The Newly Born Woman', in Susan Sellers (ed.), *The Hélène Cixous Reader* (London: Routledge, 1994), pp. 35–46.

Finnegan, Nuala, 'Reproducing the Monstrous Nation: A Note on Pregnancy and Motherhood in the Fiction of Rosario Castellanos, Brianda Domecq, and Angeles Mastretta', *The Modern Language Review* 96.4 (2001), 1006–1015.

Finnegan, Nuala, *Ambivalence, Modernity, Power: Women and Writing in Mexico since 1980* (Bern: Peter Lang, 2007).

Foster, David William, and Reis, Roberto (eds.), *Bodies and Biases: Sexualities in Hispanic Cultures and Literature* (Minneapolis; London: University of Minnesota Press, 1996).

Foucault, Michel, 'Nietzsche, Genealogy, History' (1977), in Paul Rabinow (ed.), *The Foucault Reader* (1984) (London: Penguin, 1991), pp. 76–100.

Grosz, Elizabeth, *Volatile Bodies: Towards a Corporeal Feminism* (Bloomington: Indiana University Press, 1994).

Horner, Avril, and Keane, Angela (eds.), 'Introduction', in *Body Matters: Feminism, Textuality, Corporeality* (Manchester; New York: Manchester University Press, 2000), pp. 1–14.

Lavery, Jane, 'The Physical and Textual Bodies in the Works of Ángeles Mastretta and Elena Poniatowska', *Romance Studies*, 19.2 (December 2001), 173–186.

Llarena, Alicia, '*Arráncame la vida* de Ángeles Mastretta: El universo desde la intimidad', *Revista Iberoamericana*, LVIII.159 (Abril-Junio 1992), 465–475.

Mastretta, Ángeles, *Arráncame la vida* (1985) (New York: Random House, 1997).

Nuñez-Méndez, Eva, 'Mastretta y sus protagonistas: Ejemplos de Emancipación Femenina', *Romance Studies*, 20.2 (December 2002), 115–128.

Oropesa, Salvador A., 'Popular Culture and Gender/Genre Construction in *Mexican Bolero* by Ángeles Mastretta', in David William Foster and Roberto Reis (eds.), *Bodies and Biases: Sexualities in Hispanic Cultures and Literature* (Minneapolis; London: University of Minnesota Press, 1996), pp. 137–164.

Pearson, Carol, 'Resistance from Within: Feminism and Politics in the Work of Angeles Mastretta', *Confluencia*, 18.2 (Spring 2003), 83–94.

Schaefer, Claudia, *Textured Lives: Women, Art and Representation in Modern Mexico* (Tucson; London: University of Arizona Press, 1992).

Smith, Sidonie, 'Identity's Body', in Kathleen M. Ashley, Leigh Gilmore, and Gerald Peters (eds.), *Autobiography & Postmodernism* (Boston: University of Massachusetts Press, 1994), pp. 266–292.

Wolf, Naomi, *The Beauty Myth* (1990) (London: Vintage, 1991).

Zajdermann, Paule (Dir.), *Judith Butler: Philosophe en tout genre*, Documentaire Arte France & Associés (2006).

6 La nada cotidiana/Yocandra in the Paradise of Nada *by Zoé Valdés* (1995)

Zoé Valdés's *La nada cotidiana*, the last and also the most recent of the all works studied within the triadic framework of this book, shares with *Arráncame la vida* a post-revolutionary setting and the evocation of the female body as a vehicle for resistance. It also, however, shares with the works studied in Parts One and Two an intentional uncovering of the myths and archetypes serving as the foundations of female gendered selfhood, and an overt and deconstructive critique of the binary oppositions informing patriarchal social arenas. Subsequently, the social critique presented via the protagonist is more overt when contrasted with that seen in my study of Mastretta's novel. She takes a step forward from what might be termed the 'accidental' feminism of Catalina by being fully engaged in a deconstruction of the national, political and cultural arena in which her *Bildung* occurs.

This is clearly a consequence of Valdés's own highly politicized outlook, and it is valuable to acknowledge the autobiographical underpinnings of this nonetheless fictional narrative—a key feature of this being that the author portrays her protagonist being born in the same year as she was: 1959. The life of both is thus completely aligned with the Cuban nation's post-Revolution years. As part of the *Generación de los 80*, the first Cuban generation of artists and intellectuals to be born and come of age within the socialist state,[1] Valdés pertains to a peer group that Cuban poet Oswaldo Sánchez has described as the

> 'children of the Utopia' [who] discovered that it wasn't particularly stimulating to be the 'docile wage-workers of official thought'. So it was that in the early 1980s, the State began to feel increasingly threatened by the critical discontent and the political distrust shared by the youngest members of the intelligentsia, whose obsession with turning Cuba's social reality into a truly liberating enterprise was to disclose, eventually, all the moral atrophy and the ideological contradictions of a system based on simulacra, manipulation and inefficiency.[2]

In line with this, in 1997 Catherine Davies described Valdés as an author who had by then 'made a reputation for herself by criticizing the Cuban government and writing novels that some would call erotic and others pornographic'[3]—a pithy assessment of the author's career and literary output then and to date that pulls to the fore the connections made in *La nada cotidiana* between the gendered body and the body politic. Valdés wrote the novel while still living on the island, 'during the most intense moment of the Postmodern revolt' led by the Generation-80 which, in the words of Madeline Cámara Betancourt, is 'the only generation, to date, that has been marked by a clear accent of political dissidence, while creating a new and vigorous art that reacted against the moral bankruptcy and spiritual repression into which the country had sunk'.[4] Two copies of *La nada cotidiana* were smuggled off the island before Valdés left in early 1995: one put on a raft leaving the island for Miami, another sent with a journalist to France, the country that would become her permanent home in exile.[5] Identifiable as a Bildungsroman for its tracing of the arc of the female protagonist's life from birth until the fictional present, and because of its account of key rites of passage akin to those explored by the other works considered in *Gender and the Self*, this text nonetheless tests the orthodox limits of the genre most stringently: a form born as a framework for the depiction of a normalized selfhood really only responsive to white, male, bourgeois, capitalist, European individualism is reformulated here to speak of and for a female selfhood that must 'grapple in contemporary terms with the paradoxical identity of [its] third world, socialist, western and mestizo [home] country'.[6] Fascinatingly, the genre's engagement with the formative dialogue between self and society takes on new meanings when placed within the socialist context and functions as an ideal vehicle for Valdés's postmodern interrogation of selfhood in the Cuban sociocultural arena of her time.

The role of the female body in this critical process is the main concern of this, my final chapter. For from the very first of hers, Valdés foregrounds that body and the complicated web of discourses that position it within Cuba's post-revolutionary nationalist ideology. Adopting a knowing, critical viewpoint regarding the impact of the island's Socialist regime on the formulation of gendered selfhoods, she reveals a subjugated biological platform for identity akin to that described by Foucault: 'power relations have an immediate hold upon it; they invest it, mark it, train it, torture it, force it to carry out tasks, to perform ceremonies, to emit signs'.[7] She does not, however, outline that body only to leave it in such a passive state, instead rewriting it as a site of self-definition essential to the formation of her protagonist's individuality *and* to the possibility of her social belonging.

TIME INTRODUCED INTO WOMAN: SOCIAL CONTEXT AND THE POLITICAL BODY

The title of this subsection infers one of the key aspects of Bakhtin's work on the Bildungsroman, discussed in the Introduction and mentioned in reference to *Arráncame la vida* also, where he describes one of the genre's main characteristics as the 'introduction of time into man'. Similarly, in

La nada cotidiana we encounter the story of a woman very much of her time, but also of her place. The appearance of the novel in 1995 means that it was written during the 'Special Period in Times of Peace' (1990–1995), as it was termed by Fidel Castro, during which Cuba suffered a period of intense economic hardship in the wake of the collapse of the Soviet Bloc. As Davies has described, during this period the 'Cuban population underwent conditions (acute shortages of all materials, foodstuffs and energy) not unlike those experienced in a war zone'.[8] As I have argued elsewhere, and as we will see here, it is therefore not surprising that notions of lack are very present in the text, just as is the seeking out of excess as a response to paucity.[9]

The English translation of the title (*Yocandra in the Paradise of* **Nada**) holds onto the notion of nothingness, but obfuscates the negation of the proverbial 'daily bread' that is very obvious in the original reference to a '*Daily Nothingness*'. This phrase invites reference to religious discourses that are fitting to the Latin American context and obviously problematized in the Cuban one specifically, but given a place at the start of the narrative nonetheless:

> *Ella viene de una isla que quiso construir el paraíso. El fuego de la agresividad devora su rostro. Los ojos casi siempre húmedos, la boca suplicante como la de una estatua de bronce, la nariz afilada.*
>
> *Ella es como cualquier mujer,* ***salvo que abre los ojos a la manera de las mujeres que habitan las islas:*** *hay una tranquila indiferencia en sus párpados. También el cuerpo tenso, en contradicción con sus pupilas demasiado fluidas* [my bold text].[10]

> *She comes from an island that wanted to create Paradise. The fire of aggression devours her face. The eyes almost always humid, the mouth supplicating like that of a bronze statue, the nose narrow.*
>
> *She is like any other woman,* ***except that she opens her eyes in the manner of island women:*** *there is a tranquil indifference upon her eyelids. And she has a tense body, a contrast to her too-fluid pupils.*

La nada cotidiana thus begins with a pseudo-religious account of an 'out-of-body' experience, in a chapter that itself exists outside the main body of the text (and whose postmodernist and poststructuralist qualities are in open opposition to the doctrine of socialist realism as the ideal artistic form with which to communicate socialist revolutionary aims). Chapter One presents a surreal episode set in a timeless and placeless place that closely echoes Puerto Rican novelist Edgardo Rodríguez Juliá's notion of '"tedium vitae", a post-colonial condition in which the soul is suspended in indecision, trapped between a "precarious past and an uncertain future".[11] A condition of "suspended self[hood]", at once nostalgic and anticipatory, [that] opens up the apparently closed-ended structure of allegorical signification'.[12] Here, 'space is transformed into cloud, white and pure'.[13] As the chapter progresses, the reader realizes that the setting is purgatory, and therefore the woman presented to us is in a liminal space somewhere between life and death, embodiment and disembodiment. Aesthetically distinguished from the following chapters by its rendering in italics, this section is also written from a third person narrative point of view that contrasts with the first person perspective of the rest of the novel. Carmen Faccini has described it as an 'oneiric, hallucinated' beginning that immediately 'forwards, from the perspective of the narrator, the Cuban Revolution as a failed project'—she comes from an island that *wanted* to create paradise.[14] And Faccini conjectures that the reader 'thus anticipates not a kind of literature that accurately depicts a referential reality, but rather a kind of literature that projects a reality partially perceived or, at least, retextualized by Valdés'.[15] Beginning the novel with a third person voice grants the writing a more objective, critical edge not usually associated with the implicitly subjective 'I' through which the protagonist will recount her story of *Bildung* from this point on. Yet, at the same time, because this introductory chapter is a metatextual, fictionalized and mythologized literary creation by Yocandra, the female *Bildungsheld* whose own story is the main thrust of the narrative, it also instils within the 'I' that will follow a critical tendency that is continued throughout the text in the ironic tone of the narrator-protagonist's recounting of key formative events in her life. It teaches the reader that she is capable of such a perspective; that her story is one of individual selfhood, yes, but still one of a contextualized selfhood informed by an unblinkered view on her social context. In sum, Chapter One is used by Valdés as a clever introduction of reader to protagonist: we learn that she is creative, insightful, willing to examine, keen to write.

It also makes very clear for us that the female body will function as a prism for the exploration of female selfhood in the contemporary Cuban context, of what it means to be '*cubana*', through its detailed depiction of the woman's physical appearance and the implied interconnection of that to national identity. In contrast to Faccini's and my interpretations of this chapter, other critics, such as Dinora Cardoso and Ynés Oggel, have equated the nameless female with Yocandra rather than reading her as a fictional character created by the fictional protagonist.[16] Similarly to them, although still acknowledging the chapter as a mise-en-abyme and thereby understanding Yocandra as the author of it, Cristina Ortiz Ceberio suggests that 'the narration of *La nada cotidiana* is situated in the moment prior to the existence of the narrator/protagonist, who begins her narrative by returning to a moment preceding her own life', and that 'this focalization of the discourse through a moment before the "worldly" existence of the character [prepares] the reader [...] for the fact that they are going to encounter a discourse that itself departs from a moment prior to cultural conditioning'.[17] I would argue, though, that a number of aspects of the chapter challenge this view, including the religious inferences that underline the impossibility of a space outside of discourse. For example, the air around the figure is described as 'white, pure'—a highly orthodox equation of color with quality that engages the vocabulary of the symbolic order. Rather than prove that *La nada cotidiana* is a story rooted in a moment 'prior to' the acculturation of the individual, then, these scenes articulate a liminal space in terms that expose the impossibility of outsideness, thus to demonstrate that to be free from discourse is to cease to be defined, to become invisible, but that to be able to *read* discourse so as to *rewrite oneself* through the revision and rearticulation of its own vocabulary, is empowering.[18]

In essence, the novel's Chapter One advances a take on the body that accepts it as never freed of the meanings that are inscribed upon it, because, as Butler has elucidated in *Bodies That Matter* (1993), without those meanings it simply ceases to exist:

> The process of that sedimentation or what we might call *materialization* will be a kind of citationality, the acquisition of being through the citing of power, a citing that establishes an originary complicity with power in the formation of the 'I'.
>
> In this sense, the agency denoted by the performativity of "sex" will be directly counter to any notion of a voluntarist subject who exists quite apart from the regulatory norms which s/he opposes. The paradox of subjectivation (*assujetissement*) is precisely that the subject who would resist such norms is itself enabled, if not produced, by such norms. Although this constitutive constraint does not foreclose the possibility of agency, it does locate agency as a reiterative or rearticulatory practice, immanent to power, and not a relation of external opposition to power.[19]

Butler's formulations of the body and its relationship to or role in agency are crucial to the proper reading of Valdés's work, for it is an analytical position that denies neither the materiality of the body, nor its fundamental role in the establishment of orthodox gendered identities via the elision of the sex/gender distinction, nor the possibilities of redefining the meanings with which the body is invested. In this sense, Butler's articulation of agency is one that negates the need for a moment prior to cultural conditioning such as that envisaged by Ortiz; a moment that might otherwise seem a prerequisite for the rewriting of bodily meanings and the subsequent redefinition of resultant identities. The idea of an 'outside' that is not itself defined by its relationship with the 'inside' becomes untenable in this view, as is the possibility of any truly exterior position. In short, Valdés show us here that the relationship between discourse and the body is reciprocal: at the same time as the discourses of gender (and nationality) require an interface upon which to make their presence felt, the body is also only made 'visible' due to the meanings invested in it by those discourses. Power and agency are configured through an equal recognition of, first, the permanent interiority of all identities to hegemonic systems and, second, the chance to play with the very codes with which those identities are construed; through a postmodern approach that exchanges 'either/or' for 'both'. Rearticulated in the analytical vocabulary of this study, this is a form of synthesis encapsulated by the dualism of the liminal space that Yocandra dreams up in her creative text and whose adoption can be empowering for the marginalized individual. It is a synthesis of the knowledge of the discursive underpinnings of identity such as those examined in Part One of this study, with the radical rejection and critique of those underpinnings explored in Part Two. The female body takes its place here in Part Three as the nodal point of that knowledge; as evidence of the effects of discourse and as the tool for its critique.

NOT EITHER/OR. BOTH/AND.

As previously mentioned, Faccini describes Valdés's first chapter as a projection of the narrator-protagonist's view of the Cuban Revolution as a failed project. She also points out that the fact of the novel's first line reappearing as its last line gives the text a closed, circular form; one that, I argue, concretizes the representation of the Revolution as a failed attempt at social change by returning the reader right back to where we began, and implying via the trajectory of the text that nothing has changed during the period depicted. In a similar vein, Madeline Cámara Betancourt classifies *La nada cotidiana* as a picaresque novel rather than as a Bildungsroman because 'like the male picaresque antiheroes, Yocandra cannot grow, and she cannot put forward any project'.[20] But I would argue that reading the novel through the prism of the body and the role it is given in the story challenges this idea. The sexed, and subsequently gendered body described in Chapter One is not imbued with the sense of limitation that we might take from the novel's circular trajectory. The narrative is not one of finite hopelessness even if it is not an openly optimistic text, and it would be erroneous to take this apparently negative perception of the Revolution as a disparaging reflection on the fruitlessness of any kind of resistance. For this reason, I would agree more with Isabel Alvarez Borland's observation that the picaresque genre serves as a useful frame of reference for Valdés's writing because of its 'dissident aesthetics' in which first person narratives give voice to 'transgressors and outlaws who emerge transformed by their power of witnessing what has happened in Cuba'.[21]

Again the anonymous figure in Yocandra's writing hints at this, in her calling to mind of the Eve archetype whose presence has been recurrent throughout this study. Linked as she is to the notion of failed paradise, she incites an imagining of Cuba as the Garden of Eden, full of promise but ultimately a project that failed in light of human error. Described in a poststructuralist manner, such human error is the author of discourses that entrap and disempower but which, for the very fact of their artifice and subsequent lack of permanence, can be reimagined. And in a way reminiscent of the eponymous protagonist of Allende's *Eva Luna*, the possibility of a fresh start comes to be symbolized here by the female body: 'She moves her head to look down at her bare breasts. She is completely naked and *does not feel ashamed*' [emphases mine].[22] Just as Allende's protagonist was not weighed down by the legacy of her socially unorthodox conception, by the 'sin' of her mother, the body of the nameless female of this episode is written in terms that refuse the association of her naked sex, which she openly studies in a mirror as she awaits her judgment, with shame or guilt.[23] The presence of the discourse requiring such self-shame is not artificially removed in the scene, for its notion remains acknowledged. But the response of the woman implies a knowing refutation of such ideology.

Just before the angel who will arbitrate over her fate, and who introduces himself as 'the one who decides',[24] casts his final judgment upon her, the woman 'thinks about how there is always, everywhere, this "who decides". And that it has never been her, precisely, that has decided for herself'.[25] Ultimately, and tellingly, though, the angel's judgment is problematized by the fact that she has earned equal 'points' towards entrance into both heaven and hell, so that he is confronted with a female figure who is 'half serene, half impetuous'.[26] That she is not condemned to either form of death by him, but instead 'obliged to return to her island' leaves the reader with an ambiguous female figure who although still commanded by the 'higher' powers whose existence she has been able to acknowledge, is nevertheless in possession of a body that is portrayed as a vessel for new possibilities of redemption, thus negating the association of the female body with passivity.[27]

Hence, at the end of the oneiric first chapter, this positivity remains a feature of her embodiment as she once again takes up an earthly presence. She awakens on a beach, 'still naked, laid out on the sand, the sea caressing her fevered skin'.[28] The sea washing over her, yet another appearance of a motif recurrent in the literature studied here, takes on a symbolic role, signifying a fresh start—much like that implied in the Cuban tradition of throwing a bucket of water from the balcony on December 31, as a kind of cleansing ritual with which to initiate the New Year.[29] Miguel González-Abellás has interpreted the portrayal of the sea in Valdés's works as the depiction of it as a source of hope for Cubans, in that it presents a possible escape route.[30] Yet here it is the sea that carries the woman back onto the island, and thus, in a sense, prevents her escape. Instead it is she who brings hope to an island that 'wanting to create paradise has created hell',[31] thanks to the potentiality for critique and resistance with which she has been invested throughout the dreamscape. This is the beginning of the novel's persistent and meaningful alignment of woman with nation in revised terms, and if at any time we should read the anonymous figure as Yocandra herself I would say that it is here, in her reembodiment and return to a more recognizable, referential 'reality'. Juxtaposed with this metatextual advancement of the novel's deconstructive take on identity politics, the main narrative becomes yet more clearly identifiable as an account of the experiences and life lessons by which the female protagonist has gained her critical perspective on identity formation. It also implies, Myriam J. Clancy rightly posits, a belief on the part of Valdés and in spite of her own status as exile, that Cuba needs not 'to be abandoned but that spaces for personal liberty and the expression of free desire (through the art of life) need to be created within it, especially for the most repressed sector of that society, women'.[32] Because '[c]ontemporary Cuba will only save itself by constructing something new with the participation of those who have remained'.[33]

Within the frame of its Cuban setting this deconstructive approach takes on a historically and socioculturally specific meaningfulness by enabling the discombobulation of sets of binaries that are central to the 'Cuban condition', to borrow the title of Gustavo Pérez Firmat's seminal study:[34] the formulation of the islanders' identity in terms of here/there, home/exile, individualist/socialist, capitalist/communist, Cuban/Un-Cuban. Perhaps most neatly encapsulated by Fidel Castro's infamous 1961 speech 'Words to the Intellectuals'—'within the Revolution everything, against it nothing'—in this view Cuban identity is formulated via, but also permanently split by, a series of articulations of interiority/exteriority that Valdés has her protagonist depict, but unpick.

One particularly striking moment in the novel that portrays the limited choices for personal identity and social identification that such Manichean thinking elicits sees her father shamed for publicly announcing that the government-set goal to achieve a ten-million ton sugar harvest between 1963 and 1970 would not be reached.[35] A fervent supporter of Revolutionary ideals who, until then, had succeeded in gaining respect and status as one of the top-ranked sugar harvesters and through his work with the 'Committee for the Defense of the Revolution', when officially reprimanded for this 'subversive' comment Carlos suffers a kind of mental breakdown and begins to wander around Havana 'as if demented',[36] eventually ending up at the Mazorra insane asylum. Gripping the railings at the front of the building and shouting 'Get me out of here!', Yocandra recounts, he confuses the

> exterior con el interior de la clínica, para él los locos eran transeúntes normales, y los transeúntes eran enfermos, y las calles, en su afiebrada histeria, devinieron celdas. No estaba muy desacertado. Fue internado de inmediato.[37]

> the outside with the inside of the clinic. For him the asylum patients were normal passers-by, the passers-by were patients, and the streets, in his fevered stated of hysteria, became cells. He wasn't completely mistaken. He was immediately detained.

In this scene, the oppositions Cuban/Un-Cuban and Sane/Insane are placed in dialogue with one another. However, the ironic comment that her father was not actually wrong undercuts the powerful, assumed fixity and certainty of the oppositional thinking foundational to grand narratives, enabling another vision of the world; one in which the dynamics of power and subjugation might be reversed by the validation of subversive thinking: Cuban/Insane, Un-Cuban/Sane.

Her father's brush with 'insanity' as a challenger of the regime clearly remains as a lesson learned for Yocandra, given it features in her story of self-development, whereas for him it is an incident whose impact is quickly assuaged by the award of an 'insignificant decoration' when his prediction comes true.[38] His total reinsertion into the regime is summarized by his activities in retirement, where he spends his days carving little wooden figurines of sugar harvesters, all identical, all male, all emulative of the basing of the regime upon constancy and sameness, and all directly countering the role that the female body is given to play by Valdés in this narrative, as shall be seen. Very intriguingly, this scene seems to speak directly back to a key revolutionary text by echoing the words of Che Guevara in his essay 'Socialism and Man in Cuba' (1965), a speech that, along with Castro's above-cited 'Words to the Intellectuals', threw down 'a theoretical and practical gauntlet for Cuban artists and writers for the better part of two decades' via their articulation of the roles and obligations of the creative figure in revolutionary society, as writes Paul B. Miller.[39] Given this, it is clear that Valdés must be familiar with the essay's content. In it, Guevara says about the role of *el pueblo*, the people in the revolutionary project:

> In the history of the Cuban Revolution there now appeared a character, well defined in its features, which would systematically reappear: the mass. This multifaceted being is not, as is claimed, the sum of elements of the same type (reduced, moreover, to that same type by the ruling system), which acts like a flock of sheep.[40]

As a textually encoded engagement with the issue of individuality, Valdés's narrative here recalls psychologist Fernandez González Rey's findings (published the same year as *La nada cotidiana*) that 'Cuban society does not offer enough room for individual freedom of opinion, which instils a fear that leaves people dependent on a homogenous official discourse'.[41] Yet even without these extratextual frames of reference, it is difficult to ignore the contradiction of the social 'mass' as envisioned by Guevara that is carried out by the uniformity of the figurines and her father's apparently mindless compulsion to continue reproducing the same model over and over again.

This depiction of a member of the older generation engaged in the perpetuation of a failed ideology—the sugar harvester figurines come to stand for the failure he predicted and thus to speak metonymically of the failure of the Cuban Socialist State as a whole—invokes the presence of the Bildungsroman and its thematic foci as generic frame of reference: in line with its investment in youth as symbolic of change and progress—a notion foundational also to the rhetoric of the Revolution[42]—it is Yocandra as representative of her generation that is imbued with agency. The gendered dimension of this argument is underpinned by the depiction of her mother, also a member of the generation that saw in the socialist regime. Aida's mind and body first begin to deteriorate in response to her devastation at the assassination of 'El Che'. She becomes nicknamed 'La Ida' by the neighbors—a playful merging of the sound of her name and the meaning of 'ida' in Spanish (the past participle of 'go', thus she is 'the one who is gone'). Yocandra describes her mother, a middle-class art student prior to the Revolution, as living in the past that she embodies, persistently recalling her previous homes and foodstuffs no longer available, and increasingly physically feeble, too. Dry-mouthed, teeth chattering despite the tropical heat, as light as 'a sack of feathers', she is seen falling asleep, 'rigid, eyelids quivering, gaze turned towards the traitorous bastard Elegguá'—a statue of the Santería god of roads and doors. The implication is, therefore, that he has allowed Cuba to take a wrong turn, and so again, here, Guevara's seminal essay is invoked:

> The pipe dream that socialism can be achieved with the help of the dull instruments left to us by capitalism […] can lead into a blind alley. **When you wind up there after having traveled a long distance with many crossroads, it is hard to figure out just where you took the wrong turn.** Meanwhile, the economic foundation that has been laid has done its work of undermining the development of consciousness. To build communism it is necessary, simultaneous with the new material foundations, to build the new man and woman. [Emphasis mine.][43]

The contrasts between this description of the socialist project and that embarked upon by Valdés in *La nada cotidiana* are fascinating and surely informative of a proper reading of her narrative. As a member of Generation-80 she came of age witnessing what award-winning Cuban Blogger Yoani Sánchez has described as the turning out of 'the lights on culture' that occurred during the 'so-called Five Grey Years (1971–1975) […] as Socialist Realism clipped the wings of our creativity and reduced us to triumphalist stories whose protagonist was always the never-realized "New Man"'.[44] *La nada cotidiana* reads as an attempt to reinitiate that formulation of the 'new man', when taken to mean the post-revolutionary Cuban national subject, through a focus on the empowerment of the 'new woman', and via exploration of the residue left behind in post-revolutionary Cuban culture of antiquated gender and identity politics. To my mind, the book's project is not a total rejection of community in favor of an individualist outlook, but an attempt at forwarding a revised project of inclusion that departs from a feminist perspective and, again, echoes but reframes the words of Che: 'What is important […] is that each day individuals are acquiring ever more consciousness of the need for their incorporation into society and, at the same time, of their importance as the motor of that society'.[45] One last valuable point to make regarding these intertexts is that they further deny any sort of seeking of 'outside' discourse as a way forward in the novel's engagement with identity politics and the *Bildung* of gender as a dimension of that. Rather, they quite literally bring revolutionary rhetoric into the narrative and, again very literally, manipulate that discourse by means of its recontextualization, so as to make it speak *against itself*.

'¡AY QUÉ ORGULLO SIENTO DE SER CUBANA! ¡AY, QUÉ TERROR SIENTO DE SER CUBANA!'[46]/HOW PROUD I FEEL TO BE CUBAN! HOW TERRIFYING TO BE CUBAN!

In essence, what Valdés proposes via her configuration of the female body as a vehicle for agency and thus for the promotion of growth and change both personal and social, is a new direction for Cuban nationhood, enacted via the participation of a woman protagonist whose embodiment is grasped as presence, and whose increasing self-presence is as vital a project as that of the drive for change on a social level—in fact, the two are absolutely intertwined just as was intended to be the case, but failed to be so, in the revolutionary project. In this way, nationhood and selfhood are aligned, but within a dynamic very different from that imposed by patriarchal discourses which, in the socialist context, 'are transferred from the hands of Father and Husband and into those of the State'.[47] From here on in the role of the female body in this text will be explored via the rites of passage that are key to the story of female *Bildung*, themselves read within the meanings attributed to them by the specificities of the Cuban context.

Returning us to a thoroughly embodied female selfhood and instigating the quest for a workable *cubanidad*, Chapter Two of *La nada cotidiana* recounts what Yocandra ironically refers to as her 'Heroic Birth'. It engages the issues of pregnancy and motherhood touched upon in relation to Mastretta's novel in the previous chapter, as well as establishing the alignment of the protagonist with the inauguration of a new regime and a subsequent new identity for her country:

> Cuenta mi madre que era el primero de mayo 1959, ella tenía nueve meses de embarazo, ya sabía que yo era niña. Cuenta que caminó y caminó desde La Habana Vieja hasta la Plaza de la Revolución para escuchar al Comandante. Y en pleno discurso comencé a cabecearle la pelvis, a romperle los huesos. La tuvieron que sacar en hombros hacia la Quinta Reina. Antes de salir de la concentración multitudinaria, al pasar por delante de la tribuna, el Che le puso la bandera cubana en la barriga.[48]

> My mother recounts that it was May 1 1959. She was nine months pregnant, and she already knew I was a girl. She tells how she walked and walked from Old Havana to Revolution Plaza to hear the

> *Comandante*. And in the middle of his speech I began to head-butt her pelvis, to break her bones. She had to be carried shoulder-high to the Quinta Reina hospital. Before she was lifted out of the thronging crowd and as she passed in front of the leaders' platform, Che placed the Cuban flag over her stomach.

The scenes that follow are noteworthy for my interest in the female body in this text because of their portrayal in 'visceral and potentially obscene detail' of the experience of childbirth.[49] As Thea Pitman has observed, Yocandra is 'outspoken' about 'the medicalization of birth and the dehumanization of the mother-to-be', emphasizing 'the grubbiness of the hospital, the lack of privacy and the disruption of the family network' through the enforced absence of her father during the birth.[50] A depiction that has also been highlighted by Faccini as a further aspect of Yocandra's critique of the regime and its failures, because of the importance of the health care system as one of pillars of the Revolution.[51] Her mother's body is shown to be mistreated by the State and turned into a passive entity with things 'done to' it, at the same time as Yocandra's own body is symbolically manipulated by nationalist discourse even *before* she is born. As a result, these scenes bring to bear the Foucauldian notion, expressed in 'Nietzsche, Geneology, History' (1971) of the body as

> the *inscribed surface* of events (traced by language and dissolved by ideas), the *locus* of a dissociated self (adopting the illusion of a substantial unity), and *a volume in perpetual disintegration* [my emphases].[52]

His words here clearly evoke the physical body, and thus present the body as something that is made tangible through the effects of history upon it, and only made visible by the meanings with which discourse invests it. Further to this, Foucault refers in that essay to a need for 'the [exposition] of a body totally imprinted by history' that is neatly encapsulated by the image depicted of Aida's pregnant belly swathed in the emblem that itself encapsulates and stands in for national ideals.[53] And yet more tellingly, this is furthered by the fact that as soon as she is born Yocandra is immediately wrapped in the same flag.

Now figuratively enveloped in all of the historical, cultural, and nationalistic meanings that the flag carries, and made legible as social subject through that symbolism, Yocandra's corporeality is invested with the responsibility of signifying the new nation state. In this way, the portrayal of the events of Yocandra's birth come to depict in the narrative Ania Loomba's assertion that

> [n]ational fantasies [...] play upon and with connections between women, land or nations [so that] the nation-state or its guiding principles [are] often imagined literally *as* a woman.[54]

Loomba goes on to discuss how '[a]s mothers to the nation, women are granted limited agency',[55] and are controlled as 'the "site" rather than the subjects of certain historical debates'.[56] This denial of access to power is highlighted by Yocandra's mother's experience, for while she begins the painful labor that will fulfil what patriarchal thought defines as woman's most valuable social role, Castro's political speech continues undeterred, rendering visible in the text the obstacles put in place between women, access to political discourse, and therefore social presence. Moreover, because neither her physical nor her symbolic absence from the speech impedes the completion of his discourse, this woman and her experiences can be read as symbolic of the limited impact of the Revolution on the lives of Cuban women: Davies remarks that the material conditions and legal rights of the vast majority of Cuban women did improve in post-Revolutionary society,[57] however, Valdés clearly insists through this episode (through the novel as a whole), that their symbolic status and the limits that it imposed upon their daily reality evolved very little. Rather, she underlines the fact that the 'universal socialist subject [is] implicitly male',[58] meaning that revolutionary ideals produced a society still based on the traditional hierarchy of gender that prioritizes the male subject. The role of women continued to be a functional one justified by their biological makeup; allowing them to 'to be incorporated into the workforce', 'protected as mothers (and children) in the heterosexual nuclear family' and thus seen as 'producers and reproducers'.[59]

The baby girl's envelopment in the symbology of the Cuban nation is then advanced yet again through the name that is chosen for her. Yocandra is, in fact, a name that the protagonist chooses for herself later on in life. Her given name, Patria, is chosen by her father, in an attempt to compensate for his profound disappointment at learning she was born just minutes into May 2, so not on May 1, the Day of the revolutionary Workers. In her retrospective account, Yocandra shows herself to be fully aware of the reason for his dissatisfaction:

> Yo aún era un bultico baboso del unto materno envuelto en la bandera cubana y ya comenzaban a reprocharme el no haber cumplido con mi deber revolucionario.[60]
>
> I was still a little lump sticky with afterbirth and wrapped in the Cuban flag, and they were already reproaching me for not having fulfilled my revolutionary duty.

Her father finds solace in the prospect of choosing a name for his new daughter, and seizes the opportunity to vicariously emphasize his own conformation with national ideals:

> —Pues mire… Me gustaría ponerle Victoria… o mejor, mejor… ¡Patria!… ¡Patria es un nombre muy original!… ¡Soy el padre, el padre de Patria,

> de la Patria! ¡El padre de la Patria! ¡Carlos Manuel de Céspedes! ¡El primero que libertó a sus esclavos! ¡Qué par de cojones, qué toletón![61]
>
> —Well let's see… I would like to name her Victoria… or better, better… Patria! Patria is a very original name!… I'm the father, the father of Patria, father of *la Patria*! The father of *la Patria*! Carlos Manuel de Céspedes! The first one to liberate his slaves! What balls, what a guy!

The meaningfulness of this name comes into view here both as a straightjacket for his daughter and for its potentially useful ambiguity in symbolic terms (although this is not adopted by her, given she eventually rejects the name). Borrowed from the nationalist slogan '¡Patria o Muerte!', 'Homeland or Death', 'Patria' is ambiguously gendered in grammatical terms: rooted in the Latin 'pater' it clearly means fatherland, but the normalized conceptualization of nations as female adds a pleasing level of dualism to its meanings both in Spanish and in translation, and it can be rendered as 'motherland', as 'fatherland', or neutrally as 'homeland'. Reflecting on the important gendered associations that surround the word *patria*, Kaminksy writes:

> The ideological divisions that align woman with private spaces (house/home) and man with public space (*país/patria*) play out in interesting ways around these linguistic and affective divides. Surely both men and women partake of the benefits of both home and *patria*. Surely, too, they have differential access to those benefits. But the gender divide cuts across these terms in another way: the affective (home/*patria*) is associated with the feminine, and the objective (house/*casa*/country/*país*) with the masculine. Yet this second formulation doesn't work so smoothly either. On the one hand, the domesticity of the house and conventional notions of masculinity do not easily coincide; on the other, *patria*, with its masculine root, is unbounded space to which women have traditionally been denied access.[62]

These observations emphasize the complex and contradictory associations set up between the individual and his or her social context through language and naming. Of particular interest here, though, is Kaminsky's final statement, where she emphasizes the etymology of the name originally given by Valdés to her main character, for given the novel's alignment of protagonist and nation, 'Patria' is a nomenclature that threatens to deny her access to her 'self'. Regardless of his assertions to the contrary ('a very original name'), the reader is led to understand that her father has not chosen this name for a uniqueness that could reflect his daughter's individuality, but because it will fully subsume her within the body politic of the nation while simultaneously investing her selfhood with the role of embodying the values by which that body politic is held together. In sum, this politically loaded name functions as a signifier that turns her body into a metaphor of the state; an apparatus of power to be manipulated and controlled by the dominant forces of patriarchal logic. Patria/Yocandra's decision to change her name thus comes into view as a refusal to be defined by the terms of the national, cultural and political discourses that dominate in her social context.

Focusing on the relationship between power and language, Nanne Timmer terms this name change as the enacting of a desire to 'name' instead of 'being named', and establishes a connection between this self-christening and her attribution of nicknames to all of the other characters in the novel.[63] One example of this giving of aliases, which serve to reveal to the reader the qualities most key to our being able to situate the characters in question within the Cuban context, appears in an early episode that also serves as an opportunity for the direct articulation of Yocandra's own feelings about the implications of her given name: when she crosses paths with an old school acquaintance, who she calls *La Militonta* (a pun mixing the term 'militant' and with word for 'stupid' (tonto/a) that ironically turns the name into a pointed accusation of unthinking conformity), the girl tries to get Yocandra's attention by shouting her old name:

> —Oye, Patria, ¿estás sorda? ¿No te acuerdas de mí?
> —Es que me cambié el nombre. Ahora me llamo Yocandra.
> La Militonta estudia de cabeza a pies mi indumentaria, su rostro se vuelve desconfiado, pregunta desafiante:
> —¿Y eso por qué, tú? ¿No te sentías orgullosa de tu nombre?
> [...]
> —Creo que no merezco ese nombre, no estoy a la altura. Era demasiado para mí...
> —¿Tú no te habrías vuelto «gusana», de esas de los derechos humanos?[64]

> —Hey Patria! Are you deaf? Don't you remember me?
> —I changed my name. I'm called Yocandra now.
> The *Militonta* looks me suspiciously up and down, from head to toe, and pointedly asks:
> —And why would you do that? Weren't you proud of your name?
> [...]
> —I don't think I deserve that name, I'm not good enough for it. It was too much for me...
> —You haven't become a *Gusana* [a 'worm'; traitor of the Revolution], one of those types that go on about human rights, have you?

Pedaling furiously away from the encounter on her Chinese bicycle, Yocandra monologues to herself in anger and frustration at the *Militonta*'s interrogation of her motives:

> Y no me llamo más Patria porque siempre odié ese nombre, porque en la primaria se burlaban de mí, porque en el fondo respeto profundamente

el significado de esa palabra. Pero además, ¿qué sentido tiene llamarse así?[65]

I'm not called Patria anymore because I always hated the name, because I was teased for it in elementary school, because deep down I really respect the meaning of the word. But also: what sense does it make to be named that?

Very noteworthy here is the fact that the way in which her rhetorical question is asked in Spanish is then revealed as ambiguous when translated into English: it could be translated as above, but just as easily as 'What *does it mean* to be called that?' The obviously anti-revolutionary connotations that her rejection of the name has for the suspicious mind of the *Militonta* answers that query. And within the terms of the narrative, given all that it has already been shown to stand for in terms of the female role in patriarchal and nationalist discourses, the fact of changing her name can and should be perceived as a symbolic rejection of the masculinized ideals, brought to bear on the world through language, by which national identity for both genders is defined. Lastly, and importantly, this scene also serves to underscore Yocandra's position vis-à-vis her sociopolitical setting: she does not outrightly and unquestioningly reject *cubanidad* per se, but she does challenge its rigid configuration through the socialist discourse of the regime.

CUBANA: BECOMING THE NEW WOMAN

As I have already begun to infer, what Yocandra does gradually come to challenge most specifically and more forcefully, is the role of gender in the formulation of *cubanidad*. And this is made evident in part, just as in *Arráncame la vida*, by using the institution of marriage to distill and reveal the persistently gendered social order in which Yocandra comes of age. In fact, the similarities between the portrayals of this event in both authors' works/protagonists' lives are remarkable. Three years into her love affair with an older man she only ever refers to as *el Traidor*—the Traitor—Yocandra recalls, he pulls up next to her in a car as she is walking down the street, exclaiming:

—Oye, tenemos que casarnos, hoy mismo, ya lo arreglé todo, hace falta que nos casemos... Necesito una mujer, digo, una «compañera»... Me dan un puesto importante en un país lejano, en Europa, y tengo que ir casado.[66]

—Listen, we have to get married, today. I've already arranged everything, we must get married... I need a wife, I mean a '*compañera*'... They've given me an important post in a faraway country, in Europe, and I have to be married to go.

Already very reminiscent of Andrés's abrupt appearance at Catalina's family home and emotional blackmailing of her father in order to secure her as his bride, the likeness continues here when all sentimentality is removed from the ceremony itself by *El Traidor* paying the lawyer conducting it to skip straight to the vow of commitment. Yocandra describes in hindsight what she *imagined* saying to the judge; a telling contrast to the 'Yes, I accept him as my husband' that she eventually utters:

> 'mire, compañera abogado, yo lo conocí menor, pero ya pasaron tres años de encierro, y soy mayorcita y sé lo que hago. Y lo que hago es lo que él ordene, porque él es un hombre del mundo y sabe lo que hace, y siempre le ha salido bien. Él va por el camino correcto y yo detrás. Para eso soy su novia, o amante, o secretaria o criada –no, perdón, la compañera que trabaja en la casa, las criadas no existen desde que la Revolución triunfó – o...'[67]
>
> 'Look, comrade lawyer, I met him when I was young, but three years of imprisonment have gone by, and I'm older now and I'm aware of my actions. And what I do is what he tells me to do, because he is a man of the world and he knows what he's doing, and it's always worked out well for him. He is walking on the right path and I am following behind him. That's why I'm his bride, or lover, or secretary or maid—no, sorry, the comrade who works in his house, because maids don't exist since the triumph of the Revolution—or...'

The clear similarities between this speech and that by made Catalina and discussed in the previous chapter, when she attempts to define her role in Andrés's life, are emphatic of the subordination of women within the marriage unit and the sex-gender system at large as a common experience for women in post-revolutionary Mexico and Cuba alike. The points of comparison also, then, point to deeply embedded patterns in gender relations and gender identity politics as a strand of social structures far more resistant to change than other dimensions of sociopolitical and symbolic orders. And, of course, additional connections are to be found here, too, in the fact that the political backdrop of Valdés's novel is personified by *el Traidor* and his obvious commitment to a regime that Yocandra is bluntly critical of, as expressed in his insistence on deploying socialist rhetoric in his self-correction and labeling her '*Compañera*', above. Yocandra, however, unpicks this political terminology so as to reveal the identities for which it can stand as a façade when she searches for an appropriate label for her role in his life and can only produce obvious gendered associations and attached social roles.

So just as Andrés serves to embody the corrupt machismo of post-revolutionary Mexico, the Traitor is created to embody the hypocrisy and machismo of post-revolutionary Cuba—some critics have suggested, in fact, that he might be intended as a stand-in for Castro himself.[68] As all the male characters in the novel, even those favored by Yocandra (*el Lince*/the Lynx and *el Nihilista*/the Nihilist), he is left underdeveloped and only really given meaning in terms of his impact on the narrator-protagonist. If she embodies the nation, he embodies the regime that is seen as harmful to *cubanidad*. Although he claims to be creative, and is accepted by the authorities as an eminent Revolutionary writer, he produces nothing of substance. In fact, quite the opposite: when they move to France following their impromptu wedding he insists on having their apartment to himself all day long in order to be able to focus on his masterpiece, so Yocandra is forced to spend her days wandering the streets of her adoptive land with nothing to do and nowhere to go—the ever-perturbing *nada* follows her on her journey and the Traitor is thus implicated in its perpetuation.

But as Dorado Otero rightly underscores, the continuation of her subaltern status in exile also plays into the critique of gendered identities forwarded by the novel because it makes clear the responsibility of patriarchy at large, not just its Cuban incarnation, in the subjugation of women.[69] Yocandra has no better opportunities for self-development in Europe than she has in Cuba—her personal growth is again only stimulated there by the continued revelation of the Traitor's total lack of substance. Hence, furthermore, these facets of the text counterpoint 'Cubanness' as an innate quality—embodied by her and anchored in her desire to see her country in an improved situation—with 'nationality' as bureaucratic label,[70] personified by the one-dimensional Traitor. The Europe episode thus feeds into a redrawing of the lines of national borders by evincing the sustainability of *cubanidad* beyond geographical lines in the sand (a point I shall return to later).

Ultimately, this is encapsulated in the moment of Yocandra's eventual discovery that all her husband has produced in these hours of seemingly dedicated writing is a manuscript repeating the same paranoid sentence over and over again: 'Everyone is harassing me. I cannot write because everyone is harassing me'.[71] In his repetition of this meaninglessness, this nothingness, he is at last revealed as a fraud and his nickname comes to take on a depth of meaning sustainable from every ideological angle: he betrays the Revolution by failing to properly embrace and promote its ideals through his work and by abusing his privileged position to carry out a masturbatory project underpinned by the egotistical pursuit of individualism; he betrays the counter-Revolution represented by Yocandra by failing to challenge the limitation it imposes on creativity via censorship and the demarcation of artistic genres in terms of their social value, and he betrays Yocandra herself by abusing her mind (she becomes a kind of research assistant for him, learning more than he about the topics he is supposed to be an expert in) and her body, which he subjects to the tyranny of his own fantasies and perceived needs, with no regard at all for hers.

BILDUNG, SEX, AND SEXUALITY: RITES OF PASSAGE AND THE RECLAIMING OF THE SELF

Above all, then, the key role played by the Traitor is to stimulate Yocandra's resistance, even if this begins with his crushing of her autonomy under the weight of his own narcissism. If he personifies the Castro regime then he also provides the impetus for her eventual understanding and gradually more articulate characterization of its flaws, and for her desire to speak out against it. His role in her education is a complex dimension of the narrative because of his negative character portrayal and the need for this to be reconciled with his simultaneous role as provider of experiences that become fundamental to our protagonist's self-formulation—the achievement of which is the most positive message carried by the text. Through him, Yocandra is enabled access to opportunities that would not otherwise have been hers via her sexualized body: the opportunity to travel abroad that would have been extremely difficult for her to procure without marrying him, and the opportunity to learn about literature and the arts in the way that she does, which is made possible by the Traitor's willingness to lie to her parents and to use his money and government connections to get certificates 'proving' that she had attended an exclusive boarding school and gained a degree in Physical Education.[72] These narrative threads are also key to the novel's critique of the Revolution in their combination with the negative portrayal of the health service, seen above. Together, these generate a disparaging portrayal of the sanitary and educational services whose value and success is a mainstay of the Revolutionary government's self-representation.[73]

In this way, the Traitor provides a space within the framework of the Revolution for Yocandra to develop her anti-Revolutionary stance. Not educated as part of 'the mass' and not participative of the official program of education via which the future of the country was to be invested in its youth, Yocandra describes how the formation she received was 'very different from those idiots at school',[74] so whilst she does actually go to Ciudad Libertad (the school set up in Havana by Castro in 1959), 'three months were enough for me to realize that what was taught in those classrooms had nothing to do with knowledge'.[75] In terms of the Bildungsroman as generic frame here, the Revolution's investment in youth is very interesting, for it adds a layer of sociocultural specificity to Valdés's reworking of the genre. Yocandra rejects the dialogue between self and society as it is construed via the regime, instead seeking out, as all the protagonists considered in this study have, a form of self-elected education that pushes beyond the boundaries of what is assumed relevant in the terms of established power structures.

It is noteworthy that in her relationship with the Traitor, Yocandra bears comparison to her friend *la Gusana*, the *jinetera* who escapes to Spain by marrying a man she is neither attracted to nor loves even platonically, essentially serving as his legalized prostitute. For both women use their sexuality as a means by which to gain opportunities otherwise not available to them, and which challenge official discourses on sex and gender. In line with this, Chancy underscores the importance of the novel's reclaiming of sexuality most especially in light of Yocandra's functioning as synecdoche for the nation state, and in context of the government's decision post-1989 to reinitiate trade tourism and the subsequent reappearance of the sex trade on the island. This, she explains, has led to 'sex [replacing] sugar as the staple choice for foreign exploitation'. Thus, by 'asserting control over her sexuality and her body, Yocandra claims *la patria's* desire to be free of such exploitation'.[76] The frequently exploited female body has its role reversed in this way, coming to represent not the passive ground of invasion but the active ground of resistance to subjugation, and the potential implications of that reversal are made to play out at a number of ideological levels, interconnecting the individual and personal with the communal and political.

This move also becomes important, therefore, for its nuancing of any accusation that could be leveled at Valdés that her own critique of the socialist regime is Manichean. Despite her writing partaking in the shift from questions of "who are we?" to "who am I?" that Nanne Timmer identifies in recent Cuban literature, she does not reject the fundamental socialist interest in community.[77] Rather, Valdés creates a character who embodies the nation and then takes the time to reincorporate into her narrative of selfhood a series of marginalized figures representative of the Cuban experience of community as diasporic: *la Gusana*, *el Lince*, the expelled homosexual sculptor whose house her family is given, the 'so-and-sos' and 'what's-his-names' who are now living in Miami, Mexico, France and Spain, are all invoked through the prism of Yocandra's sense of loss in order to be given presence.[78]

Vitally, though, all of these interconnected readings are made possible by the laying of the foundations of the novel's reclaiming of the female body as the site for identity construction early on in the narrative/protagonist's life, beginning with a critique of the upholding of virginity as a valued marker of 'successful' femininity. As we saw in Mastretta's novel in the previous chapter, the rite of passage of losing one's virginity is depicted in *La nada cotidiana*, too, although in a very different tone—a marker equally of the narrative's more contemporary setting and of the author's more radical take on gender. Unlike Catalina's innocence in this regard, even as a young girl Yocandra refuses to perceive her virginity as something sacred that must be protected, and she underlines the arbitrariness of its social symbolism by pointing out that 'I was a *señorita* as far as my vagina was concerned, but not where other 'c-anal-s' were'.[79] This statement indicates a rebellious exploration of sexual pleasure in ways that might still be socially condemned, but which are not endowed with the same relevance to female gendered identity and its imposed parameters,[80] thus emphasizing the arbitrary nature of this symbolic economy. Serving to underscore the critique of this method of regulating female sexuality, *el Traidor* actually refuses to sleep with her because he 'was incapable, he couldn't stand virgins, he wouldn't dare to break something as delicate and humid' as a hymen.[81] Yocandra ironically points out, in hindsight: 'How could I have suspected that later on, and very frequently, he was going to tear into far more sensitive parts of me: my dignity, my soul, and all that crap so important for us women',[82] engaging in a critique of the ideological control of the physical body as taking place to the detriment of recognition of individual psychological and emotional development.

At the time, however, she is determined to get what she wants by complying with the older man's singular perspectives on her body and responses to the social mores that labeled that particular part of her as 'delicate' (he reverses the usual socially inculcated veneration of female sexual purity). She writes with verve about how she left his house with the intention of purposefully ridding herself of her virginity:

> Me abrió la puerta y por ella salió, no una jovencita asustada, sino un himen criminal. Un himen dispuesto a matar el primer pene que se atravesara en su camino.[83]

> He opened the door for me and out stepped not a frightened young woman, but a criminal hymen. A hymen ready to kill the first penis that crossed its path.

Throughout this episode we see the female character in a double bind, one in which she pursues her own desires by conforming to those of *el Traidor*. Nonetheless, her language here expresses not passivity, but action: her virginity is not something that will be taken from her, nor will it be offered up by her as a signification of her femininity and compliance with gender roles, but it will be put to use in the pursuit of *her* present desires. In this way, even while the limitations of hegemonic powers, symbolized by *el Traidor*, are not inescapable, her desire serves as a drive to resistance against the social definition of her being. Her body is transformed from being the foundation upon which her identity is constructed, into the means by which she might be able to gain self-definition. Again this recalls Butler's emphasis on the ever-present possibility of 'reaction' against dominant discourses, even as the subject continues to be defined by his or her relationship with such ideologies. And in fact, Yocandra's name change, discussed earlier, also indicates this dualistic and therefore complex positioning both within and against discourse, for while she removes herself of the weighty expectations inherent to her given name, and chooses a new name that, as Perla Rozencvaig rightly asserts, encompasses the term 'Yo'—'I',[84] she nonetheless takes this name from one of her lover's muses in the hope that it will make her more attractive to him.

As this key episode unfolds, the description of the way in which Yocandra effectively deflowers *herself*, continues the reconfiguration of gender codes. She recounts that leaving the house of *el Traidor* she comes across some 'long-haired guy' high on marijuana and drunk on rum, 'who had no idea of his destiny'.[85] She effectively kidnaps the stupefied man, hitchhikes a ride in a General's car (which she halts by exposing her breasts), and takes him to a nightclub:

> Le di cuatro bofetones, lancé dos jarras de agua fría en su imbécil cara y comencé a besarlo para no perder la costumbre del romanticismo. En el pullman descosido y sudoroso, escuchando un bolero en la propia voz de José Antonio Méndez, él se abrió la portañuela, y se

> sacó el pito bien tieso. Yo ya tenía el blúmer por los tobillos. Evoqué la guillotina, y de un tirón me senté en la cabeza del rabo. Él chilló de dolor, yo no había lubricado lo suficiente. Costó trabajo, pero lo decapité. Sólo hubo un mínimo ardor y una aguada sangrecita. Mi himen había cumplido su cometido: matar a un tolete.[86]

> I gave him four slaps around the face, threw two jugs of cold water in his imbecile's face and began to kiss him so as not to do away altogether with romance. On the threadbare, sweaty sofa, listening to a bolero sung by José Antonio Méndez, he unzipped his fly and took out his erect prick. I already had my panties round my ankles. I was like a guillotine, and in one fell swoop I sat down on the head of his cock. He cried out in pain; I wasn't wet enough. It took some effort, but I beheaded him. I only felt a slight burning sensation and there was a little watery blood. My hymen had fulfilled its mission: to kill a penis.

The total contrast of this portrayal to orthodox narratives on the theme of a young girl's first sexual encounter—a more normalized version of which is provided in *Arráncame la vida*, where, as Jane Lavery has observed, Catalina is rendered passive by lack of knowledge and dehumanized by Andrés's objectification of her—is obviously very purposeful.[87] Valdés empowers her protagonist, placing her in control of the event from the outset and, more than this, recounts the scene in such a way as to clearly evoke a rape scene of reversed gender roles. Her drugged, drunken accomplice, whereas evidently not an unwilling accomplice and therefore not a disempowered victim, is nonetheless turned into the passive element in this scenario. And there is an aggression to the scene that is stereotypically masculine. The analogy drawn between Yocandra and a guillotine is recourse to violent imagery that places her in the role of perpetrator of this sexual act; as a female castrator. It is also recourse to a chain of signification by which the reader is encouraged to recall the Revolution (tracing back through the French Revolution), so that the active female body becomes intertwined with the symbology of both resistance and power in a highly politicized manner.[88]

It is worthwhile commenting that in the increasing body of criticism available on Valdés's work, this scene, the chapter that I will now move on to discuss, and the recognized eroticism of her work more generally are very often foregrounded, and this is significant because despite the open-minded stance such studies take in respect of this feature of her oeuvre, we must continue to see as noteworthy our continued investment of it with meaning. This surely says something about the tardiness of shifts in social thinking vis-à-vis female sexuality and women's ownership of that. For the fact is that for such a narrative strategy to remain functional and contemporary as a mode of speaking out against the repression/appropriation of female selfhood—which it does, for we do not need to historicize Valdés's portrayals of this theme within the Cuba of the Special Period in order for them to retain their 'shock value'—neither that selfhood nor its sexuality can have been fully reclaimed.

As far as the character of Yocandra is concerned, protagonism in her sexual life is something that truly comes to the fore as a fulfilling area of her existence when her active enjoyment of her body is represented and explored in the text through her relationship with the man she nicknames *el Nihilista*—a fellow dissident whose own work as a cinema director is made subject to censorship by the authorities.[89] Her portrayals of the physical relationship she shares with the Nihilist are a continuation of the sense of presentism and immediate gratification that she seeks out in the scene just discussed, and which Cámara Betancourt has remarked are part of a broader strategy for survival depicted in the novel.[90] The fact of an active female sexuality, again as opposed to a female body that bears a relationship to sex only through its reproductive function, is emphasized in the scenes where he is present through the literary evocation of a female gaze, recalling Catalina's close observations of Carlos's body in Mastretta's text. Much more explicit than that portrayal, however, Yocandra eulogizes the physical beauty of her lover, and expounds at length upon their sexual activities on the night they first met and also during one evening that she refers to as 'our *Nine and a ½ Weeks*'.[91] Their shared rejection of the limitations imposed by dominant ideologies is translated into their sexual relationship through the trope of excess. In particular, this is called forth by the focus on the number of orgasms that Yocandra has each time they are together,[92] and on bodily fluids—saliva, sperm and vaginal fluids—that tap into the metaphorics of liquidity connected to female gendered identity by Elizabeth Grosz and discussed in the previous chapter.[93]

What is more, this superfluity stands out greatly in a novel that focuses, to a large extent and as indicated by the title, on the limitations of daily life in Cuba. Indeed, these quotidian limitations are directly connected to the body, and then pointedly juxtaposed with the open-endedness that comes to characterize the main sex-scene through the description of the meager meal the two share beforehand:

> Devoramos las pizzas, las tripas resuenan indecentes, protestando porque no quedan del todo satisfechas, sino más bien ahorcados [...] Apuramos la botella y nuestras cabezas apenas dan una media vuelta, entonces nos damos cuenta de que el vino no alcanza para desordenar al máximo nuestros sentidos y simulamos la deliciosa borrachera que suponemos debería acontecer.[94]

> We devoured the pizzas, our stomachs gurgling indecently, protesting because they had not been satisfied, only somewhat placated [...] We finished the bottle and our heads barely spun at all, so we realized that the wine wasn't going to be enough to properly disorder our senses and we simulated the delicious drunkenness that we believed should have come about.

The vibrant description of the sex scene as a follow-on to this renders sex visible as a form of compensation for a feeling of lack in other areas of life. Yocandra's and *el Nihilista*'s crossing of the boundaries of each other's bodies is thus bound up in the novel with a redefinition of individuality (by their coming together) and experience (plentitude provided by their interrelationship) through the materiality and pleasures of the body. This is a different form of bodily politics, in which the human form becomes the tool by which to react against sociopolitical and cultural limitations of a number of different kinds. There is an attempt at the destruction of bodily limits thus to enable a more fulfilled life; one not defined by the body and permissive of its use as a tool of subjugation, but instead by the enabling of the embodied subject via the body's capacity to feel and do. To paraphrase Dorado-Otero, this is eroticism as a form of transcendence.[95] Or, in the words of González Abellás, 'this overflowing sexuality is also an alternative discourse to the precariousness of life in Cuba during the Special Period, and to the official discourse that is, "grey", serious, political'.[96]

'WRITING BEYOND THE ENDING'

For these reasons it is significant that at this stage, with two chapters remaining, the narrative takes on a highly self-referential style reminiscent of the metatextual beginning of this work. The penultimate chapter begins:

> 'Parece que los capítulos ocho de la literatura cubana están condenados a ser pornográficos.'
>
> Así se expresará el censor cuando lea estas páginas. El censor que me toca por libreta, porque cada escritor tiene un policía designado to them.[97]
>
> 'It seems that all chapter eights in Cuban literature are condemned to be pornographic.'
>
> That's what the censor will say when he or she reads these pages. My own personal censor, because each writer has one designated to them.

The direct references to the censorship of literature by the State, because made at the start of the chapter in which she most explicitly portrays sex and sexuality, serve to comment in an equally explicit manner on political control of bodies both textual and sexual. As Chancy puts it, Yocandra 'adopts a sexuality that is considered amoral and therefore counter-revolutionary'.[98] Yocandra highlights the intimate connections between the physical body, the body of writing in which she describes it, and the body politic of which both are constituent parts. Put another way, as a result of her blatant confrontation with the established rules of censorship through her narrativization of the body, the body of the text takes on the same task of questioning the discursive regulation of identity as

Yocandra performs through her own physical form. It is thus that she condemns the censorship of female desire and its regulation via sociopolitical and cultural discourse.

Rozencvaig notes that one of Yocandra's responses to the frustration of her job as editor of a cultural magazine—a task made obsolete by numerous unfulfilled material requirements and by the time delay in receiving items that could serve as content for the magazine—is to replace the creation of text in that role with sex.[99] And, in line with the role given to sex in the novel, as elucidated, this is true. But it only makes the self-referential reappearance of 'text' at the end of the narrative more meaningful. This stylistic choice has a twofold importance: first, it underlines the text as linguistic construction, and therefore as social comment rather than as a simpler form of realist narrative—the kind of escapist literature whose limitations have been negatively associated with women's writing. The second, is that it seems to take the energy and excess of the sex scenes as impetus for the creative act of writing, injecting a story that focuses on stagnation and frustration with momentum, for the final chapter of the work is narrated in a tumbling of words and thoughts. The more considered, structured account and analysis of her life up until this point is changed as the story moves into the present moment—forcing the reader to join Yocandra in the 'presentism' noted above—and she finds herself confronting a wave of reflections, worries, concerns, and the presence of both the Nihilist and the Traitor who meet here for the first time, and with both of whom she continues to have a physical relationship. Again defying genre codes, then, the simplistic romance plot that Valdés might have opted for is rejected. The simplification of the complexities of life via the portrayal of her happiness with the Nihilist and their emotional, ideological and physical unity is present, but then undermined. If we take their pairing as a form of binary opposition, for the story to conclude with their 'happy ending' would undermine the deconstructive approach taken throughout the novel. Instead, Yocandra seems to remain trapped in a bifurcation between *la nada* and *el todo*—the plurality or excess through which she has sought comfort:

> No me pueden ocurrir tantas cosas al mismo tiempo. Y sin embargo, parece como si nada ocurriera, como si desde nací hiciera lo mismo, callarme, estallar, llorar. Callarme, estallar, llorar. He roto mi pasividad. Ser melancólica es mi protesta, la huelga que soy capaz de hacer para independizar mi tristeza de la tristeza colectiva.[100]

> All this can't happen to me at once. And yet it seems that nothing ever happens, as if since I was born I've been doing the same thing: be quiet, explode, cry. Be quiet, explode, cry. I have broken my passivity. Being sad is my protest, the strike I am able to carry out in order to separate my individual sadness from the collective one.

The clearly evoked sense of entrapment here threatens to end the novel at a point of stagnation and it will require the creative force of writing to avoid this fate. The last pages of the text are voiced in a revelatory tone in which Yocandra's consciousness seems heightened, as she contemplates the world from windows of her hexagon-shaped bedroom:

> Suspiro, inhalo el humito del café [...] Hay mucho sol y sin embargo un aire fresco bate mi pelo. El mar está azulísimo, encima hay un jardín de girasoles, tulipanes, adelfas, siemprevivas, mar-pacíficos, orquídeas, jazmines, margaritas, y todas, todas las flores del planeta. El cielo está despejado y menos teñido que el mar. Es bella, hermosísima, esta combinación de luz y color. Lo nunca visto. ¿Pero son flores o ataúdes? ¿Es un jardín o un cementerio? ¡Yo quiero un jardín, me urge un jardín!
>
> I breathe, I inhale the smell of coffee [...] It is really sunny and yet there is a cool breeze that ruffles my hair. The sea is so blue, and above it there is a garden of sunflowers, tulips, rosebays, sempervivums, hibiscus, jasmine, daisies, and all, all of the flowers of the world. The sky is clear and a lighter blue than the sea. This combination of colour and light is so, so beautiful. As never seen before. But are they flowers or markers of tombs? Is it a garden or a cemetery? I want a garden, I need a garden!

In terms of the tenets of the Bildungsroman as discussed in the Introduction, and in relation to the triadic form of this study, itself adapted from Hegel's threefold dialectic mode, this scene reads as the closest depiction in any of the novels discussed here of the notion of 'Absolute Knowledge'. The heightened senses, the clear recognition of at once the good and the bad, Yocandra's self-presence and consciousness of the world in which she is located are at their greatest at this point in the story; at the culmination of her narrative of female gendered *Bildung*. And it is at this moment in her life that she chooses to take up her pen, despite her lack of confidence: 'I am facing a lined notebook', she writes, 'racking my brains'.[101]

> Busco cualquier pretexto [...] para no seguir pensando más. Para no comprometerme con algo que no sé si podré hacer, si tendré ovarios: describir la nada que es mi todo [...] Yo sé que no será genial. No me sobrevaloro. Soy un producto semántico de pésimas maestras de español. No me sobrestimo. Tengo dudas con la construcción de frases largas, hago choricera de palabra superflua. No soy la campeona de las declinaciones, nadie tiene que decírmelo. [...]
>
> Invoco a mis orishas. ¡Denme fuerzas! ¿Tal vez debería ir a lavarme los dientes? [...] ¿Por qué estoy tan ceremoniosa? [...] Para impedirme comenzar. Para evitarme iniciar la frase. Para autocensurar las palabras que, como unas locas, unas putas, unas hadas, unas diosas,

> explotan desaforadas con la tinta de la pluma que mis dedos aprietan. Porque hay amigos que se fueron y otros que se quedaron. Todos aquí, dentro de mí. Dentro de las palabras que no sé más si soy yo quien las escribe. O si son ellas las que me escriben a mí:
>
> *Ella viene de una isla que quiso construir el paraíso...*

> I look for any excuse [...] not to think any more. To not commit myself to something that I don't know if I will be able to do, if I'll have the ovaries for it: describe the nothingness that is my everything [...] I know it won't be great. I don't over-estimate myself. I am a semantic product of the worst Spanish teachers. I don't give myself more credit than I'm due. I have doubts about the construction of long sentences, I string together unnecessary words. I am not a champion of declensions, no one needs to tell me that. [...]
>
> I invoke my Orishas. Give me strength! Maybe I should clean my teeth? [...] Why am I being so ritualistic? [...] To stop myself from starting. To avoid beginning the sentence. To self-censure the words that, like crazy women, some whores, some fairies, some goddesses, explode boundlessly with the pen and ink that my fingers are holding. Because there are friends who have left and there are friends who have stayed. All of them are here, within me. Within these words, which I can't tell if I'm writing or not anymore. Or if instead they are writing me:
>
> *She came from an island that wanted to create paradise...*

Following as they do the fact of State censorship of literature, the comments made in this section about writing as a matter of life or death become weighty. And juxtaposed with these comments the fear of writing, of claiming a voice and speaking out about her life experiences, takes on both ideological and gendered dimensions. Read within the frame of my interest in women's writing, this thrust of the reader towards the end of the narrative is of great interest for its open engagement with issues whose overcoming has been vital to the formulation of a female canon. The lack of confidence and the fear of one's own voice; the fear of denouncing an all-powerful, masculinized system. And so then the overcoming of that fear through the personification of words, of language itself, as female, functions to reclaim language for precisely the kind of story Yocandra initiates at the narrative's end. In this way, her last passages seem to draw together and push beyond the limitations imposed by gender, on female *Bildung*, and on women's self-expression through both sexual and textual bodies.

Throughout the novel Valdés has created a protagonist who narrates her own *Bildung* by placing the physical body *en relief*, and subsequently defies imposed limitations on self-expression thematically, politically and in terms of genre. In a sense, and as is concurrent with the novel's postmodernist tenets, this pushing forth, beyond preestablished boundaries and towards self-expression, is a movement also necessarily envisaged as a kind of excess, an overflow from one space into another; a blurring of lines and demarcations. In other words, it is a movement towards synthesis, whereby previously separated forms and characteristics are forcibly drawn together. The dynamism of this shift is mirrored in the growth towards agency that, I have argued, is encapsulated, metaphorized and performed in *La nada cotidiana* through the female physical form.

More broadly, within the terms of the threefold structure of this book, arrival at the point of agency is, however, arrival at an end point that does not signify an ending *per se*. As with all of the novels studied here, Yocandra's narrative ends without ending, projecting forward into the future. Whereas not perhaps an optimistic final sentence, hers is nonetheless a final paragraph that, through the image of the words being written or writing her, suggests continuation and potential, because if we assume that her oneiric Chapter One is actually begun here, then it does not belong at the start of the story we have read, but rather here, at that story's end. This makes the last lines of Chapter One the last lines of Valdés's novel, and so the work ends with a rhetorical question that, although indicative of an ongoing dilemma, does not generate closure: '*She doesn't know what to do. Why swim? Why drown?*'[102]

Again as a connection between the necessary challenge made by women writers to the tenets of the traditional Bildungsroman and the Cuban post-Revolutionary setting of Yocandra's coming-to-be, the possibility of rearranging the story's constituent parts in this way interrogates the teleological tendencies of both genre and regime. For just as in the Bildungsroman's potentially conservative aim to depict the protagonist and guide the reader to find their place in the social order, so does Cuban Revolutionary discourse invest in the 'linear progress of enlightenment'.[103] In contrast, we find here the text's postmodern ability to be reordered, and subsequent capacity to remove Yocandra from the 'perpetual present' of the Special period that she depicts so viscerally.[104]

In the end, then, the female body in this novel is made visible as a site of identity that is, to borrow Butler's words, 'both constrained by certain kinds of cultural forces but not determined by them, and also open to improvisation and malleability and repetition and change'.[105] And it is transformed into a productive force through a focus on it as a vehicle of, not just a vessel for, language and writing. The possibility of continuity is invoked by the use in its final line of the strategy that Rachel Blau DuPlessis has termed 'writing beyond the ending'; a 'transgressive invention of narrative strategies [...] that express critical dissent from the dominant narrative'.[106] Here, the dominant narratives in question are those grand narratives by which gendered identity formation is shown to be governed and explored, but also the grand narrative of the classical Bildungsroman. Through this formal technique, therefore, the protagonist's *Bildung* is shown not to end here, with accommodation into her sociohistorical context. Rather, to borrow the words of Adrienne Rich, this narrative is driven beyond its own pages by 'the energy of desire, summoning a different reality'.[107]

NOTES

1. Roberto Tejada, 'In Relation to the Poetics and Politics of Cuba's Generation-80', http://writing.upenn.edu/library/Tejada-Roberto_Cuba-Generation-80.pdf, p. 1 of 12 [Accessed 21/02/2015]. Other critics, such as Isabel Alvarez Borland in the article referenced later on in this chapter, include Valdés in the *Generación de los 90*, focusing on the time at which she began writing as opposed to the time of her own coming of age.
2. Oswaldo Sánchez, 'Children of Utopia', cited in Tejada, 'In Relation to the Poetics and Politics of Cuba's Generation-80', p. 1 of 12. As Tejada explains, Sánchez makes a 'sidelong reference' here to Ernesto Che Guevera's essay 'Socialism and Man in Cuba' (1965), available at https://www.marxists.org/archive/guevara/1965/03/man-socialism.htm. And as will be discussed, there are moments of Valdés's own text that also seem to speak to this essay.
3. Catherine Davies, *A Place in the Sun?: Women Writers in Twentieth Century Cuba* (London; New York: Zed Books, 1997), pp. 223–224.
4. Madeline Cámara Betancourt, *Cuban Women Writers: Imagining a Matria* (London: Palgrave Macmillan, 2008), p. 121. Cámara Betancourt also notes that the novel was illicitly circulated on the island, despite State censorship, receiving mixed reviews.
5. Larry Rohter, 'Arts Abroad; Living with a Shortage of Everything but Desire', *New York Times* (January 7, 1998), http://www.nytimes.com/1998/01/07/books/arts-abroad-living-with-a-shortage-of-everything-but-desire.html [Accessed 03/28/2015].
6. Sánchez, 'Children of Utopia', cited in Tejada, 'In Relation to the Poetics and Politics of Cuba's Generation-80', p. 33.
7. Michel Foucault, *Discipline and Punish: The Birth of the Prison* (1975), 2nd edn. (London: Vintage Books, 1995), p. 25.
8. Davies, *A Place in the Sun?*, p. 223.
9. See Emma Staniland, 'Fighting the Opposition: Lack and Excess in Cuban and Cuban-American Narratives of Selfhood', *Comparative American Studies*, 12.3 (September 2014), 190–204.
10. Zoé Valdés, *La nada cotidiana* (1995) (Barcelona: Publicaciones y Ediciones Salamandra, 2004), p. 13. All further citations are taken from this edition and all translations are my own.
11. Cited in Paul B. Miller, 'The Prison-House of Allegory: Reflection on the Cultural Production of the Cuban 'Special Period', *INTI*, No. 59/60, 'Cuba: Cien Años de Alejo Carpentier' (Primavera 2004—Otoño 2004), 195–206, p. 201.
12. Miller, 'The Prison-House of Allegory', p. 201.
13. Valdés, *La nada…*, p. 14. 'El espacio se transforma en nube blanca, pura'.
14. Carmen Faccini, 'El discurso político de Zoé Valdés: *La nada cotidiana* y *Te di la vida entera*', http://www.lehman.cuny.edu/ciberletras/v07/faccini.html, p. 1 of 7. 'Este onírico, alucinado Capítulo Inicial adelanta, desde la perspectiva de la narradora, la Revolución como proyecto fracasado'.
15. Faccini, 'El discurso político de Zoé Valdés', p. 1 of 7. 'Se anticipa así no una forma literaria que delate cabalmente una realidad referencial, sino una forma literaria que proyecta una realidad parcialmente percibida o, al menos, así retextualizada por Valdés'.
16. Dinora Cardoso and Ynés Oggel, 'Self-Actualization as Paradise: *La nada cotidiana* by Zoe Valdés', *Journal of Caribbean Literatures*, 6:2 (Fall 2009), 65–75, p. 66.

17. Cristina Ortiz Ceberio, 'La narrativa de Zoé Valdés: Hacia una reconfiguración de la na(rra)ción cubana', *Chasqui: revista de literatura latinoamericana*, 27.2 (1998), 116–127, p. 122. 'De esta manera, la narración de *La nada cotidiana* se sitúa en el momento anterior a la existencia de la narradora/protagonista, quien al iniciar su narración se retrotrae a un momento previo a su propia vida'; 'Con esta focalización del discurso en un momento anterior a la existencia "terrena" del personaje, se apunta al lector que se va a enfrentar a un discurso que parte de un momento previo al condicionamiento cultural'.
18. The bodily details portrayed in the scene also challenge a reading of the nameless figure as Yocandra, for the woman points out scars on her body that have resulted from childbirth and we know that Yocandra has not had children.
19. Judith Butler, *Bodies That Matter: On the Discursive Limits of Sex* (1993) (London: Routledge, 2011), p. xxiii.
20. Madeline Cámara Betancourt, *Cuban Women Writers: Imagining a Matria* (London: Palgrave Macmillan, 2008), p. 125.
21. Isabel Alvarez Borland, 'Fertile Multiplicities: Zoé Valdés and the Writers of the '90s Generation', in Andrea O'Reilly (ed.), *Cuba: Idea of a Nation Displaced* (New York: State University of New York Press, 2007), pp. 253–266, p. 255.
22. Valdés, *La nada…*, p. 16. 'Dirige su cabeza hacia sus senos al aire libre. Está completamente desnuda y no siente vergüenza'.
23. Valdés, *La nada…*, p. 14
24. Valdés, *La nada…*, p. 17. '¡Él que decide!'.
25. Valdés, *La nada…*, p. 18. 'Ella piensa que siempre hay, en todas partes, ese "que decide". Y que nunca ha sido ella, precisamente, quien ha decidido por sí misma'.
26. Valdés, *La nada…*, p. 18. 'mitad sereno, mitad impetuoso'.
27. Valdés, *La nada…*, p. 19 'La han obligada a volver a su isla'.
28. Valdés, *La nada…*, pp. 18–19. 'Esta todavía desnuda, acostada en la arena, el mar alrededor de ella acariciando su piel afiebrada'.
29. Award-winning Cuban blogger Yoani Sánchez wrote about this tradition in the *Huffington Post* in January 2011, placing the ritual in the context of stagnating hopes for change on the island: http://www.huffingtonpost.com/yoani-sanchez/the-buried-revolution_b_803348.html [Accessed 02/28/2015].
30. Miguel González Abellás, '"Aquella Isla": Introducción al universo narrativo de Zoé Valdés, in *Hispania*, 83.1 (March 2000), 42–50, p. 45.
31. Valdés, *La nada…*, p. 19. 'Esa isla que, queriendo construir el paraíso, ha creado el infierno'.
32. Myriam J. Chancy, *From Sugar to Revolution: Women's Visions of Haiti, Cuba, and the Dominican Republic* (Waterloo, ON: Wilfred Laurier University Press, 2012), p. 147.
33. Chancy, *From Sugar to Revolution*, p. 147.
34. Gustavo Pérez Firmat, *The Cuban Condition: Translation and Identity in Modern Cuban Literature* (Cambridge: Cambridge University Press, 1989).
35. See Manuel R. Moreno Fraginals and Teresita Pedraza Moreno, 'The Ten Million Ton Sugar Harvest', http://faculty.mdc.edu/tpedraza/MMF-Ten%20Million%20Ton%20Harvest.htm for a useful summary of this government aim and its failed achievement. [Accessed 20/02/2015].
36. Valdés, *La nada…*, p. 94. 'como un demente'.
37. Valdés, *La nada…*, p. 94.
38. Valdés, *La nada…*, p. 94.

39. Miller, 'The Prison-House of Allegory', p. 197.
40. Che Guevara, 'Socialism and Man in Cuba' (1965), in *The Che Guevara Reader*, David Deutschmann (ed.), 2nd Revised edn., (Melbourne: Ocean Press, 2003), pp. 212–229, p.213
41. Discussed in Nanne Timmer, 'Dreams That Dreams Remain: Three Cuban Novels of the 90s', in Theo D'Haen and Pieter Vermeulen (eds.), *Cultural Identity and Postmodern Writing* (Amsterdam: Rodopi, 2006), pp. 185–205, p. 191.
42. See Che Guevara, 'Socialism and Man in Cuba', in David Deutschmann (ed.), *The Che Guevara Reader*, pp. 212–229.
43. Guevara, 'Socialism and Man', in Cuba p. 217.
44. Yoani Sanchez, 'The Buried Revolution', *The Huffington Post*, 01/02/2011, http://www.huffingtonpost.com/yoani-sanchez/the-buried-revolution_b_803348.html [Accessed 02/28/2015].
45. Guevara, 'Socialism and Man in Cuba', p. 218.
46. Valdés, *La nada...*, p. 183.
47. Madeline Cámara, 'Femenismo vs. Totalitarianismo: Notas para un estudio de textos y contextos de mujeres en Cuba contemporánea (1989–1994)'. Cited in Timmer, 'Dreams That Dreams Remain', p. 195.
48. Valdés, *La nada...*, p. 21.
49. Thea Pitman, '*En Primera Persona*: Subjectivity in Literary Evocations of Pregnancy and Birth by Contemporary Spanish-American Women Writers', *Women: a Cultural Review*, 17.3 (2006), 355–377, p. 357.
50. Pitman, 'En Primera Persona', p. 358.
51. Faccini, 'El discurso político', p. 2 of 7.
52. Michel Foucault, 'Nietzsche, Genealogy, History' (1971), cited in Lois McNay, *Foucault and Feminism: Power, Gender and the Self* (Cambridge, UK: Polity Press, 1992), p. 15.
53. Foucault, 'Nietzsche, Genealogy, History', cited in McNay, *Foucault and Feminism*, p. 15.
54. Ania Loomba, *Colonialism/Postcolonialism* (London: Routledge, 1998), p. 215.
55. Loomba, *Colonialism/Postcolonialism*, p. 218.
56. Loomba, *Colonialism/Postcolonialism*, p. 222.
57. Davies, *A Place in the Sun?*, p. 118.
58. Davies, *A Place in the Sun?*, p. 119.
59. Davies, *A Place in the Sun?*, p. 119.
60. Valdés, *La nada...*, p. 26.
61. Valdés, *La nada...*, p. 27.
62. Amy Kaminsky, *After Exile: Writing the Latin American Diaspora* (Minneapolis: University of Minnesota Press, 1999), p. 4.
63. Nanne Timmer, 'La crisis de representación en tres novelas cubanas: *La nada cotidiana* de Zoé Valdés, *El pájaro, pincel y tinta china* de Ena Lucía Portela y *La última playa* de Atilio Caballero' in *Revista Iberoamericana*, LXXIII.218–219 (enero–junio 2007), 119–134, p. 126.
64. Valdés, *La nada...*, p. 35.
65. Valdés, *La nada...*, p. 36.
66. Valdés, *La nada...*, p. 57.
67. Valdés, *La nada...*, pp. 58–9. 'Sí, lo acepto por esposo'.

68. Chancy, *From Sugar to Revolution*, p. 142.
69. Ángela Dorado Otero, *Dialogic Aspects of the Cuban Novel of the 90s* (Woodbridge, UK: Tamesis Press, 2014), p. 218.
70. Dorado Otero, *Dialogic Aspects*, p. 223.
71. Valdés, *La nada…*, p. 66. 'Todos me persiguen. No puedo escribir porque todos me persiguen'. It is also possible to translate 'perseguir' as 'to persecute', however given that the Traitor is protected by his government connections, hence the move to France in the first place, it makes more sense to interpret this as his feeling 'harassed', because it falls in line with his narcissistic characterization.
72. Valdés, *La nada…*, pp. 48–56.
73. As also mentioned by Faccini, 'El discurso político', p. 2 of 7.
74. Valdés, *La nada…*, p. 52. 'Recibí una preparación muy diferente a las bobaliconas de la escuela'.
75. Valdés, *La nada…*, p. 53. 'Cuando meses después entré por la puerta de Ciudad Libertad, me bastaron tres meses para darme cuenta de que sus aulas nada tenían que ver con el conocimiento'.
76. Chancy, *From Sugar to Revolution*, p. 148.
77. Timmer, 'Dreams that Dreams Remain', p. 191. That said, Valdés does not seem concerned about such accusations, for she has explained in interview that criticism of her characters as Manichean caricatures merely acknowledges her intentions: 'Quise marcar la caricatura y el maniqueísmo de los personajes porque provienen de una realidad caricaturesca y maniquea. Esos son los personajes que produce esa sociedad'. Interview with Enrico Mario Santí, 'Plante con Zoé Valdés', cited in Elena Lahr-Vivaz, 'Timeless Rhetoric, Special Circumstances: Sex and Symbol in *La nada cotidiana*', *Revista Canadiense de Estudios Hispánicos*, 34.2 (Invierno 2010), 303–321, fn. 26, p. 318.
78. Valdés, *La nada…*, p. 176.
79. Valdés, *La nada…*, p. 44. 'era señorita por la vagina, pero no por otros c«anal»es'.
80. See Lois Smith and Alfred Padula, *Sex and Revolution: Women in Socialist Cuba* (New York: Oxford University Press USA, 1996).
81. Valdés, *La nada*, p. 44. 'Él no era capaz, él no soportaba a las vírgenes, él no se atrevía a romper algo tan delicado y húmedo, ¡el himen!'.
82. Valdés, *La nada*, p. 44. ¿Cómo iba a sospechar que mucho tiempo después, y muy a menudo, iba a desgarrar zonas más sensibles en mí: la dignidad, el alma, y toda esa mojonería tan importante para nosotras?'.
83. Valdés, *La nada…*, p. 45.
84. Perla Rozencvaig, 'La complicidad del lenguaje en *La nada cotidiana*, *Revista Hispánica Moderna*, 49.2 (December 1996), 430–433, p. 431.
85. Valdés, *La nada…*, p. 46. 'que no tenía idea de su destino'.
86. Valdés, *La nada…*, pp. 46–7.
87. Jane Lavery, 'The Physical and Textual Bodies in the Works of Ángeles Mastretta and Elena Poniatowska', *Romance Studies*, 19.2 (December 2001), p. 174.
88. With reference to Cuban literature especially, the reader is reminded here of Alejo Carpentier's *El siglo de las luces* (1962), in which the guillotine features strongly as a revolutionary symbol.
89. Valdés, *La nada…*, p. 146.
90. Cámara Betancourt, *Cuban Women Writers*, p. 125.
91. Valdés, *La nada…*, p. 162. 'nuestra *nueve semanas y media*'.

92. Valdés, *La nada...*, p. 151.
93. Valdés, *La nada...*, pp. 153, 154, 159, 162, 161.
94. Valdés, *La nada...*, p. 158.
95. Dorado Otero, *Dialogic Aspects*, p. 228.
96. Miguel González Abellás, *Visiones de exilio: Para leer a Zoé Valdés*, cited in Dorado Otero, *Dialogic Aspects*, p. 204. 'esta sexualidad desbordante es también un discurso alternativa a la precariedad con que se vive en la Cuba del periodo especial y el discurso oficial 'gris', serio y político'.
97. Valdés, *La nada...*, p,144.
98. Chancy, *From Sugar to Revolution*, p. 145. Chancy says this as part of her interesting analysis of a scene in Chapter Five, where Yocandra's family inherits the house of an exiled gay sculptor, and posits that the amoral sexuality attributed to the protagonist is her own personal inheritance from him; her appreciation of his artwork implying her taking up of his place in the social order. The scene is also the first textual representation of her sexuality, for she examines in detail the statues of naked males that fill one room and has her 'first kiss' with one of them. Then, in the detailed and admiring description she gives of the Nihilist's body she compares his mouth to that of a statue (p. 151).
99. Rozencvaig, 'La complicidad del lenguaje', p. 432.
100. Valdés, *La nada...*, p. 173.
101. Valdés, *La nada...*, p. 183.
102. Valdés, *La nada...*, p. 19. '*Ella no sabe qué hacer. ¿Para qué nadar? ¿Para qué ahogarse?'.*
103. Timmer, 'La crisis de representación', p. 188.
104. Miller, 'The Prison-House of Allegory', p. 203.
105. Jill Stauffer, 'Interview with Judith Butler' in *The Believer*, May 2013, http://www.believermag.com/issues/200305/?read=interview_butler, pp. 1–8, p. 7. [Accessed 02/28/2015].
106. Rachel Blau DuPlessis quoted by Danny J. Anderson, 'Displacement: Strategies of Transformation in *Arráncame la vida* by Ángeles Mastretta', *The Journal of the Midwest Modern Language Association*, 21.1 (Spring 1988), 15–27, p. 16. Anderson applies this terminology in his own discussion of the ending of Mastretta's novel, however it is equally and usefully applicable also to Valdés's text as discussed here.
107. Adrienne Rich, *What is Found There: Notebooks on Poetry and Politics*, cited by Jennifer Browdy de Hernandez in *Women Writing Resistance: Essays on Latin America and the Caribbean* (Cambridge, MA: South End Press, 2003), p. 9.

BIBLIOGRAPHY

Alvarez Borland, Isabel, 'Fertile Multiplicities: Zoé Valdés and the Writers of the '90s Generation', in Andrea O'Reilly (ed.), *Cuba: Idea of a Nation Displaced* (New York: State University of New York Press, 2007), pp. 253–266.

Anderson, Danny J., 'Displacement: Strategies of Transformation in *Arráncame la vida* by Ángeles Mastretta', *The Journal of the Midwest Modern Language Association*, 21.1 (Spring 1988), 15–27.

Browdy de Hernandez, Jennifer, *Women Writing Resistance: Essays on Latin America and the Caribbean* (Cambridge, MA: South End Press, 2003).

Butler, Judith, *Bodies That Matter: On the Discursive Limits of Sex* (1993) (London: Routledge, 2011).

Cámara Betancourt, Madeline, *Cuban Women Writers: Imagining a Matria* (London: Palgrave Macmillan, 2008).

Cardoso, Dinora, and Oggel, Ynés, 'Self-Actualization is Paradise: *La nada cotidiana* by Zoe Valdés', *Journal of Caribbean Literatures*, 6:2 (Fall 2009), 65–75.

Chancy, Myriam J., *From Sugar to Revolution: Women's Visions of Haiti, Cuba, and the Dominican Republic* (Waterloo, ON: Wilfred Laurier University Press, 2012).

D'Haen, Theo, and Vermeulen, Pieter (eds.), *Cultural Identity and Postmodern Writing* (Amsterdam: Rodopi, 2006).

Davies, Catherine, *A Place in the Sun?: Women Writers in Twentieth Century Cuba* (London; New York: Zed Books, 1997).

Dorado Otero, Ángela, *Dialogic Aspects of the Cuban Novel of the 90s* (Woodbridge, UK: Tamesis Press, 2014).

Faccini, Carmen, 'El discurso político de Zoé Valdés: *La nada cotidiana* y *Te di la vida entera*', http://www.lehman.cuny.edu/ciberletras/v07/faccini.html [Accessed 02/28/2015].

Foucault, Michel, *Discipline and Punish: The Birth of the Prison* (1975), 2nd edn. (London: Vintage books, 1995).

González Abellás, Miguel, '"Aquella Isla": Introducción al universo narrativo de Zoé Valdés, *Hispania*, 83.1 (March 2000), 42–50.

Guevara, Che, 'Socialism and Man in Cuba' (1965), in David Deutschmann (ed.), *The Che Guevara Reader*, 2nd Revised edn., (Melbourne: Ocean Press, 2003), pp. 212–229.

Gustavo Pérez Firmat, *The Cuban Condition: Translation and Identity in Modern Cuban Literature* (Cambridge, UK: Cambridge University Press, 1989).

Kaminsky, Amy, *After Exile: Writing the Latin American Diaspora* (Minneapolis: University of Minnesota Press, 1999).

Lahr-Vivaz, Elena, 'Timeless Rhetoric, Special Circumstances: Sex and Symbol in *La nada cotidiana*', *Revista Canadiense de Estudios Hispánicos*, 34.2 (Invierno 2010), 303–321.

Lavery, Jane, 'The Physical and Textual Bodies in the Works of Ángeles Mastretta and Elena Poniatowska', *Romance Studies*, 19.2 (December 2001).

Loomba, Ania, *Colonialism/Postcolonialism* (London: Routledge, 1998).

McNay, Lois, *Foucault and Feminism: Power, Gender and the Self* (Cambridge, UK: Polity Press, 1992).

Miller, Paul B., 'The Prison-House of Allegory: Reflection on the Cultural Production of the Cuban 'Special Period', *INTI*, No. 59/60, 'Cuba: Cien Años de Alejo Carpentier' (Primavera 2004–Otoño 2004), 195–206.

Moreno Fraginals, Manuel R., and Pedraza Moreno, Teresita, 'The Ten Million Ton Sugar Harvest', http://faculty.mdc.edu/tpedraza/MMF-Ten%20Million%20 Ton%20Harvest.htm [Accessed 02/20/2015].

Ortiz Ceberio, Cristina, 'La narrativa de Zoé Valdés: Hacia una reconfiguración de la na(rra)ción cubana', *Chasqui: Revista de literatura latinoamericana*, 27.2 (1998), 116–127.

Pitman, Thea, '*En Primera Persona*: Subjectivity in Literary Evocations of Pregnancy and Birth by Contemporary Spanish-American Women Writers', *Women: a Cultural Review*, 17.3 (2006), 355–377.

Rohter, Larry, 'Arts Abroad; Living with a Shortage of Everything but Desire', *New York Times* (January 7, 1998), http://www.nytimes.com/1998/01/07/books/

arts-abroad-living-with-a-shortage-of-everything-but-desire.html [Accessed 03/28/2015].

Rozencvaig, Perla, 'La complicidad del lenguaje en *La nada cotidiana*', *Revista Hispánica Moderna*, 49.2 (December 1996), 430–433.

Sanchez, Yoani, 'The Buried Revolution', *The Huffington Post* (01/02/2011), http://www.huffingtonpost.com/yoani-sanchez/the-buried-revolution_b_803348.html [Accessed 02/28/2015].

Smith, Lois, and Padula, Alfred, *Sex and Revolution: Women in Socialist Cuba* (New York: Oxford University Press USA, 1996).

Staniland, Emma, 'Fighting the Opposition: Lack and Excess in Cuban and Cuban-American Narratives of Selfhood', *Comparative American Studies*, 12.3 (September 2014), 190–204.

Stauffer, Jill, 'Interview with Judith Butler', *The Believer* (May 2013), http://www.believermag.com/issues/200305/?read=interview_butler [Accessed 02/28/2015].

Tejada, Roberto, 'In Relation to the Poetics and Politics of Cuba's Generation-80', http://writing.upenn.edu/library/Tejada-Roberto_Cuba-Generation-80.pdf [Accessed 02/21/2015].

Timmer, Nanne, 'Dreams That Dreams Remain: Three Cuban Novels of the 90s', in Theo D'Haen, and Pieter Vermeulen (eds.), *Cultural Identity and Postmodern Writing* (Amsterdam: Rodopi, 2006), pp. 185–205.

Timmer, Nanne, 'La crisis de representación en tres novelas cubanas: *La nada cotidiana* de Zoé Valdés, *El pájaro, pincel y tinta china* de Ena Lucía Portela y *La última playa* de Atilio Caballero' *Revista Iberoamericana*, LXXIII.218–219 (enero–junio 2007), p119–134.

Valdés, Zoé, *La nada cotidiana* (1995) (Barcelona: Publicaciones y Ediciones Salamandra, 2004).

*In*conclusion

Towards Agency: From Uncharted Lives to Uncharted Futures

LOOKING BACK

This book began with two primary critical interests: first the Bildungsroman as a genre of literature whose gender-based theoretical delineation has both echoed, and threatened to exacerbate, a parallel restriction of self-definition on the part of women, but which offers nonetheless an extremely pertinent framework for Spanish American women's writing. The second, correlative interest, was a curiosity about the ways in which disparate texts from within the broad field of Spanish American women's writing engage with the genre's central narrative concern—the journey towards a workable selfhood that must take place in dialogue with the protagonist's social context—in particular as a means of exploring the sociocultural construction of gendered identities.

As a way of engaging with these concerns, the structure of my study was inspired by the Hegelian dialectic and its stages of thesis, antithesis, and synthesis—each of which constitutes one necessary step on a longer journey towards a desired goal—due to the recognized similarities between Hegel's philosophical mode of enquiry and the narrative trajectory of the Bildungsroman. Here, I have adopted that triadic form as an analytical framework that enables a critical reading of the process of *Bildung*, or self-development, as expressed in the novels I have examined. In this way, I began with an exploration of the narratives individually, considering the ways in which they adopt and adapt, borrow and recontextualize, reject or rearticulate the rites of passage through which *Bildung* is understood to take place for the two genders. But in addition, I was interested in how the works collectively voice a cross-corpus narrative depicting the *Bildung* of gender itself, and the subsequent contributions they make to our cognizance of the discursive formulation of gendered selfhoods. For this reason, I have made use of a double retextualization of Hegel's three phases in terms more directly germane to gender studies and the study of Post-Boom Spanish American women's writing: as stages exploring and/or contributing to the 'construction', 'deconstruction', and finally 'reconstruction' of gendered identities, articulated through the six authors' thematic and stylistic investment in the literary topoi of fairy tales and mythical archetypes, exile, and the female body. What is crucial about this overarching narrative, though, is its mapping onto a dialectically-rendered journey towards a form of agency characterized by the (female) self coming to know itself *as social construction,* and to thereby be enabled to (re)articulate itself in terms not limited to the vocabulary of the patriarchal representational order.

It was therefore within this critical framework that I explored Isabel Allende's *Eva Luna* (1987) and Laura Esquivel's *Como agua para chocolate* (1989) in terms of the two writers' return to archetypal figures in their portrayals of female self-development, and considered both the usefulness and the limitation of such reference points to a broader critique of gendered identities. Overall, what came into view was an ambiguity in their portrayals that allowed for a reading of the two novels as neither presenting a radical reappraisal of the question of gender and its social role, nor fully conforming to hegemonic models of femininity and masculinity. The importance of these texts for this project is, therefore, twofold. It stems from their insistent revelation of the archetypal foundations of social codes that govern gendered identity formation in the Spanish American context, and of the difficulty of untethering notions of selfhood from those anchors. But it also stems from their indication of the possibilities for reworking this symbolic material in the name of more liberated, more liberating, sociocultural perspectives on gender roles. In particular, both texts share an interest in issues of legacy—in the inheritance at a social level of accepted codes for the governance of identity politics, and the ways in which each generation (especially of women, in these novels) can positively impact the next by handing down an improved understanding of possibilities and strategies for subversion of the social script. In essence, they point towards the more far-reaching gender critique presented in the next phase of the journey, and are vital for doing so.

In Part Two, Exile served as the topos for the exploration of what might be considered the more radical phase of this dialectical *Bildung*, that of 'deconstruction', in which hegemonic structures and discourses on identity formation are most forcefully confronted. The exploration of this stage through exile literature is apt, because in such texts traditional organizational structures are thrown into disarray through the experience of expulsion, leading to a similar crisis at the level of individual identity. The protagonists of the works studied in this chapter, Equis from Cristina Peri Rossi's *La nave de los locos* (1984) and the anonymous female writer-protagonist of Sylvia Molly's *En breve cárcel* (1981), present a challenge to dominant discourses on identity formation through their 'problematic' sexualities—he as an impotent male and she as a lesbian. And so the journeys of these characters demarcate pathways and rites of passage necessarily very different to those normalized within the hegemonic order that they both, by their very existence, undermine. I have posited that for this reason these highly deconstructive works can be read as 'anti-Bildungsromane'—they portray not a journey towards social integration, but an exploration of the world 'outside' the accepted order that entails an unpicking of the ideological threads by which that order is constituted. This is most neatly evoked by the motif of the

'Tapestry of the Story of Creation' in Peri Rossi's novel, but echoed in Molloy's writer-protagonist and her psychological unraveling through nightmarish dreamscapes. Through such narrative features and facets, the works expose an unorthodox selfhood that even in exile continues to be defined by its relationship with the 'inside', and thereby expose also the role of gender in the formation and workings of the binary system by which hegemonic power bases are structured, informed, and sustained. The protagonists of these texts are crucial in their revelation of the hidden but inherent interstices of the grand narratives of the phallocentric order, and begin in those spaces of exile an exploration of selfhood that forcefully signals the possibility of their reconfiguration in more dynamic terms—the theme of the final analytical chapter of this book.

In Part Three I focused on the female body as the epicenter of identity, exploring its potential as the location of the self-reflexive, self-knowing genderedness that characterizes the intended destination of this figurative developmental journey. In my study of Ángeles Mastretta's *Arráncame la vida* (1985) and Zoé Valdés's *La nada cotidiana* (1995), I examined the portrayal of the female body in these Bildungsromane as site of performative agency; a dualistic location upon and through which the material and the symbolic come together. By considering the themes and events through which these two writers depict female *Bildung*, and the constant presence of the body within those representations, I emphasized the role of the female body as the point of synthesis of the dialectic, in which the knowledge gained regarding both the mythical construction and the exilic deconstruction of gendered identities can be understood to meet in the reconstruction of an active, not passive, female body. I have argued in these chapters that agency is located in the body precisely as a result of the writing 'I''s newly achieved recognition of its simultaneous, dualistic, and paradoxical location: marked by hegemonic discourses and implicated in the perpetuation of the same, but existent nonetheless as a site of resistance and potential self-(re)definition. It is a body whose now greater prescience confounds the mind/body split, and thereby empowers us to prioritize the possibility of difference over the formulation of categories of Otherness. In Mastretta's text these understandings are more external to the narrative, given that her historically realist early twentieth-century protagonist is not the overt feminist that Valdés creates in her protagonist, Yocandra. But both works emphasize the centrality of the body in the formulation of gendered identities, and lead their reader to grasp its potential as a site from, and through which to refute hegemonic discourses.

THINKING FORWARD

This newly prescient body seems a most apt point of culmination for the journey towards self-knowing, and most especially because the stage of 'synthesis' within which I have framed it is not actually conceived of as a final destination. For the dialectical structure is understood here as a continuum, enacted each time through the three constitutive stages, but always taking its own conclusion as the starting point for a new critical process. This intrinsic dynamism chimes with the Post-Boom, poststructuralist, postmodern mentalities of the novels, and informs their responsive textual engagement with sociocultural contexts themselves undergoing change—post-Revolutionary Mexico; the various political regimes of early twentieth-century Venezuela; the meanderings of the Uruguayan and Argentine exile seeking the way 'home', and the Special Period in post-Revolutionary Cuba. Moreover, it echoes the operation of Latin American feminist women's writing, in the important words of Debra A. Castillo, 'within a field of sinuous and shifting positionalities rather than from a single, fixed position.'[1] A quality most clearly evinced in the works discussed here because as a natural extension of their varied approaches to exploring the processes and practices inherent to the discursive construction of gendered selfhoods, they represent also the developmental journey of feminist practice in their region.

And whereas the panoramic view of the narratives opened up by this triadic analytical structure reveals all of the topoi studied to be vital material in the task of outlining, and challenging assumptions about orthodox gendered identities in the national and regional contexts in question, because each appears to some extent in all of the works considered, the role of the body in identity formation and oppression is ever visible. Its implication in the constraints of gender, as well as what it has to offer to the project of emancipation from the binds of the phallocentric order, are made absolutely evident, and very many of the body-related issues portrayed by these women writers remain, by necessity, key foci for feminist endeavors today. In all of the novels the female body is depicted as an instrument of female oppression, or as a means of symbolizing that oppression. In *Como agua para chocolate* Tita stares dumbfounded at her own hands when, for the first time, they are not required by the patriarchal order that her ruthless mother embodies to *do* anything in particular. Eva Luna's dominantly safe passage through life, protected by the fairy tale optimism with which Allende imbues her story, finds herself in real physical danger only once—and it is precisely her body that is attacked; burned with cigarettes, beaten, and threatened with rape. Peri Rossi has her character Graciela travel to Africa to write a report on Female Genital Mutilation (markedly, instead of taking a job as a door-to-door cosmetics saleswoman). Sylvia Molloy's pseudo-autobiographical writer-protagonist envisages her physical body fragmenting into its constituent elements of flesh, blood, and bone, as part of the delirium of depression that makes her choose to retreat into a lonely one-roomed world. Mastretta and Valdés, as discussed in the chapters on their novels, highlight a female body subordinated to the male gaze, and serving as the site of a national identity that fails to attribute subjectivity to the citizens by whose bodily form it comes to be symbolized. Further examples include the numerous depictions of coerced marriage and its transformation of women into material possessions, the perpetuation and/or abuse of women's unknowing relationship with their capacity for sexual pleasure, and the absolutely fundamental place of the maternal body and its correlative social role in the formation of Spanish American female genderedness.

In this way, the novels' relationship to one another comes to be characterized by fluidity, as narrative interests wash back and forth among them, and this also finds expression in the open-endedness that is one of the key narrative, and ideological, strategies of these works. Through it, they mirror the perpetuity of the dialectic; the way that it refuses closure and insists on an implicit future; one that will respond to the past and present by which it is informed, but which awaits, nonetheless, definition. Perhaps most meaningful, however, is the way that this non-closure is encapsulated above all in the continued relevance of their challenge to gender as a constraining, repressive category. Published between twenty and thirty-four years ago at the time of my writing, the extent to which the issues depicted in these textual explorations of gendered selfhood remain utterly anchored to contemporary lived realities, is remarkable. In this, they fully emphasize the task of women's liberation and self-definition, as well as that of all other identities circumscribed by the Manichean order of the sex-gender system, as an enduring project.

If there is anything, then, that I wish to emphasize in this *In*conclusion (it seems contradictory and counterproductive to call it anything else given the insistence here on the importance of dynamic open-endedness), it is the role of the female body as the focal point of this final stage of dialectic *Bildung*, but therefore also as the point of departure for the next triadic push forwards; as a tangible site upon and through which Spanish American feminism can, and does, ground itself. This is usefully exemplified via Amy Kaminsky's discussion, in *Reading the Body Politic: Feminist Criticism and Latin American Writers* (1993), of a particular conceptualization of the notion of 'presence' borrowed from Spanish American political discourse; one which neatly interacts with the trajectory of my study and its culmination at this point of gendered embodiment, and which she posits as a valuable focal point for feminist critics. This kind of 'Presence', she explains, 'does not rely on a psychoanalytic explanation of coherence', but

> is rather a notion that posits the sense of self in the quest for transformation. Consciousness-raising is part of this process—it is transformative, collective, and can make for crucial changes in self-definition. This conscious positioning, enabling choice and agency, is what is at stake; not some (as of today) irreconcilable and unanswerable questions about the stability of the psychological subject or the subject as language effect. Presence is created in history and through language; it represents and is represented, but it also acts on material reality.[2]

Significantly, Kaminsky's summary makes use of a number of terms and concepts—'quest for transformation', 'consciousness-raising', 'transformative', 'agency'—central to the analytical vocabulary through which this project, too, has been elucidated. Thus, whereas she takes these terms from a broader field of Latin American political practice, here they can be adopted to articulate 'presence' as the necessary, ongoing, and equally political goal of Spanish American female *Bildung*.

For this reason, whereas the narratives studied in *Gender and the Self in Latin American Literature* are, as narratives of selfhood, necessarily more inwardly than outwardly focused, and whereas they portray frustrated and frustrating social participation more than they can be said to depict widespread social change as a result of proactive female intervention and/or political activism, I nonetheless insist on the fact that these novels have impact at a political level. Their recuperation and re-expression of the narrative trajectory of the Bildungsroman is a vital step towards longer-term aims, for it firmly establishes the quest for female self-definition within the regional canon, and thereby promotes women's social visibility—their 'Presence'. In this way they enact the socially engaged didacticism inherent to the novel of development by communicating important messages to their readership about the positive changes that must be established as goals towards which to work, even while they embrace the open-endedness of that task; the need to be malleable and progressively minded in our confrontation with the challenges that lay ahead. Ultimately, alongside the stories they relate, the novels studied here also tell us much about what Spanish American literary feminism has achieved, needs to achieve, and can achieve by continuing to '[string] out bridges of words into the uncharted future'.[3]

NOTES

1. Debra A. Castillo, *Talking Back: Towards a Latin American Feminist Literary Criticism* (Ithaca, NY; London: Cornell University Press, 1992), p. xxii.
2. Amy Kaminsky, *Reading the Body Politic: Feminist Criticism and Latin American Women Writers* (Minneapolis; London: University of Minnesota Press, 1993), p. 25.
3. I borrow once more here the words of Jennifer Browdy de Hernandez in her Introduction to *Women Writing Resistance: Essays on Latin America and the Caribbean* (Cambridge, MA: South End Press, 2003), p. 9.

BIBLIOGRAPHY

Castillo, Debra A, *Talking Back: Towards a Latin American Feminist Literary Criticism* (Ithaca, NY; London: Cornell University Press, 1992).

Kaminsky, Amy, *Reading the Body Politic: Feminist Criticism and Latin American Women Writers* (Minneapolis; London: University of Minnesota Press, 1993).

Browdy de Hernandez, Jennifer (ed.), 'Introduction', *Women Writing Resistance: Essays on Latin America and the Caribbean* (Cambridge, MA: South End Press, 2003).

Index

For Product Safety Concerns and Information please contact our EU representative GPSR@taylorandfrancis.com
Taylor & Francis Verlag GmbH, Kaufingerstraße 24, 80331 München, Germany

www.ingramcontent.com/pod-product-compliance
Lightning Source LLC
Chambersburg PA
CBHW071515110726
47908CB00003B/845

* 9 7 8 1 1 3 8 5 4 7 6 7 4 *